The Philosophy
of the American Revolution

Other Books by Morton White

The Philosophy
of the
American Revolution

MORTON WHITE

OXFORD UNIVERSITY PRESS
Oxford New York Toronto Melbourne

Oxford University Press

Oxford London Glasgow

New York Toronto Melbourne Wellington

Nairobi Dar es Salaam Cape Town

Kuala Lumpur Singapore Jakarta Hong Kong Tokyo

Delhi Bombay Calcutta Madras Karachi

First published by Oxford University Press, New York, 1978

First issued as an Oxford University Press paperback, 1981

Library of Congress Cataloging in Publication Data

White, Morton Gabriel, 1917-
The philosophy of the American Revolution.
Includes index.
1. Philosophy, American—History. 2. United States
—Intellectual life—18th century. I. Title.
B878.W48   191   77-18081
ISBN 0-19-502381-1
ISBN 0-19-502891-0 pbk.

Printed in the United States of America

To
Harold Cherniss

A Note
to the Galaxy Edition

The publication of the paperback edition has provided me
with an opportunity to include two substantive points brought
to my attention by colleagues since the original publication of
this book in 1978.

On pages 62–63, after expressing doubt as to whether
Jefferson relied on Cicero while employing the concept of
self-evident truth in the Declaration, I explicitly refrain from
denying that Jefferson was influenced by a famous passage in
De republica in which Cicero speaks of unchangeable and
everlasting law. I have since been informed, first by my colleague Professor J. F. Gilliam, and independently by Professor
David S. Wiesen, that Jefferson could not have read that passage in *De republica* itself before writing the Declaration since
the part of *De republica* in which the passage appears was not
discovered before 1820.

I am very grateful to these scholars and also to Professor
H. L. A. Hart, who has informed me that the part of John
Lind's *An Answer to the Declaration of the American Con-
gress* that I discuss on pages 75–76 and page 208 below, was

written by Jeremy Bentham. This is evident in a letter from Bentham to Lind of September 1776, reprinted in *The Correspondence of Jeremy Bentham*, Volume I, pp. 341–344 (ed. T. L. S. Sprigge) in *The Collected Works of Jeremy Bentham* (London, 1968). The reader should also consult Professor Hart's luminous article, "Bentham and the United States of America," which appeared in *The Journal of Law and Economics*, Volume XIX (1976), pp. 547–567.

May 19, 1980   M. W.

Acknowledgments

In writing this book and preparing it for publication, I have incurred many debts that I wish to acknowledge with gratitude.

My research has been greatly facilitated by the libraries of The Institute for Advanced Study, of Princeton University, and of Princeton Theological Seminary. And I should like to add a special word of thanks for the hospitality I have enjoyed at two homes for scholars away from home, the Huntington Library in San Marino, California and the Villa Serbelloni in Bellagio, Italy.

These institutions have permitted me to read material that I should have understood much less well and to write material that others would have understood much less well if I had not had the benefit of many conversations at the Institute for Advanced Study with my friend and colleague Harold Cherniss. He has sent me to passages in ancient philosophy which were relevant to my concerns, taken pains and precious time to interpret them for me, and helped me to clarify my own views on the later thinkers I treat in this book. And since Jefferson was one of these thinkers, I have often called on my neighbor Julian Boyd, who invariably gave illuminating answers to my questions about the author of the Declaration of Independence.

I have been lucky to have had Richard Hudelson as my research assistant. He has been agile enough to gather a multitude of books for me from local libraries, and he has helped me mine them for material that has been of great use to me. He has, moreover, read and commented on various versions of what I have written, and labored loyally to help me produce a clearer and more coherent work than I should have written without his help. My secretary, Rose T. Murray, was another loyal and stalwart aide. She too helped me gather books, and after meticulously typing whatever I might present to her, would cheerfully and ingeniously alter the typescript to accommodate any afterthought that I might develop during what turned out to be a long and arduous period of revision.

Often such an afterthought would be prompted by conversation with my wife, Lucia White, who has helped me enormously in all stages of my research and writing. She has encouraged me to find felicitous as well as clear and true words—as she always has during the more than thirty-five years in which we have worked together. This time, however, she was not the only member of my family to come to my assistance. I have had the good fortune to have discussed many of the ideas in this book with my son Stephen D. White, who made several suggestions of great value to me, and with my son Nicholas P. White, who carefully examined the work and persuaded me to alter it in ways that have greatly improved it.

In conclusion I wish to thank a number of academic institutions which have afforded me the honor and the opportunity to give lectures in which I have presented some of the ideas developed here. In April, 1974, I delivered the Everett

W. Hall Lecture at the University of Iowa in Iowa City; in April, 1975 the Orestes Brownson Lecture at Sacred Heart University in Bridgeport, Connecticut; in September, 1975, a lecture inaugurating a series on the Bicentennial at the College of Notre Dame of Maryland in Baltimore, where Clare Fitzgerald, Conrad Johnson, Robert Sokolowski, and Garry Wills served as designated commentators on my talk; in November, 1975, the Humanities Lecture at the University of Kansas in Lawrence, Kansas; in February, 1976, the W. T. Jones Lectures at Pomona College; in March, 1976, a lecture under the auspices of the Department of Philosophy of Tokyo University at International House in Tokyo; and in October, 1976, a lecture before the First Plenary Session of the Bicentennial Symposium in Philosophy, held at the Biltmore Hotel in New York City under the auspices of the Graduate Center of the City University of New York. To the colleges and universities that sponsored these lectures I am grateful for presenting me with occasions on which I could air my ideas publicly and benefit from questions and criticisms.

In expressing my gratitude to so many persons, libraries, and institutions of learning, however, I do not wish to implicate any of them in the writing of this book. I give thanks and praise to all of them for what they have done for me, but so far as the book is concerned I have no one to blame but myself.

Princeton, New Jersey   M. W.
August 1977

Contents

The Philosophy
of the American Revolution

Prologue
The Changeable Philosophy
of the Immutable

In this study of the fundamental philosophical ideas associated with the American Revolution, I focus on the Declaration of Independence and refer on many occasions to other American revolutionary writings of the eighteenth century in an effort to analyze the epistemology, metaphysics, philosophical theology, and ethics upon which the revolutionaries rested their claim to independence. Since they leaned heavily on transatlantic thinkers whom we may rightly call the founding forefathers, I frequently refer to the views of those foreign moralists and jurists whose ideas were used by rebels seeking to justify the steps they took at Philadelphia in 1776. Now that we have passed from celebration in 1976 to sober cerebration, we may repeat what scholars have always known, and what the most candid rebels always admitted, namely, that they did not invent a single idea that may be called philosophical in the philosopher's sense of that word. The self-evidence that the revolutionaries applied to their truths when they used an old term of epistemology, the essence or nature of man to which they appealed in their metaphysical

3

moods, the concept of equal creation that loomed so large in their theology, the unalienable moral rights they defended, and the happiness they were so bent on pursuing as individuals and as a people—all of these ideas were familiar to distinguished Western philosophers and jurists before they were used in the political slogans of American revolutionaries. But we cannot understand how the revolutionaries used these ideas without detailed probing of their writings and of those writings from which they borrowed.

In spite of being philosophical borrowers, the revolutionaries deserve to have their philosophical reflections read carefully because they seriously used philosophical ideas while leading one of the great political transformations of history. Though they wrote their philosophy as they ran, many of them were men of considerable intellectual power, trained in the law and fully capable of grasping most of what they read in the writings of distinguished moralists and jurists. Historians of the twentieth century may speak of the "pragmatism" of Franklin Roosevelt or John Kennedy, but no one can suppose this to mean that those politicians seriously applied the technical doctrines of William James to public affairs. On the other hand, when historians speak of the impact of the doctrine of natural law on Jefferson, Hamilton, Adams, and James Wilson, they most certainly call attention to the influence of technical philosophy on politicians. It is obvious that Jefferson made far more serious use of the writings of Locke than Roosevelt or Kennedy made of the papers of Peirce or the works of any other philosopher for that matter. And for this reason I shall not be recording what the philosopher F. H. Bradley once called "an unearthly ballet of bloodless categories." Such categories as I shall study here were enshrined in the Declaration by a man who wrote that "the tree of liberty must be refreshed from time to time with the blood of patriots and tyrants." But in order to understand what Jefferson understood by words like "liberty," I shall try to fill a gap which has been left in the history of the Revolution by a failure to study the revolutionary understanding of such words with care, to examine the epistemological, metaphysical, and ethical borrowing by the colonists from more distinguished thinkers, and to reflect on the uses to which the philosophical ideas they borrowed could be and were put.

I should make clear, however, that my discussion of Locke or Burlamaqui—to take two of the more important influences on the revolutionaries—is not offered merely to show that they influenced the Americans, for that goes without saying. I aim to improve our understanding of what the Americans believed by exposing the Lockean or Burlamaquian antecedents of their beliefs and not simply to answer the question: "Who got what from whom?" The present work is not a mindless history of American revolutionary thought in which names of pre-Revolutionary thinkers are rattled off *seriatim,* as if that alone could be expected to produce the requisite knowledge of how terms like "self-evident truth," "unalienable right," and "the nature of man" were used in the philosophical literature that American revolutionaries studied and imitated. Merely dropping the names of Locke, Burlamaqui, Hooker, Hobbes, Grotius, Pufendorf, Aquinas, Aristotle, Wolff, Vattel, Richard Price, Cicero, Francis Hutcheson, and other figures in the history of Western thought will do very little to clarify the views of Jefferson, Adams, Hamilton, or Wilson. That is why there is an opportunity for a historian of philosophy to say something new and useful on a topic which has attracted so many opaque pages to itself.

Let me emphasize that in taking this opportunity, I do not intend to restrict myself to the exposition of texts. I shall expound some, to be sure, but not uncritically. I shall not confine myself to translating what Revolutionary and pre-Revolutionary thinkers say into terms that are more comprehensible. When it is hard or impossible to make what they say more comprehensible, I shall not hesitate to assert or to conjecture that they are *in*comprehensible. Nor will I hesitate to call attention to ambiguity or indefiniteness in their writings, especially ambiguity or indefiniteness which may have political significance. Let me also emphasize that by concentrating on the philosophical writings of the revolutionaries I do not wish to imply that those writings contain within themselves a complete causal explanation of the Revolution which makes it unnecessary to deal with the society, the economy, and the politics of eighteenth-century America and Britain.[1] I believe, however, that the philosophy of the rebellious colonists was one causal factor in a conjunction that led to the Revolution and that we shall not be able to explain the Revolution unless we understand that philosophy in more than a superficial way.[2]

This brings me to the theme expressed in the title of this

1. I wish to emphasize that in concentrating on the explicit philosophical language of the revolutionaries, I am not committed to the view that their philosophical beliefs by themselves "explain" why the Revolution occurred. By contrast, Bernard Bailyn has concluded after studying the pamphlets of the American Revolution that they were eminently "explanatory." See his book, *The Ideological Origins of the American Revolution* (Cambridge, Mass., 1967). Bailyn thought that he had discovered confirmation for his "rather old-fashioned view that the American Revolution was above all else an ideological, constitutional, political struggle and not primarily a controversy between social groups undertaken to force changes in the organization of the society or the economy" (*ibid.*, p. vi). However, I must confess to being unable to understand as well as I should wish Bailyn's statement that the Revolution was *"above all else"* or *"primarily"* an ideological, constitutional struggle, nor do I find any further statement in his study which improves my understanding of these difficult words. In this connection, see my review of Richard Hofstadter's *The Progressive Historians,* in *American Historical Review,* 75 (December 1969): 603; reprinted in my *Pragmatism and the American Mind* (New York, 1973), p. 208. See also my *Foundations of Historical Knowledge* (New York, 1965), Chapter IV, "Causal Interpretation."

2. See my article "Why Annalists of Ideas Should Be Analysts of Ideas," *The Georgia Review,* XXIX (Winter 1975): 930–947.

Prologue, one that will appear at different times throughout this work. I shall try to record it here with enough clarity to give the reader some idea of what to expect, and that may best be accomplished by means of an illustration which will receive fuller treatment later on. It concerns the idea of self-evident truth, which, as we shall see, is so conspicuous in the epistemology of the doctrine of natural law accepted by the revolutionaries. There is an old philosophical tradition according to which a truth may be self-evident to some people but not to others, a tradition which goes at least as far back as Aquinas, who emphasized that a learned man can see as self-evident a truth which an ignorant and rude man cannot see as self-evident. The idea appears in Locke, and it also appears in a slightly different form in Burlamaqui. But what about their revolutionary disciples in America? The answer to this question is not altogether clear if only because Jefferson and his associates did not write as fully on such topics as Burlamaqui and Locke did. Yet the fact that the Americans did not abandon the terminology of the older writers and announced the self-evidence of certain truths suggests that they operated within a philosophical tradition according to which the power to see self-evidence was attributed to a restricted group and not to every person. Therefore, the American revolutionaries were working with a terminology that could sanction various forms of élitism even though some of the revolutionaries professed great admiration for the people.

Such ambiguity and indefiniteness were not limited to epistemology. Turning to metaphysics, we may ask how the revolutionaries conceived of the nature or essence of man, a notion notorious for being identified by different philosophers in different ways. Much in the theory of natural law depended on how the essence or nature of man was identified, since the ends and inherent rights of man were supposedly derived from that mysterious entity which Jefferson came to disparage in later life but whose existence he assumed when he spoke of "inherent" rights in the Rough Draft of the Declaration. And it must always be remembered that the essence of man, as conceived by most philosophers of natural law, was created by a God whose purposes in creating man could have been identified differently by different philosophers. Those who held that God created man with a desire for happiness as part of his essence could regard the pursuit of happiness as an *inherent* duty and right of man, but those who held otherwise could not regard the pursuit of happiness as an *inherent* right of man. Moreover, if the essence of government was identified with the purpose proposed for it by God, then one philosopher who saw God's intentions in one way might define government so that it was obliged to *aid and abet* man in the pursuit of happiness, whereas another might think it obliged only to *protect* man's right to pursue happiness—a crucial difference in political philosophy.

I have listed these examples in a sketchy manner in order to give the reader a glimpse of one thread that will run through my discussion, a thread which links my efforts at purely philosophical interpretation of philosophical ideas with reflections on the political uses to which those ideas may be put. However, I should add that a considerable part of this book may gain the assent of readers who cannot agree with my reflections on what may be called the politically exploitable ambiguities of the Revolutionary version of the doctrine of natural law. I can imagine my readers treating this work much as they would a loose-leaf book, discarding the pages they deem false or indefensible and saving what they regard as remnants of truth, but needless to say, I hope that they will not find themselves tearing out many pages.

Self-evident Truth and Democracy

Since one of my main concerns in this volume is to expound and analyze the fundamental philosophical ideas of the American Revolution, I shall concentrate in the opening three chapters on a question in the theory of knowledge that interested many of the revolutionaries: How do we know that the truths of morality or of natural law are true? In this first chapter I shall present some of the antecedents of their doctrine that we can know some of them to be true by the use of reason; in Chapter 2 I shall show the influence of that doctrine on the revolutionaries, especially by considering their famous announcement in the Declaration of Independence that they held certain moral truths to be self-evident; and in Chapter 3 I shall focus on their attitudes toward the rival moral theory of the eighteenth century which asserted that we have a faculty called "the moral sense" and that it, rather than reason, was the faculty or power men exercised in discovering the moral truths that underlay the proposition that the American colonists had a right, in fact a duty, to rebel against Britain.

Although I shall begin my investigations by examining the epistemology of the revolutionaries, my reason for doing so is not obvious. So let me admit at once that other historians of Revolutionary philosophy might prefer to begin with the ethics and the metaphysics of the revolutionaries, to tell us first *what* the revolutionaries thought they knew, and *then* to tell us how they thought they knew it, whereas I shall turn to the more substantive beliefs of the revolutionaries in later chapters. In my opinion, however, if one begins with some understanding of Revolutionary epistemology, one is better able to see why the American Revolution was, among other things, a chapter in the Age of Reason or Enlightenment. Furthermore, once the reader sees that many of the revolutionaries adopted a rationalistic theory of knowledge, the reader will be better prepared to see why the revolutionaries thought they knew certain propositions in metaphysics about the essence of man and certain propositions in ethics about the rights of man.

The Courage To Use One's Own Reason

The first thing to observe about the notion of self-evident truth in the Declaration is this: if Jefferson and other signers had been challenged to say how they knew that some propositions were true, each might have thought it proper to reply, "I know it by intuition." Such a reply is equivalent to saying that the truth expressing the knowledge in question is self-evident. As we know, the signers of the Declaration assert very early that when "it becomes necessary for one People to dissolve the Political Bands which have connected them with another"—in short, to make a revolution—"a decent respect to the opinions of mankind requires that they should declare the causes which impel them to the separation." And then, in their effort to persuade *mankind,* for whose opinion they expressed so much respect, of the rightness of their cause, they start laying down their axioms or the truths which they hold to be self-evident. If asked by mankind: "How do you know that all men are created equal, that they are endowed by their Creator with certain unalienable Rights, and that among these are Life, Liberty, and the Pursuit of Happiness?", the signers might have been quite content to answer that they knew these propositions by intuition, that they could not give *arguments* for them, that these propositions were like the mathematical axioms that the whole is greater than any part and that things equal to the same thing are equal to each other. Whether they were justified in giving such an answer is, of course, another question. The revolutionaries were under the influence of a theory of knowledge which John Locke had defended, and I focus on him because he was the most eminent philosopher whom the American colonists were likely to take as an authority in such matters. However, the tradition behind this theory stretches very far back into the history of philosophy, being linked with the ancient claim that one can search only so far for premises when one is trying to prove something, and that at a certain point one must stop and say that some propositions—one's axioms—are known to be true without being deducible from anything else. And this claim is also present in Aquinas and in the rationalism of Descartes, Leibniz, and Spinoza.

We shall have occasion later to concentrate on Locke's and Aquinas's views of self-evident truth as they figured in their doctrines of natural law, but we should bear in mind that the idea that there are self-evident principles of natural law was espoused by a number of less famous but nonetheless important figures in the history of that doctrine who likened such principles to elementary truths of mathematics, simple truths of logic, or so-called essential predications which are true by definition. This was the position even of thinkers who held that the natural law was decreed by God and that it was revealed by God to a chosen few. The great Grotius likened some principles of natural law to the proposition that two times two make four, and he insisted that even God could not make that proposition false. Grotius supported this proposition by citing a passage in the second book of the *Nicomachean Ethics* where Aristotle says that "Some things are thought of as bad the moment they are named," meaning that the very names of certain acts and feelings which do not admit of observance of a mean connote evil and that they are therefore blamed without attention to whether they exhibit an excess or deficiency of something. "It is impossible," Aristotle added, "ever to go right in regard to them—one must always be wrong." And although Pufendorf takes issue with Grotius and Aristotle on this point because he fears that Grotius minimizes the role of God as legislator and Aristotle the role of moral principle (because Aristotle does not appeal to the principle of the mean) in the examples mentioned above, Pufendorf also regards the fundamental principles of natural law as necessarily true dictates of reason.[1] Nathanael Culverwel, who influenced Locke, wrote in his *Discourse of the Light of Nature* (1652) that the principles of natural law "have so much of certainty in them, that they are near to a tautology and identity; for this first principles are."[2] The "judicious Hooker," as Richard Hooker was called by Locke and others, characterized all of the allegedly obvious propositions of natural law by saying, as Locke came to say, that as soon as they are "proposed the mind doth presently em-

1. See Hugo Grotius, *De jure belli ac pacis*, trans. F. W. Kelsey et. al. (Oxford, 1925), Book I, Chapter I, Part X, Section 5, p. 40. The passages in Aristotle to which Grotius refers may be found in *Nicomachean Ethics*, trans. H. Rackham, Loeb ed., II, vi. For Pufendorf's views see *De jure naturae et gentium*, trans. C. H. and W. A. Oldfather (Oxford, 1934), Book II, Chapter III, and especially p. 203. For his discussion of Grotius and Aristotle on the point in question, see pp. 29–30.

2. Nathanael Culverwel, *Discourse of the Light of Nature*, ed. John Brown (Edinburgh, 1857), p. 127. See W. von Leyden's Introduction to Locke's *Essays on the Law of Nature* (Oxford, 1954), pp. 39–43.

brace them as free from all possibility of error, clear and manifest without proof."[3]

This appeal to intuition or self-evidence was made in many different fields of intellectual activity. It was most frequently made in philosophical comments on mathematics, usually by appealing to the method of geometers like Euclid. It was also made in the discussion of theology, though less frequently in the eighteenth century after the great inroads that empiricism had made in that century. And it was made in moral philosophy, which contains the theory of natural law and natural rights that appears in the Declaration. Moral philosophy, in a way that may strike some contemporary readers as odd, has often been a field in which mathematics has been looked up to as a logical model, even by so-called empiricists like John Locke. And to make matters more interesting, mathematics was used as a model by moralists who sought to justify popular revolutions. But how, it might be asked, could democrats think that such an appeal was democratic in effect? To some readers it might appear incompatible with what they might think of as the spirit of the Age of Reason or the Enlightenment. They might think, as John Stuart Mill and John Dewey thought, that appealing to self-evidence and intuition was hardly compatible with being prepared to de-

3. Richard Hooker, *Laws of Ecclesiastical Polity* (Everyman ed., 1954), Volume I, p. 177. The work originally appeared in 1593–1597. Just before saying this, Hooker calls upon the authority of Theophrastus, whom he translates as asserting: "They that seek a reason of all things do utterly overthrow Reason." Hooker himself says in this same paragraph that "to make nothing evident of itself unto man's understanding were to take away all possibility of knowing any thing." Gabriel Towerson, one of Locke's friends, writing well before Locke's *Essay* appeared, refers to the "judicious Hooker" as one who had observed that "all knowledge is at length resolved into such things as are clear and evident of themselves," *An Introduction to the Explication of the Decalogue,* Part II of *An Exposition of the Catechism of the Church of England,* Discourse I, "Of the Law of Nature," p. 2. This *Explication* was published in 1676, according to von Leyden, *op. cit.,* p. 36, note 2. I have used an edition of *An Exposition of the Catechism* published in London in 1681.

fend one's views to all of mankind since both Mill and Dewey
identified the appeal to intuition and self-evidence as conservative, undemocratic, and authoritarian because it implied
the existence of a faculty which was employed only by a few
who might seek to impose their views on the many. One can
even find signs of such an attitude in a very famous essay by
Immanuel Kant. In 1784, between the Declaration and the
Constitutional Convention, Kant looked at the times in
which he lived and published "What Is Enlightenment?" In
that essay Kant complains: "I hear on all sides, 'Do not
argue!' The officer says: 'Do not argue but drill!' The tax-
collector: 'Do not argue but pay!' The cleric: 'Do not argue
but believe!' "[4] In the light of this complaint one may ask:
Did the signers expect mankind to believe their self-evident
truths without argument? It would appear that they did if
only because they used the word "self-evident" in the final
version of the Declaration. But it must be remembered that
in the Rough Draft, Jefferson first called his truths "sacred
and undeniable" rather than "self-evident," and later on we
shall see that the revolutionaries might have been better off if
they had not used the word "self-evident," since it would appear that some of them really accepted their so-called self-
evident truths on the basis of an argument that they did not
make explicit in the Declaration. That argument, which I
shall present in a later chapter, rested on other premises that
would have been regarded by them as self-evident so long as
they retained their belief in a certain form of moral rationalism. Therefore, so long as they accepted *any* truths as self-
evident, they would have been forced to say "Do not argue
but believe!" at some point. And if they did so by resting on
premises that the majority of the people could not expect to

4. A translation of this essay by L. W. Beck appears in Immanuel Kant,
Critique of Practical Reason, And Other Writings in Moral Philosophy
(Chicago, 1949), p. 287.

understand, much less believe, one might well ask how this was compatible with the American revolutionaries' being men of the Enlightenment, which, according to Kant, was the age in which *the people* were to be encouraged to use their own reason.[5]

Innate Principles and Dictators

To answer these questions we must turn first to the philosophy of Locke and call attention to a number of things that he bequeathed to the eighteenth century. First of all, he believed that there was a fundamental contrast between what he called *innate principles,* the existence of which he was determined to refute, and *self-evident principles,* the existence of which he confidently asserted. Secondly, Locke regarded the doctrine of innate principles as conservative, whereas he regarded the doctrine of self-evident principles as very different just because he thought it encouraged the people to use their own reason. But there are, he held, two kinds of reason, one intuitive and the other discursive. The first was used to see the truth of self-evident principles and the second to deduce theorems from them. And, as we shall see, Locke held in some places that just to the extent that intuition was a branch of the faculty of God-given reason, an ordinary man had the power to exercise it if some "dictator of principles" should try to palm something off on him as true which he himself did not intuit or see as true. To use one's own intuition, Locke held, was to use a faculty that God had given to *all* men for their use whereas, according to the doctrine of innate principles, one would be forced to *swallow,* as he put it, a lot of principles without checking them oneself. When he spoke in this way, Locke saw the doctrine of self-evident principles as a great advance, from a

5. Kant, *op. cit.,* p. 286.

political point of view, on the doctrine of innate principles but as we shall see, he said other things which pointed in another political direction.

Since I believe that in the Declaration the use of the word "self-evident" was directly or indirectly influenced by John Locke's use of the word,[6] I want to present a more detailed exposition of Locke's views on this matter. Having pointed out that Locke distinguished sharply between what he called "innate principles" and what he called "self-evident principles," and that one of the main tasks of his *Essay Concerning Human Understanding* (1690) was to demolish the idea that there are innate principles, I do not intend to linger too long over what Locke meant by "innate principles." However, I want to say enough about his view of them to explain why he tried to distinguish them from self-evident principles both for epistemological and political reasons. In the opening book of his *Essay* Locke argues vehemently against what he calls an established opinion amongst "some men"—and his failure to mention the men in question launched a vast literature of speculation as to the men he had in mind—that there are in the understanding certain innate principles, some primary notions which, like characters, are *stamped* upon the mind of man, and "which the soul receives in its very first being, and brings into the world with it."[7] And although many of Locke's critics have held that there is virtually no

---

6. For an interesting discussion of an indirect route whereby Locke's concept of self-evidence exerted an influence on the Declaration, see W. S. Howell, "The Declaration of Independence and Eighteenth-Century Logic," *William and Mary Quarterly*, Third Series, XVIII (October 1961): 463–484. Howell emphasizes the importance of certain books on logic which Jefferson had in his library, notably William Duncan's *Elements of Logick*, first published in London in 1748. Howell believes "that Jefferson must certainly have studied the *Logick* [of Duncan] when he was enrolled at William and Mary between 1760 and 1762" (p. 471).

7. John Locke, *Essay Concerning Human Understanding* (1690), Book I, Chapter I, Section 1, ed. A. C. Fraser (Dover Publications, New York, 1959); often referred to below as "*Essay*."

difference between Locke's conception of an innate principle and his conception of a self-evident principle, Locke himself certainly believed there was. For him an innate principle would have to be "imprinted on the soul" from birth, and if it were so imprinted on the soul, it would have to be perceived and understood from birth. "No proposition," he held, "can be said to be in the mind which it never yet knew, which it was never yet conscious of."[8] So, for example, principles of logic like "Whatsoever is, is" and "It is impossible for the same thing to be and not to be," the strongest candidates for innateness, so to speak, *cannot* be innate because they, Locke holds, cannot be imprinted on the minds of children from birth since infants surely "have not the least apprehension or thought of them."[9]

On the other hand, Locke insists that these logical truths are self-evident. But what is a self-evident truth? In one place he says that "universal and ready assent upon hearing and understanding the terms is . . . a mark of self-evidence,"[10] and it would appear from his use of the word "mark" that he is not giving a definition of "self-evident" but merely a characteristic that all self-evident truths possess. But later in the *Essay*, it would seem that he defines the idea of self-evidence and goes beyond a mere "mark" of it when he discusses the "degrees of evidence" for a proposition and tells us that "sometimes the mind perceives the agreement or disagreement of two ideas *immediately by themselves*, without the intervention of any other: and this I think we may call *intuitive knowledge*."[11] Here, Locke goes on to say, the mind is at no pains in *proving* or examining, but sees the truth "as the eye doth light, only by being directed toward it."[12] In illus-

---

8. *Ibid.*, Book I, Chapter I, Section 5.
9. *Ibid.*
10. *Ibid.*, Book I, Chapter I, Section 18.
11. *Ibid.*, Book IV, Chapter II, Section 1.
12. *Ibid.*

trating self-evidence, Locke also offers the propositions that
white is not black, that a circle is not a triangle, that three
exceeds two, and that three equals two and one. He adds that
"such kinds of truths the mind perceives at first sight of the
ideas together, by bare intuition; without the intervention of
any other idea: and this kind of knowledge is the clearest and
most certain that human frailty is capable of. This part of
knowledge is irresistible, and, like bright sunshine, forces
itself immediately to be perceived, as soon as ever the mind
turns its view that way; and leaves no room for hesitation,
doubt, or examination, but the mind is presently filled with
the clear light of it. *It is on this intuition that depends all the
certainty and evidence of all our knowledge;* which certainty
every one finds to be so great, that he cannot imagine, and
therefore not require a greater."[13]

After drawing this purely epistemological contrast between
innate principles and self-evident, intuitively seen principles,
Locke proceeds, as some present-day thinkers might say, to
"politicize" his preference for self-evident principles over
innate principles. Once he has finished his epistemological
argument, Locke tells his reader that he has just done him a
great political favor by destroying the politically pernicious
doctrine of innate principles. Locke held that the doctrine
that certain propositions are inscribed on the mind from
birth discouraged men from using their own powers of reason and encouraged them to take allegedly innate principles
"upon trust without further examination." "In which posture of blind credulity," he goes on to say, "they might be
more easily governed by, and made useful to some sort of
men, who had the skill and office to principle and guide
them." Summing up his political opposition to the doctrine of
innate principles, Locke said: "Nor is it a small power it
gives one man over another, to have the authority to be the

13. *Ibid.*

dictator of principles, and teacher of unquestionable truths; and to make a man swallow that for an innate principle which may serve to his purpose who teacheth them."[14]

Locke's main political point is that because innate principles are allegedly *stamped* by God on man's mind at birth, and hence not arrived at by the *exercise* of man's reason, the doctrine of innate principles is, or certainly can be, a tool of dictators. According to Locke, the nefarious nativist or innatist first persuades his unwitting dupe that principles which are really self-evident are innate. Hence the dupe is prevented from seeing that he himself sees the truth of the self-evident principle through the use of intuitive reason. Once the dupe has been led this far, he is supposedly sunk. For now the nativist will get him to accept what Locke calls a principle of principles, namely, "that principles must not be questioned." So, as soon as the dupes are fallaciously persuaded that some of their beliefs—which are really self-evident and hence testable by the exercise of reason—are *innate*, the dictators of principles can persuade them to stop using their own reason and judgment and to take what the dictators say on trust. Once that happens, "no small power" over the people is given to the dictators of principles.

It will be recalled that I asked earlier how a democrat could appeal to intuition and to self-evident principles without the sort of concern that developed later in the writings of Mill and Dewey. And the answer I have so far offered on behalf of Locke is that a self-evident principle must be certified by a man's intuitive reason. *He* had to see the truth of the principle immediately upon understanding its terms; therefore, he could not be forced to swallow principles "upon trust without further examination," and he could not be forced into a "posture of blind credulity" which would allow others to govern him, to guide him, and to "principle" him.

14. *Ibid.*, Book I, Chapter III, Section 25.

Aquinas on Self-evidence:
The Learned and the Ignorant

The answer offered above might be acceptable to complaining democrats were it not for a certain tradition within the history of the doctrine of natural law, the tradition of insisting that only a certain kind of person could see self-evidence. We shall see that Locke himself was part of this tradition, but he was anticipated by Thomas Aquinas, one of the most influential theorists of natural law. Aquinas held that a person who did not have certain ideas or who did not know the meanings of certain words would not—indeed, *could not*—see that certain propositions were self-evident. Aquinas made two distinctions in his treatment of the matter. His first was between a proposition's being self-evident "in itself" and its being self-evident "in relation to us." To be sure, the concept of being self-evident *in itself* is not an easy one to understand, but apparently what Aquinas had in mind was that there are certain concepts between which certain objective relations hold and that when a proposition asserts that such a relation holds, the proposition is self-evident in itself. For example, he thinks that *Man is a rational being* is a proposition which is self-evident in itself. It is self-evident quite apart from what anyone thinks about it just as it is *true* that snow is white quite apart from what anyone thinks about it. But what does it mean to say that a proposition is self-evident in itself? It means, according to one translation of Aquinas, that it is a proposition whose "predicate is contained in the notion of the subject."[15] In other words, the notion of being rational is objectively *contained* in the notion of being a man. Therefore, by its very nature, the proposition is self-evident, according to Aquinas.

On the other hand, Aquinas says: "to one who does not

15. See note 16 below.

know the definition of the subject, such a proposition is not self-evident. For instance, this proposition, *Man is a rational being,* is, in its very nature, self-evident, since who says *man,* says *a rational being;* and yet to one who does not know what a man is, this proposition is not self-evident."[16] But, Thomas goes on to say, "certain axioms or propositions are universally self-evident to all; and such are the propositions whose terms are known to all."[17]

For us, the most important implication of what Aquinas has to say here is that certain terms are understood by all, whereas some, as he puts it, are understood only by the learned and are not understood by the ignorant. Aquinas, in the context I have been discussing, uses a theological example: ". . . to one who understands that an angel is not a body, it is self-evident that an angel is not circumscriptively in a place." But it is not self-evident to the ignorant because they do not grasp the fact that an angel is not a body. The point he stresses in this context is that self-evidence will not be perceived by one who fails to know the essence of something.[18] In other places, however, he seems to adopt a view not unlike Locke's when he is identifying a proposition which is self-evident.[19] Thus, in a discussion of the question whether the existence of God is self-evident, Aquinas writes in response to an objection which he is considering: "those things are said to be self-evident which are known as soon as the terms are known."[20] Aquinas seems to accept this formulation of what is meant by "self-evident," which anticipates

16. Saint Thomas Aquinas, *Summa Theologica,* First Part of the Second Part, Question XCIV, Second Article. See A. C. Pegis (ed.), *Basic Writings of Saint Thomas Aquinas* (New York, 1945), Volume II, p. 774. Aquinas's Latin for a proposition "whose predicate is contained in the notion of the subject" is *"cuius praedicatum est de ratione subiecti."*
17. *Ibid.*
18. *Ibid.*
19. Aquinas's Latin for "self-evident" is *"per se nota."*
20. *Summa Theologica,* Part I, Question II, First Article; Pegis, *op. cit.,* Volume I, p. 18.

the mark of self-evidence mentioned by Locke. And in Aquinas's statement that some terms are known to or understood by *all men*, a statement for which he finds authority in Boethius, we also find the basis for Boethius's and Aquinas's view that "certain axioms or propositions are universally self-evident to all." Note that they are not only *believed* by all, but they are *self-evident* to all. Among the illustrations of propositions said to be self-evident to all, we find Aquinas citing two given by Boethius, namely, the mathematical axioms, "Every whole is greater than its part" and "Things equal to one and the same are equal to one another." He lists a third which is a logical principle he takes from Aristotle, namely, "That the same thing cannot be affirmed and denied at the same time," and a fourth which is a precept of natural law, as Aquinas calls it, namely, "Good is to be done and promoted, and evil is to be avoided."[21]

Taking as my point of departure Aquinas's idea that some truths are self-evident only to the learned, I want to turn now to Locke's own statements on self-evidence and allied topics in order to show the extent to which he subscribed to similar views—views that make it easier to see how the doctrine of *self-evident* principles might also be exploited by

21. *Summa Theologica*, First Part of the Second Part, Question XCIV, Second Article; Pegis, *op. cit.*, Volume II, p. 774. It is important to note that although for Aquinas some self-evident propositions like "Man is a rational being" are essential predications and what Locke later called "trifling propositions," such propositions did not exhaust the class of self-evident propositions for Aquinas or, at any rate, it would be difficult for Aquinas to argue successfully that they did. It is worth noting that Aquinas argues as follows: ". . . the first principle in the practical reason is one founded on the nature of the good, viz., that *good is that which all things seek after*. Hence this is the first precept of law, that *good is to be done and promoted and evil is to be avoided*" (*ibid.*). The difficulty here is that if the *nature* or essence of the good is that which all things *seek* after ("rationem boni, quae est, *Bonum est quod omnia appetunt*"), it is hard to see how Aquinas can extract from the notion of the good as that which is *in fact* sought after, the notion of being that which *ought to be* done and promoted.

those whom Locke had called dictators of principles. This procedure is justified on historical grounds because Locke was indebted—directly or indirectly—to Aquinas for some of the views to be found in the English philosopher's *Essays on the Law of Nature*,[22] to which I now turn for further light on what power the people allegedly had to see the rational truths of natural law.

How Democratic Was Locke's Appeal to Self-evidence?

It will be recalled that Locke, when describing self-evident truth and intuitive knowledge in the *Essay,* said that such knowledge was irresistible, and it forced itself like bright sunshine *"as soon as ever the mind turns its view that way."* The qualification I have emphasized was interestingly exploited by Locke in his unpublished *Essays on the Law of Nature*, a work which shows that he held that truths of reason were not self-evident to *all*. Locke's figurative reference to light and the mind turning its view in the proper direction makes it easy for him to say that some men did *not* turn their minds or eyes in the proper direction, that some men were blind, that some men did not open up their eyes, and so on. Therefore, he responds to certain critics of his rationalistic doctrine of natural law as follows:

> Some people here raise an objection against the law of nature, namely that there is no such law in existence at all, since it can nowhere be found, for most people live as though there were no rational ground in life at all nor any law of such a kind that all men recognize it; on the

22. John Locke, *Essays on the Law of Nature: The Latin Text with a Translation, Introduction, and Notes, Together with Transcripts of Locke's Shorthand in His Journal for 1676,* ed. W. von Leyden (Oxford, 1954). See von Leyden's Introduction, p. 36, for comment on the relationship between Locke's views and those of Aquinas.

contrary, on this point men appear to disagree most of all. If indeed natural law were discernible by the light of reason, why is it that not all people who possess reason have knowledge of it?

My answer to this is, first, that as in civil affairs it does not follow that a law does not exist or is not published, because it is impossible for a blind man, and difficult for one who sees badly, to read a legal notice displayed in a public place, so, in other circumstances, a man who is occupied is not free, nor an idle or bad man disposed, to lift his eyes to the notice board and learn from it the nature of his duty. I admit that all people are by nature endowed with reason, and I say that natural law can be known by reason, but from this it does not necessarily follow that it is known to any and every one. For there are some who make no use of the light of reason but prefer darkness and would not wish to show themselves to themselves. But not even the sun shows a man the way to go, unless he opens his eyes and is well prepared for the journey. There are others, brought up in vice, who scarcely distinguish between good and evil, because a bad way of life, becoming strong by lapse of time, has established barbarous habits, and evil customs have perverted even matters of principle. In others, again, through natural defect the acumen of the mind is too dull to be able to bring to light those secret decrees of nature. For how few there are who in matters of daily practice or matters easy to know surrender themselves to the jurisdiction of reason or follow its lead, when, either led astray by the violence of passions or being indifferent through carelessness or degenerate through habit, they readily follow the inducements of pleasure or the urges of their base instincts rather than the dictates of reason. Who, as I might almost say, is there in a commonwealth that knows the laws of his state, though they have been promulgated, hung up in public places, are easy to read and to understand, and are everywhere exposed to view? *And how much less will he be acquainted with the secret and hidden laws of nature? Hence, in this matter, not the majority of people should be consulted but those who are more rational and perceptive than the rest.*[23]

Later on in his *Essays on the Law of Nature,* Locke says something else of importance to us. While trying to explain why some mortals lack knowledge of the law of nature and why nearly all of them think of it differently, he writes:

 . . . granted that our mental faculties can lead us to the knowledge of this law, nevertheless it does not follow from this that all men necessarily make proper use of these faculties. The nature and properties of figures and numbers appear obvious and, no doubt, knowable by the light of nature; yet from this it does not follow that whoever is in possession of mental faculties turns out a geometer or knows thoroughly the science of arithmetic. Careful reflection, thought, and attention by the mind is needed, in order that by argument and reasoning one may find a way from perceptible and obvious things into their hidden nature. Concealed in the bowels of the earth lie veins richly provided with gold and silver; human beings besides are possessed of arms and hands with which they can dig these out, and of reason which invents machines. Yet from this we do not conclude that all men are wealthy. First they have to equip themselves; and it is with great labour that those resources which lie hidden in darkness are to be brought to the light of day. They do not present themselves to idle and listless people, nor indeed to all those who search for them, since we notice some also who are toiling in vain. But if in matters that relate to the practice of ordinary life we meet but few who are directed by reason, since men only seldom delve into themselves in order to search out from thence the condition, manner, and purpose of their life, then it is not to be wondered at that of the law of nature, which is much less easy to know, men's opinions are so

23. *Ibid.,* pp. 113–115. The emphasis is mine.

different. For most people are little concerned about
their duty; they are guided not so much by reason as
either by the example of others, or by traditional customs and the fashion of the country, or finally by the
authority of those whom they consider good and wise.
They want no other rule of life and conduct, being satis-
fied with that second-hand rule which other people's
conduct, opinions, and advice, without any serious thinking or application, easily supply to the unwary. It does
not therefore follow that the law of nature cannot be
known by the light of nature because there are only few
who, neither corrupted by vice nor carelessly indifferent,
make a proper use of that light.[24]

And while we are examining Locke's view on the people's
relationship to the law of nature, let us also quote what he
says in his *Essays on the Law of Nature* about the maxim
"The voice of the people is the voice of God":

Surely, we have been taught by a most unhappy lesson
how doubtful, how fallacious this maxim is, how pro-
ductive of evils, and with how much party spirit and
with what cruel intent this ill-omened proverb has been
flung wide [lately] among the common people. Indeed,
if we should listen to this voice as if it were the herald of
a divine law, we should hardly believe that there was any
God at all. For is there anything so abominable, so
wicked, so contrary to all right and law, which the general consent, or rather the conspiracy, of a senseless
crowd would not at some time advocate? Hence we have
heard of the plunder of divine temples, the obstinacy of
insolence and immorality, the violation of laws, and the
overthrow of kingdoms. And surely, if this voice were
the voice of God, it would be exactly the opposite of that
first fiat whereby He created and furnished this world,
bringing order out of chaos; nor does God ever speak to
men in such a way—unless He should wish to throw

24. *Ibid.,* pp. 133-135.

everything into confusion again and to reduce it to a state of chaos. In vain, therefore, should we seek the dictates of reason and the decrees of nature in the general consent of men.[25]

The point of quoting these passages from Locke is to show that although he was so politically hard on the doctrine of innate principles because he thought it could be used by "dictators of principles," the political potentialities of his own doctrine of *rational* principles do not seem very different. The passage quoted earlier which begins with the words "Some people" is to some extent linked with the doctrine of Aquinas. We see that after "admitting" that all people are by nature endowed with reason and saying that natural law can be known by reason, Locke adds that from this it does not necessarily follow that natural law is known to any and every one. But then Locke goes on to list the various ways in which man can fail to use his natural endowment of reason. Some simply make no use of the light of reason. Indeed, they *prefer* darkness; and it is in describing such people that Locke observes that one must open one's eyes even to see the sun. A second group of non-seers Locke describes in moral terms. They are brought up in vice and therefore "scarcely distinguish between good and evil." A third group of non-seers resembles more closely the non-seers of self-evidence described by Aquinas. In them, "through natural defect the acumen of the mind is too dull to be able to bring to light those secret decrees of nature." No wonder, then, that Locke concludes this passage by saying that in trying to discover what the law of nature is, "not the majority of people should be consulted but those who are more rational and perceptive than the rest."

The second passage, which begins with "granted that,"

25. *Ibid.*, p. 161. The "unhappy lesson" to which Locke refers is said by von Leyden, his editor, to be "the Civil War and its aftermath."

seems even more pessimistic in its estimate of the number of people who use their reason, though it does end with some indications that this state of affairs is deplorable. I have in mind, first of all, Locke's saying that some people rely on "the authority of those whom they consider good and wise" where there is a suggestion that the emphasis should be placed on the word "consider" and therefore an implication that those relied on might *not* be so good and wise. I also have in mind the statement by Locke that people who rely on others in this way are "unwary."

The suggestion and the statement I have just mentioned are linked with Locke's later warnings about dictators of principles in the *Essay Concerning Human Understanding*. In both cases we find him worried about people being deceived or taken advantage of, but when he mentions this possibility in the *Essays on the Law of Nature* he does not mention it as an *objection* to the theory of natural law. Moreover, we should observe that in the *Essays on the Law of Nature* Locke does assert that some people are more rational and perceptive than the rest, that the former are in the minority, and that senseless crowds can advocate abominable and wicked deeds. Furthermore, when he mentions the things that prevent some people from seeing truths of natural law by the light of reason, some of these obstacles do seem insuperable even though these people have been endowed by nature with reason. Take, for example, those who are said by Locke to be too dull to bring to light the secret decrees of nature because of natural defects in their minds. It seems hard to avoid the conclusion that *they* might be just as vulnerable to a dictator of principles as the people about whom Locke is so solicitous when he worries about the political consequences of the doctrine of innate principles in the *Essay Concerning Human Understanding*. After all, the defect in question is said by Locke to be *natural* and presumably one which is not remediable, in which case those suffering from it might easily fall victim to dictators of the principles of natural law and, therefore, be incapable of questioning what those dictators had told them was a dictate of reason. And let us not forget that it was the unquestionableness of what the dictators of principles asserted that worried Locke greatly.

In the light of this, it seems that there is a very fine line between the doctrine of innate principles and the doctrine of self-evident principles if one focuses on their possible political consequences. It is true that Locke makes much of the fact that self-evident principles *can be* perceived by the exercise of reason, whereas innate principles are so construed by him that, being *inscribed* on the mind, they do not require the exercise of a God-given faculty, reason. But so many people are, for one reason or another, *unable to exercise* that faculty in Locke's own view that it seems hard to see why—leaving aside the question of the epistemological *truth* of the doctrine of self-evident principles—one might not condemn it almost as harshly as Locke condemned the doctrine of innate principles on the score of its political consequences. Later, I shall try to show that certain thinkers tried to avoid these consequences by adopting the so-called doctrine of moral sense. They abandoned ethical rationalism for a theory which attributed the power of "seeing" moral principles to a faculty which was, on their theory, more widely possessed or more easily exercised than Locke's intuitive reason. But I must not conclude this discussion of Locke without remarking on what may be viewed as the ultimate irony in Locke's *political* attack on innate principles, his own appeal to religious authority in moral matters.

In 1692, two years after the *Essay Concerning Human Understanding* appeared, Locke's correspondent, Molyneux, urged him to write a treatise on morals which would make good his claim that ethics could be developed as a demonstrative science. To this Locke replied in the same year: "Though by the view I had of moral ideas, whilst I was con-

sidering that subject, I thought I saw that morality might
be demonstratively made out; yet whether I am able so to
make it out, is another question." Molyneux repeated his
request a few years later, but Locke continued to decline the
invitation, saying in 1696: "The Gospel contains so perfect
a body of ethics, that reason may be excused from that inquiry, since she may find man's duty clearer and easier in
revelation than in herself."[26] I say that this is ironical because of Locke's contention that the doctrine of innate principles would encourage men to take allegedly innate principles "upon trust without further examination" and that
once they were in a "posture of blind credulity, they might
be more easily governed by, and made useful to some sort of
men, who had the skill and office to principle and guide
them."[27] Obviously, Locke's appeal to revelation and to the
Gospel might easily be seized on by a debating defender of
innate principles or, for that matter, by anyone bent on
questioning Locke's concern for those who might be bullied
by "dictators of principles." For here Locke seems to be taking moral principles "upon trust without further examination" from the Gospel and seems to acknowledge that even a
man of his own intellectual powers was unable to get very
far by the exercise of reason in developing a demonstrative
science of ethics. This could have meant that virtually everyone would be forced into a "posture of blind credulity" and
"made useful to some sort of men who had the skill and
office to principle and guide them"—namely, the sort of men
who claimed to be teachers of "unquestionable truths" and
who might "make a man swallow that for a *self-evident* principle which may serve to his purpose who teacheth them."
The reader will have noticed that I have simply taken one of
Locke's remarks on the dangers of the doctrine of *innate*

26. Locke, *Works* (1823; reprint ed., London, 1963), Volume IX, pp. 291, 294–
  295, 374, 377.
27. See note 14 above.

principles and replaced "innate principles" by "self-evident principles"[28] to show how easily the tables might have been turned on Locke. Once Locke himself appeals to revelation as the basis for accepting principles of morality or natural law, a critic might say that Locke resembled the cleric whom Kant described in his essay on the Enlightenment, the one who commanded: "Do not argue but believe!"

Such a critic might find even more to support his view in Locke's *The Reasonableness of Christianity, As Delivered in the Scriptures,* which appeared in 1695, the year before Locke wrote to Molyneux that the Gospel contained "so perfect a body of ethics, that reason may be excused from that inquiry, since she may find man's duty clearer and easier in revelation than in herself." For in that book he says something quite reminiscent of what he had said thirty-five years earlier in his *Essays on the Law of Nature* about the intellectual powers of the majority of men:

> The greatest part of mankind want leisure or capacity for demonstration; nor can carry a train of proofs, which in that way they must always depend upon for conviction, and cannot be required to assent to, until they see the demonstration. Wherever they stick, the teachers are always put upon proof, and must clear the doubt by a thread of coherent deductions from the first principle, how long, or how intricate soever they be. And you may as soon hope to have all the day-labourers and tradesmen, the spinsters and dairy-maids, perfect mathematicians, as to have them perfect in ethics this way. Hearing plain commands is the sure and only course to bring them to obedience and practice. The greatest part cannot know, and therefore they must believe. And I ask, whether one coming from heaven in the power of God, in full and clear evidence and demonstration of miracles, giving plain and direct rules of morality and obedience;

28. *Ibid.*

be not likelier to enlighten the bulk of mankind, and set
them right in their duties, and bring them to do them,
than by reasoning with them from general notions and
principles of human reason? And were all the duties of
human life clearly demonstrated, yet I conclude, when
well considered, that method of teaching men their
duties would be thought proper only for a few, who had
much leisure, improved understandings, and were used
to abstract reasonings. But the instruction of the people
were best still to be left to the precepts and principles of
the Gospel. The healing of the sick, the restoring sight to
the blind by a word, the raising and being raised from the
dead, are matters of fact, which they can without difficulty conceive, and that he who does such things, must
do them by the assistance of a divine power. These
things lie level to the ordinariest apprehension: he that
can distinguish between sick and well, lame and sound,
dead and alive, is capable of this doctrine. To one who is
once persuaded that Jesus Christ was sent by God to be a
King, and a Saviour of those who do believe in him; all
his commands become principles; there needs no other
proof for the truth of what he says, but that he said it.
And then there needs no more, but to read the inspired
books, to be instructed: all the duties of morality lie
there clear, and plain, and easy to be understood.[29]

Locke's *Reasonableness of Christianity,* and especially
passages in it like the one just quoted, may be regarded as
doubly ironical by a reader of his political attack on the doctrine of innate principles. For Locke not only appeals to the
Gospel as a source of morality in a way that is not altogether
in keeping with Locke's fear of dictators of principles but he
makes a sharp distinction between two kinds of readers of the
Gospel: men of improved understanding and others. By making this distinction Locke continues to provide a large loop-

29. John Locke, *Reasonableness of Christianity,* in *Works* (1823; reprint ed.,
London, 1963), Volume VII, pp. 146–147.

hole through which a human dictator might slip. For although Locke asserts that all men must rely on the Gospel, he also asserts that the few who are intellectually superior are able to confirm revealed moral truths by reason. He does this by maintaining in the *Reasonableness of Christianity* that all of us know of a great many truths which we at first receive from others, which we accept readily, and which we would not have discovered ourselves because we lacked the "strength" to have discovered them. He also maintains that Christian philosophers who read the Gospel merely give their immediate assent to principles which are revealed to them but which they do not discover.[30] This distinction between discovering a self-evident truth and merely seeing the self-evidence of a truth which Jesus discovered allows Locke to separate the "few, who had much leisure [and] improved understandings" from the day-laborers and their ilk since the latter not only could not *discover* self-evident truths but could not even see their self-evidence after they were discovered by others. This would permit one reader of the Gospel to dictate to another what it "really meant" and would be strikingly reminiscent of Aquinas's statement that the learned can see the self-evidence of the religious proposition that no angel is circumscriptively in a place whereas the rude and ignorant cannot. So, although Locke puts the many and the few on the same level by making both of them depend on revelation for their morality, he gives a decided advantage to "the most elevated understandings" over "the lowest capacities of reasonable creatures."

It must be noted, however, that the fact that men of elevated understanding may see the self-evidence or undeniability of moral truths uncovered in the Gospel is not enough to show that the Gospel contains a demonstrative science of

---

30. *Works,* Volume VII, p. 140. Locke also tells us that as soon as these principles are "heard and considered," they "can by no means be contradicted," *Ibid.*

morality. Even if it were to contain all of the axioms of such a science, it would still lack the theorems and their proofs. I emphasize this because Lord Bolingbroke, whom the youthful Jefferson admired, seems to have misunderstood Locke on this point. Seizing on Locke's statement that a "body of ethics, proved to be the law of nature, from principles of reason, and teaching all the duties of life" was not available before Christ[31] and that pre-Christian philosophers had not "from undeniable principles given us ethics in a science like mathematics, in every part demonstrable,"[32] Bolingbroke erroneously concluded that Locke held in the *Reasonableness of Christianity* that there *is* in the Gospel just such an axiomatized code of morality.[33] But Locke never says that such a systematic code is to be found in the Gospel. On the contrary, when he wrote that a philosopher must give rational assent to Christ's principles, Locke wanted to *contrast* the unsuccessful deductive method of a rationalistic philosopher like himself and that of Christ. That contrast is connected with Locke's distinction between two ways in which one can become a "dictator of rules"—itself an interesting phrase when we think of Locke's pejorative use of "dictator of principles" in his attack on innate principles. According to Locke, such a dictator "must show, that either he builds his doctrine upon principles of reason, self-evident in themselves; and that he deduces all the parts of it from thence, by clear and evident demonstration: or must show his commis-

31. *Ibid.*, p. 141.
32. *Ibid.*, p. 146. Readers of Jefferson's Rough Draft of the Declaration of Independence should note that here Locke applies the term "undeniable" to "self-evident" principles since the latter term was substituted for the former by Jefferson himself, or by Franklin, before the final version was prepared.
33. *The Works of Lord Bolingbroke* (Philadelphia, 1841), Volume III, p. 406. This appears in his *Essays on Human Knowledge,* Essay the Fourth, Section VII, parts of which were copied into Jefferson's so-called *Literary Bible,* about which we shall have something to say later. See below, Chapter 2, note 22.

sion from heaven, that he comes with authority from God, to deliver his will and commands to the world."[34] But nobody, Locke continues in a passage not fully comprehended by Bolingbroke, constructed morality in the first manner before or after Christ's time, not even Locke himself. Still, Locke held, mankind needs a complete moral code "as their unerring rule," not merely parts of the law of nature which fall short of the whole; and "such a law of morality Jesus Christ hath given us in the New Testament." However, Jesus gave it to us by revelation.[35] He gave us a rule which is "conformable to that of reason" but—and this is crucial for some critics who might wish to taunt Locke about some of his political statements concerning the doctrine of innate principles—Locke held that "the truth and obligation of its precepts have their force, and are put past doubt to us, by the evidence of [Jesus'] mission. He was sent by God: his miracles show it; and the authority of God in his precepts cannot be questioned. Here morality has a sure standard, that revelation vouches, and reason cannot gainsay, nor question; but both together witness to come from God, the great lawmaker."[36]

We now see more clearly what Locke meant when he said that he would have to rely on revelation, but we can also see why the ethics of Locke might easily be characterized as authoritarian by those who did not share his belief in Christ's miracles and his consequent acceptance of Christ as a revealer of God's law. Naturally, Locke would have insisted in reply that there was a profound difference between an ordinary human dictator and one who, by the evidence of his miracles, showed that he was a messenger of God. But if the miracles were questioned or denied, Locke's argument would collapse.

34. Locke, *Works,* Volume VII, p. 142. Note the Thomistic phrase "self-evident in themselves."
35. *Ibid.,* pp. 142–143.
36. *Ibid.,* p. 143.

And, what is more, a critic of Locke's inconsistency might well have reminded him of the passage in his own *Essay* which anticipated by almost a century Kant's exhortation, "Have courage to use your own reason," namely:

> I think we may as rationally hope to see with other men's eyes, as to know by other men's understandings. So much as we ourselves consider and comprehend of truth and reason, so much we possess of real and true knowledge. The floating of other men's opinions in our brains, makes us not one jot the more knowing, though they happen to be true. What in them was science, is in us but opiniatrety; whilst we give up our assent only to reverend names, and do not, as they did, employ our own reason to understand those truths which gave them reputation. Aristotle was certainly a knowing man, but nobody ever thought him so because he blindly embraced, and confidently vented the opinions of another. And if the taking up of another's principles, without examining them, made not him a philosopher, I suppose it will hardly make anybody else so. In the sciences, every one has so much as he really knows and comprehends. What he believes only, and takes upon trust, are but shreds; which, however well in the whole piece, make no considerable addition to his stock who gathers them. Such borrowed wealth, like fairy money, though it were gold in the hand from which he received it, will be but leaves and dust when it comes to use.[37]

Burlamaqui, the "Stupid Wretches," and Self-evidence

As we have seen, Locke's account of the light of nature and its uses was not as luminous as might be wished. But, as often happens in the history of philosophy, he acquired transmitters who would make some of his ideas more accessible to

37. *Essay*, Book I, Chapter III, Section 24.

American colonists, though they, of course, were able to read his own words in some of the works from which we have previously quoted as well as in others, notably his *Two Treatises of Government*. One of the more effective transmitters of Locke's ideas was Jean Jacques Burlamaqui (1694–1748), a Swiss-born jurist of Italian extraction who exerted a very great influence on several American founding fathers, especially on James Wilson. We know from Chinard's edition of *The Commonplace Book of Thomas Jefferson: A Repertory of His Ideas on Government* (Baltimore, 1926) that Jefferson had read and excerpted Wilson's pamphlet, *Considerations on the Nature and Extent of the Legislative Authority of the British Parliament* (1774), in which Wilson leaned heavily on Burlamaqui's *Principles of Natural and Politic Law*, first published in French in 1747. The first volume of this work was translated into English in 1748, and in 1769 Jefferson bought a copy of it in French.[38] It is fair to surmise that Burlamaqui's work was one of those "elementary books of public right" to which Jefferson referred when he described the views he was trying to "harmonize" while writing the Declaration.[39]

38. Marie Kimball, *Jefferson: The Road to Glory* (New York, 1943), p. 210.
39. Letter to Henry Lee, May 8, 1825, *The Writings of Thomas Jefferson*, ed. A. A. Lipscomb and A. E. Bergh (Washington, 1903), Volume XVI, pp. 118–119. (Hereafter this collection is sometimes referred to briefly as *"Writings."* However, the reader should not confuse this collection of Jefferson's writings with that edited under the same title by Paul Leicester Ford.) I use the word "surmise" because Jefferson refers only to the authors of these books as "Aristotle, Cicero, Locke, Sidney, etc." My surmise, therefore, is that Burlamaqui's book was one of the *cetera* to which Jefferson referred. And as to the colonists' familiarity with the works of Burlamaqui, it is of interest to find William Bradford writing James Madison in 1774 that "The Congress sits in the Carpenter's Hall in one room of which the City Library is kept & of which the Librarian tells me the Gentlemen make great & constant use. By which we may conjecture that their measures will be wisely plan'd since they debate on them like philosophers; for by what I was told Vattel, Barlemaqui [*sic*], Locke and Montesquie[u] seem to be the standar[d]s to which they refer either when

Burlamaqui's dependence on Locke's epistemology is evident in a number of respects. For example, he denies the existence of innate principles, but he believes in self-evident principles, asserting "that the most general and most important maxims of the law of nature are so clear and manifest, and have such a proportion to our ideas, and such an agreeableness to our nature, that so soon, as they are proposed to us, we instantly approve of them."[40] Burlamaqui's view about who can know these truths and how they can know them is also consonant with what we have seen in our discussion of Locke and Aquinas. It is therefore not surprising to find Burlamaqui saying that not all men are capable of discovering the principles of natural law and their consequences, and that there are some men "who, having taken a particular care to cultivate their minds, are qualified to enlighten others" by giving instructions to "the common run of mankind," who exhibit "rudeness and ignorance."

The word "rude," it will be recalled from the earlier section dealing with Aquinas's views on self-evidence, was applied by him to those who could not see the self-evidence of certain propositions, and he also speaks of them as ignorant. His Latin words are *"rudibus"* and *"ignoranti."* Locke applied similar words to those who failed to discern self-evident moral truth, even though he sometimes asserted that there were no self-evident moral principles. In a similar vein,

settling the rights of the Colonies or when a dispute arises on the justice or propriety of a measure," *The Papers of James Madison*, ed. W. T. Hutchinson and W. M. E. Rachal (Chicago, 1962–), Volume I, p. 126. For an account of the ideas of Burlamaqui and his impact on American Revolutionary thinkers, see the useful work of R. F. Harvey, *Jean Jacques Burlamaqui: A Liberal Tradition in American Constitutionalism* (Chapel Hill, 1937).

40. See Burlamaqui's *Principles of Natural and Politic Law*, trans. Thomas Nugent (Cambridge, Mass., 1807), Volume I (*The Principles of Natural Law*), p. 126. The passage appears in Part II, Chapter V, Section I of Volume I. For a French version see *Principes du droit naturel* (Genève et Coppenhague, 1762), p. 112.

Burlamaqui at one point exclaims about the "multitudes" of "stupid wretches, who lead a mere animal life, and are scarce able to distinguish three or four ideas, in order to form what is called ratiocination."[41] Can such "stupid wretches" see by the light of Locke's intuitive reason all of the truths listed as self-evident in the Declaration of Independence? It is very unlikely that they can if they have only four ideas. And if they cannot, what is to be said by the signers to someone who complains that the Declaration argues for the people's revolution from assumptions which many people cannot understand, much less intuit as true in Locke's sense? Could the signers really believe that *all men* had a sufficient grasp of *all* of the ideas in the so-called self-evident truths listed in the Declaration, "creation," "equal," "right," "liberty," and so on, so as to say that the people's knowledge of these truths was, in the language of Locke, "irresistible, and, like bright sunshine, force[d] itself immediately" upon them, leaving "no room for hesitation, doubt, or examination"? Certainly not all of the signers believed this.[42]

Burlamaqui insisted that one *"can (peut)* discover all [the principles of natural law], and deduce from them several duties, by that natural light, which to no man has been ever refused," and he added that "it is in this sense we are to under-

---

41. *Ibid.*, Part II, Chapter III, Section IV. On Locke, see below, p. 178, note 46.
42. Thus John Adams writes: "We often hear and read of free states, a free people, a free nation, a free country, a free kingdom, and even of free republics; and we understand, in general, what is intended, although every man may not be qualified to enter into philosophical disquisitions concerning the meaning, or to give a logical definition of the word liberty," *Defence of the Constitutions of Government of the United States of America, Works of John Adams,* ed. C. F. Adams (Boston, 1851), Volume IV, p. 401. The remark is relevant because of the Declaration's statement in the Rough Draft that it is undeniable that the right to preserve liberty is derived from the equal creation of man, as well as the statement in the final version that it is self-evident that men are endowed with the right to liberty. To see that this is self-evident, one would have to be able to do more than "understand, in general, what is intended" by the word "liberty." See Locke, *Essay,* Book IV, Chapter XII, Sections 14–15.

stand what is commonly said, that this law is naturally known to all mankind."[43] However, Burlamaqui's use of "can," which I have emphasized, was compatible with a man's being able to see self-evidence only after receiving "succours" from others qualified to enlighten him. It was Burlamaqui's awareness of the difficulty that some men might have in rationally perceiving the self-evidence of certain principles that led him to say that it was sufficient for some men of "middling capacities" to comprehend the principles when they were "explained" to them and "to feel the truth and necessity of the duties, that flow from them, by comparing them with the constitution of their own nature." And finally, when he confronts the possibility that there are "capacities of a still inferior order," he is compelled to say that "they are generally led by the impressions of example, custom, authority, or some present and sensible utility."[44]

It is necessary to understand Burlamaqui's use of the word "can" in his statement that every man can discover all the principles of natural law by natural light. And it is especially important to realize that although the enlightened few can and do know these principles in the strictest sense of "know" by using their own reason, the many are held responsible for knowing them even if they fail to know them for lack of intelligence or education. According to Burlamaqui, lesser minds are responsible for knowing these truths because they may receive them from more enlightened minds, even though lesser minds do not know them to be true by intuition or by deduction. According to Burlamaqui, inferior minds can also know the natural law through the impressions of example, custom, and authority, or even by seeing its utility. Therefore, Burlamaqui can support a form of élitism which says that only the few "really know" the principles of natural law and their duties and hence are able to dictate to others. And

43. Burlamaqui, *Principles of Natural Law,* Part II, Chapter V, Section 1.
44. *Ibid.,* Part II, Chapter V, Section II.

to lesser minds who say that they cannot or do not see the
self-evidence of an allegedly self-evident proposition, Burlamaqui will reply that they can have a second-class kind of
knowledge on the basis of example, custom, authority, or
utility. This makes it possible for Burlamaqui to hold that
lesser minds who cannot "really know" can know these truths
in some weaker sense of "know." Therefore, he continues, the
"law of nature is sufficiently notified to empower us to affirm,
that no man, at the age of discretion, and in his right senses,
can allege for a just excuse an invincible ignorance on this article."[45] It follows that since such people *can* know the truths
in question in Burlamaqui's second-class way, they may be
treated *as if* they know them in the first-class way that Locke
celebrated when he spoke of knowing such truths by bare intuition and being irresistibly forced to acknowledge them.
This is a practical implication of Burlamaqui's asserting that
so-called inferior capacities cannot *excuse* their ignorance of
the principles of natural law. If their ignorance is, as he says,
not "invincible," then they *can* know the principles; and if
they *can* know them, any failure on their part to perform the
duties prescribed by these principles is not excusable by an
appeal to their actual ignorance of the natural law.

Self-evidence and Utilitarianism

The upshot, then, of certain statements by Locke and by Burlamaqui is that they both depart from the anti-authoritarian-
ism so dramatically expressed in Locke's *Essay* when he says
that we may as rationally hope to see with other men's eyes as
to know by other men's understandings, and that the floating
of other men's opinions in our brains makes us not one jot
the more knowing, though they happen to be true.[46] As
we have seen in our discussion of Locke's *Reasonableness*

45. *Ibid.*
46. *Essay Concerning Human Understanding*, Book I, Chapter III, Section 24.

of Christianity, he was quite prepared to have "the day-labourers and tradesmen, the spinsters and dairy-maids" *believe without knowing* moral propositions they found in the Bible, saying: "Hearing plain commands is the sure and only course to bring them to obedience and practice. The greatest part cannot know, and therefore they must believe."[47] And Burlamaqui subscribed to essentially the same doctrine, except that he was willing to say that the day-laborers, tradesmen, spinsters, and dairy-maids *could know* propositions even if they had been led to their "knowledge" by impressions of example, custom, authority, and utility. The difference, however, between Locke and Burlamaqui on this point was purely terminological since Locke, like Burlamaqui, would have held his day-laborers and tradesmen, his spinsters and dairy-maids culpable if they violated precepts of the Scriptures, even though Locke believed that these lesser beings did not know these propositions.

It is amusing to note that pre-Christian thinkers such as Solon, Cicero, Confucius, Aristippus, Zeno, Epicurus, and Seneca were put by Locke in the same category as the day-laborers and dairy-maids simply because these great minds also failed to "know" the principles of natural law. Like the lesser beings mentioned by Burlamaqui, these great men were led to some of these principles by impressions of utility, convenience, or beauty since Locke writes: "The law of nature is the law of convenience too: and it is no wonder, that those men of parts, and studious of virtue (who had occasion to think on any particular part of it) should, by meditation, light on the right, even from the observable convenience and beauty of it; without making out its obligation from the true principles of the law of nature, and foundations of morality."[48] By contrast, as we have seen, Locke held that certain enlightened post-Christian thinkers managed to assent im-

47. *Works,* Volume VII, p. 146.
48. *Ibid.,* p. 142.

mediately to the moral precepts of Jesus, but as we have also seen, even they had not constructed a demonstrative system of morality. However, Locke tells us, the wisest of those who have read the New Testament "must acknowledge" that it presents "a complete rule of life" which "tends entirely to the good of mankind" and that "all would be happy, if all would practise it."[49] Whether this last proposition is true or not, it is not self-evident and therefore not an axiom from which Locke could have deduced theorems of morality. It is in the same category as Burlamaqui's statement that the precepts of natural law have "sensible utility" and Locke's own statement that they have "observable convenience and beauty." Locke did not believe that knowing of the happiness, utility, or convenience produced by following the precepts of natural law was tantamount to knowing the truth of those precepts. On the other hand, Locke did believe that revelation presents us with moral truths which, when they receive immediate assent, receive it only from the learned and the perceptive. And this makes it hard to defend him against the charge that his view of how moral truths are known is just as exploitable by "dictators of principles" as the doctrine of innate principles is.

Having argued that Locke, even though he believes the proposition that all men would be happy if they all lived in accordance with the natural law, does not regard this proposition as a *foundation* for morality, I want to say something now, however brief, about the question whether Locke is a utilitarian. In my opinion he is not, and it is reassuring to know that Henry Sidgwick held this opinion.[50] Some of the most striking evidence for it is to be found in the *Reasonableness of Christianity,* where Locke says quite explicitly that convenience, which I take to be equivalent to utility, *is*

49. *Ibid.,* p. 147.
50. Henry Sidgwick, *Outlines of the History of Ethics,* 5th ed. (London, 1906), pp. 175–178.

not the basis for accepting principles of natural law. Then there are all the passages in defense of the view that morality *can* be a demonstrative science and therefore that there must be axioms that are seen to be true immediately. Like Sidgwick, I admit that there are places where Locke claims that following the precepts of natural law will contribute to general happiness, but this is not enough to make him a utilitarian. I say this with full awareness of Locke's having said that "God . . . by an inseparable connexion joined virtue [the observance of natural law] and public happiness together, and made the practice thereof necessary to the preservation of society, and visibly beneficial to all with whom the virtuous man has to do."[51] Indeed, I take this as supporting the view that Locke is *not* a utilitarian because I do not regard the "inseparable connexion" to which Locke refers as showing that the predicate "true moral precept" is synonymous with "precept the following of which promotes the general happiness." According to most utilitarians, the former phrase *means the same as* the latter, whereas for Locke the "inseparable connexion" between virtue and public happiness is merely causal, a fact of nature. I reiterate that when Locke spoke of presenting the foundations of morality, he meant giving a reason why, for example, "one should do as he would be done unto," and that giving a reason why, as he says explicitly, is to prove the proposition by giving a self-evident proposition from which it may be deduced.[52] In further support of my interpretation, I should like to note that

51. *Essay Concerning Human Understanding*, Book I, Chapter II, Section 6. Also see *Essays on the Law of Nature*, Essay VIII *passim*.

52. *Essay*, Book I, Chapter II, Section 4. ". . . should that most unshaken rule of morality and foundation of all social vitrue, 'That one should do as he would be done unto,' be proposed to one who never heard of it before, but yet is of capacity to understand its meaning; might he not without any absurdity ask a reason why? And were not he that proposed it bound to make out the truth and reasonableness of it to him? . . . So that the truth of all these moral rules plainly depends upon some other antecedent to them, and from which they must be *deduced*."

if one tries to establish the golden rule by means of an argument which begins with these two premises: (1) *A moral precept the following of which promotes the general happiness is a true moral precept;* and (2) *The golden rule is a precept the following of which promotes the general happiness,* then one cannot *prove,* in the sense required by Locke, (3) *The golden rule is a true moral precept.* And the reason why Locke cannot prove or demonstrate (3) in this way is that the second premise is not self-evident or undeniable. Even if one should hold that Locke regards the first premise as self-evident—which I doubt—it would be hard to see how Locke could regard the second as self-evident. It asserts that if men were to do certain things, they would promote general happiness; and such a statement is hardly in the same category as "$1 + 1 = 2$."[53] This, I think, constitutes a refutation of one version of the view that Locke is a utilitarian and to that extent reinforces the claim that he is what is sometimes called a rational intuitionist.

Failure to see that Locke is an intuitionist has been, as Sidgwick once said, connected with the mistaken belief that "the founder of English empiricism must necessarily have been hostile to 'intuitional' ethics."[54] And this misinterpretation of Locke has been indirectly responsible for a failure on the part of some of his readers to observe the anti-democratic potentialities of his theory of morals and natural law. Perhaps the most striking example of this kind of misinterpretation is to be found in the writing of John Stuart Mill. In his essay, "Coleridge," Mill attributes to Locke the view that there are "no truths cognizable by the mind's inward light, and grounded on intuitive evidence."[55] So eager was Mill to

53. For an interesting effort to show that Locke was in some sense a utilitarian, see A. P. Brogan, "John Locke and Utilitarianism," *Ethics,* LXIX (1959): 79–93.

54. Sidgwick, *op. cit.,* p. 175.

55. J. S. Mill, *Collected Works* (Toronto, 1969), Volume X, p. 125. This volume is edited by J. M. Robson.

claim Locke as a leader of the forces who opposed Coleridge's intuitionism that Mill failed to see the intuitionistic elements in Locke's thinking. Mill tried his hardest to undermine intuitionistic rationalism in all fields by holding that all our knowledge—even our logical and mathematical knowledge— was empirical; and like Locke, Mill tried to "politicize" his epistemology by showing that those who held opposing views advocated a doctrine which stood in the way of the reformer. Mill believed firmly that the difference between the schools of philosophy which he called that of "Intuition" and that of "Experience," the latter being his own, "is not a mere matter of abstract speculation; it is full of practical consequences, and lies at the foundation of all the greatest differences of practical opinion in an age of progress."[56] Mill's main point was that the reformer must continually demand that certain established things be changed and therefore that they not be regarded as "necessary" and "indefeasible." But, Mill continues, the intuitionist, by defending the existence of necessary and indefeasible truths, becomes an object of the reformer's hostility because the intuitionist subscribes to "a philosophy which is addicted to holding up favourite doctrines as intuitive truths, and deems intuition to be the voice of Nature and of God, speaking with an authority higher than that of our reason."[57]

I wish to emphasize that insofar as Mill claims Locke as an ally in the onslaught against intuitionism Mill glossed over the sharp distinction made by Locke between innate principles and intuitive principles. Indeed, because Mill glossed over this distinction, he failed to realize that when he attacked intuitionism, he also attacked Locke, the defender of intuition, who was not, as I have argued, a utilitarian. The intellectual gulf between Mill and Locke on this issue is dramati-

56. J. S. Mill, *Autobiography*, ed. J. J. Coss (New York, 1924), pp. 191–192.
57. *Ibid.*, p. 192.

cally illustrated by Mill's statement in his essay *On Liberty:* "I forego any advantage which could be derived to my argument from the idea of abstract right, as a thing independent of utility. I regard utility as the ultimate appeal on ethical questions." But I think that in his essay on Coleridge, Mill underestimated this gulf. In subscribing to utilitarianism Mill seemed to think that he could establish moral precepts without using intuition, whereas we have seen that Locke did not think so, when he was using the word "establish" in a very strict sense. Therefore, if Mill held that appealing to intuition rather than experience made a thinker conservative and anti-democratic because such a thinker would deem "intuition to be the voice of Nature and God, speaking with an authority higher than that of our reason," Mill would have had a hard time bringing Locke into his own camp on several grounds that we have made sufficiently obvious. In effect, Mill seems to have said to the people: "Don't listen to self-appointed dictators of alleged *intuitive* principles, but do listen to experience." In effect, Locke said to the people: "Don't listen to self-appointed dictators of alleged *innate* principles, but do listen to the voice of God as revealed by Jesus, and do listen to the learned few who can come closer than you can to intuiting the moral principles revealed by Jesus and closer to forming a system of demonstrative morality than you can come."

On the other hand, even though we may contrast Locke the intuitionist and Mill the utilitarian on the grounds I have just presented, Mill's utilitarianism contained a qualification that must not be forgotten by those who might be inclined to see *him* as an epistemological tribune of *all the people*. Just after informing us that he regards utility as the ultimate appeal on ethical questions, he tells us: "but it must be utility in the largest sense, grounded on the permanent interests of man as a progressive being. Those interests, I contend, authorize the subjection of individual spontaneity to external control, only in respect to those actions of each, which concern the interests of other people."

What, we are entitled to ask, is a progressive being? But even if we cannot get an acceptable answer, we are entitled to observe that Mill's progressive being is the counterpart of Aquinas's learned man, Locke's perceptive man, and Burlamaqui's natural and undepraved man. Just as Aquinas and Locke say, in effect, that self-evidence is *self-evidence to the learned,* so Mill says that utility is *utility to the progressive.* And the reason for this is clear. Just as intuitionists don't want to have their moral principles rest on the intuitions of any being whatever, so Mill doesn't want his to rest on the utility that may be reaped by a being who lacks qualities that might well have coincided with some of those possessed by Locke's accredited seers of self-evidence. One may add that if Locke *had been* a utilitarian in the way in which he linked virtue with public happiness, he could have incorporated his political prejudices into that doctrine by a sufficiently narrow definition of the word "public."

Having spent so much time on the epistemology of the doctrine of natural law as defended by Locke, I want to assure the reader that I have not forgotten that I am writing a book on American thought. I also want to say that I am preparing the way for showing that the enunciation of "self-evident" truths in the Declaration of Independence revealed an acceptance of an epistemology of natural law which was basically Lockean and rationalistic in tendency, and that when the word "self-evident" appeared in the Declaration, it was used as it had been by Locke and by other rationalistic theorists of natural law. I have tried to show that in spite of Locke's protestations about how dictators of principles could make use of the doctrine of innate principles but could *not* make similar use of the doctrine of self-evident principles, the fact is that the latter doctrine was exploitable by the few who might seek to take advantage of the many. The theory of self-evident principles, like other theories of knowledge, contains "jokers," as they are called by card-players, which could have been used so as to favor "the *right* people" as opposed to "*the* people." So it is obviously important that we proceed to see what American revolutionaries thought about an epistemology of self-evident principles which distinguished between what was self-evident to the rational, perceptive few but not to the "multitude of stupid wretches."[58] We should not be surprised to find some of them prepared to accept an epistemology of self-evident truth which was consonant with John Adams's favorable quotation of the following passage in a note by Barbeyrac to Pufendorf's *Law of Nature and Nations:* "When we speak of a tyrant that may lawfully be dethroned by the people, we do not mean by the word *people,* the vile populace or rabble of the country, nor the cabal of a small number of factious persons, but the greater and more judicious part of the subjects, of all ranks."[59] Nor should we be surprised to find Burlamaqui using almost the same words *without* indicating that he is quoting from Barbeyrac.

Burlamaqui, who held with Aquinas and Locke that the rude, the ignorant, and the stupid could not see the truths of natural law, refused to identify *the people,* who have a right

---

58. Many of the points made in this chapter about Aquinas and Locke on self-evidence were made by me in my "Original Sin, Natural Law, and Politics," *Partisan Review* (Spring 1956): 218–236 and in an expanded version of that article which formed the "Epilogue for 1957" to a paperback edition of my *Social Thought in America* (Boston: Beacon Press, 1957). This also appears in a paperback edition published by Oxford University Press in 1976.

59. John Adams, *Works,* Volume IV, p. 82. Adams's reference is to Pufendorf, Book VII, Chapter VIII, Sections 5 and 6 as well as to Barbeyrac's note on Section 6. However, the passage I have reproduced is from Barbeyrac's note to the first sentence of Section 6.

to resist or depose a tyrant, with *"la vile populace ou la ca-naille du Païs."*[60] In the same vein, Locke's eighteenth-century editor, Thomas Elrington, argues that Locke used the term "people" "to signify only those who were possessed of such property as was sufficient to secure their fidelity to the interests of the state, and to make it probable that they were qualified to judge of those interests as far as was requisite for the due performance of the duty entrusted to them."[61] Elrington is also quick to ask a profound question after Locke has asserted that while a child lacks an understanding to direct his own will, "he is not to have any will of his own to follow: He that *understands* for him, must *will* for him too; he must prescribe to his will, and regulate his actions."[62] Elrington asks: "May not this incapacitating deficiency of understanding exist among adults as well as minors? and if any class of adults be, from inevitable circumstances, inferior in point of intellectual attainments, or any other qualities requisite to make them *competent* and *unprejudiced* judges of right and wrong in matters of polity, ought they not be in the same proportion inferior in political power?"[63]

It is hard, therefore, to avoid the conclusion that many philosophical tutors of our founding fathers built into their theories of *how we know* the natural law a requirement which was the analogue of property qualifications for voters. I say "the analogue" with confidence, but there are those who might also argue for a logically stronger proposition, namely, that these philosophical tutors and many of their American students thought (1) that there was a causal connection be-

---

60. *Principes du droit politique* (*Principles of Politic Law*), Part II, Chapter VI, Section XXIX.

61. Thomas Elrington, in his annotated edition of Locke's *Second Treatise* (Dublin, 1798), "Advertisement," p. v.

62. *Second Treatise,* Section 58.

63. Elrington, *op. cit.,* note to Section 58. See P. Laslett's reference to this note by Elrington in the former's edition of Locke's *Two Treatises of Government,* 2nd ed. (Cambridge, England, 1970), p. 324.

tween possessing the intellectual qualifications for knowing moral truths and the property qualifications for, as it were, entering electoral booths and (2) that *the people,* as distinct from the rabble, possessed both of these qualifications. Which qualification came first for these thinkers is a chicken-egg question. It is sufficient for our purposes to know that the qualifications were thought by some to be causally linked and also to know that the phrase "the people" often referred to a narrow class.[64] If the people were identified as those who possessed the intellectual capacity to see the truths of natural law, then those who held that the natural law was an instrument of the people so identified, avoided a problem that is hard to avoid when one identifies the people with *all* of the people. For if it takes intellectual qualifications that *not* all of the people possess to know the moral truths upon which the argument for government by *all* of the people rests, then some, and perhaps the majority, of the people must be asked to accept that argument on trust. They must trust the few who allegedly know moral truths that they, the majority of the people, do not know. But if the majority of the people do not know the truths allegedly known by their leaders, by what signs will they know which dictator of principles is to be trusted? We have seen that Locke thought that Jesus could be trusted to produce true moral precepts because his miracles showed that he was a messenger of God. But what miracles could the many attribute to the few who supposedly saw the moral principles upon which the rule of the many supposedly rested? The question is as difficult as it is profound for anyone who thinks about the moral foundations of a democracy of *all* of the people.

64. "By 'people' most seventeenth-century Republicans had meant people of some state and consequence in the community. Cobblers, tinkers, or fishermen were not people but *scum* to Whigs like James Tyrrell—who used the term—to Locke, Withers, and Trenchard," Caroline Robbins, *The Eighteenth-Century Commonwealthman* (Cambridge, Mass., 1959), p. 16.

I should emphasize that I am concerned with the question whether all of the people were thought by the revolutionaries to have the power to see the self-evidence of the fundamental principles of *morality,* and not with the question whether all the people have a power to see the truth of technical statements that may be involved in a democracy's coming to a vital decision. We have become accustomed to the idea that all of the people cannot be authorities in nuclear strategy and that they must rely in great measure on so-called experts in that area. But we are not accustomed to hear that according to our founding fathers, many, and perhaps a majority, of the people are incapable of seeing the self-evidence of moral truths upon which our Revolution and the formation of our government supposedly rested. Yet this was part of the epistemology of natural law as expounded by some of its most famous advocates in England and on the Continent, and the question that I shall discuss later on is whether this form of epistemological élitism was adopted by American followers of Locke and Burlamaqui. We have already seen that John Adams implicitly acknowledged that most people could not see the self-evidence of moral truths about liberty for want of a thorough grasp of what "liberty" meant.[65] But what about some of the others, for example, Jefferson, ostensibly a greater friend of all the people? To answer the query we must press on further, bearing in mind that since the Declaration appealed to a Lockean rationalism in ethics, then according to the signers, seeing self-evidence was indispensable for seeing the moral truths upon which the Revolution rested. For, like Locke, our revolutionaries were not utilitarians; they did not think that the principles of natural law were empirical propositions or that they could be established by the so-called inductive methods of certain utilitarians.

65. See above, note 42.

Locke, the Laboring Classes, and Divine Sanctions

Although I have written at length about Locke's views on rational moral truth and on their possible political impact, I should like to say a few words about the views of Professor C. B. McPherson, who has said certain things on matters that I have discussed. McPherson has focused on Locke's *Reasonableness of Christianity* mainly to show that when Locke calls attention to the utility of the Christian doctrine of rewards and punishments, he has his eye primarily on the laboring classes: "The implication is plain: the labouring class, beyond all others, is incapable of living a rational life. One can detect a shade of difference in his attitude towards the employed and the unemployed. The idle poor he seems to have regarded as depraved by choice; the labouring poor as simply incapable of a fully rational life because of their unfortunate position. But whether by their own fault or not, members of the labouring class did not have, could not be expected to have, and were not entitled to have, full membership in political society; they did not and could not live a fully rational life."[66]

In the course of coming to this conclusion, McPherson says a number of things which are compatible with or which support my own point of view, but there are certain other points on which I cannot altogether agree with him. I begin by pointing out that it is questionable whether Locke held that the laboring poor could not live a fully rational life. It is true that they might not be able to produce a demonstrative system of morality, but according to Locke, *that* would not prevent them from living a fully rational life since if it did, neither Locke nor any other mortal could lead a *fully* ra-

66. C. B. McPherson, *The Political Theory of Possessive Individualism: Hobbes to Locke* (New York, 1967, paperback), p. 226.

tional life. Furthermore, if the poor were to follow fully, in the sense of comply fully with, the moral principles of the Gospel, they *might be* said by Locke to lead a fully rational life because Locke holds that the Gospel presented them with moral principles which were rational truths, even though no one might see that they were or had as yet incorporated them in a demonstrative system. On the other hand, how can one suppose that Locke held that *anyone* could fully comply with the moral principles of the Gospel, whether he was a laborer, a merchant, or a philosopher, when Locke spoke so vehemently of man's capacity to be biased, vicious, prejudiced, and, in general, so apt to violate or fail to understand the law of nature as to make it necessary for him and his fellow men to leave the state of nature for civil society?

I infer, therefore, that living a fully rational life is identified by McPherson with *knowing the truth* of moral propositions. Yet, though I myself have asserted that according to Locke, some men of elevated understanding would immediately assent to the moral truths of Jesus, I have also pointed out that Locke held that some men of elevated understanding might not be able to *discover* those moral truths and, *to that extent,* have no advantage over a laborer in the realm of morals. Moreover, it is hard to argue that Locke singled out the laboring poor as the *only* class capable of coming to erroneous beliefs, moral or otherwise. One may see this in Book IV, Chapter XX of the *Essay,* part of which McPherson cites. There Locke, in the course of discussing the sources of error, first takes up the class of persons who fail to discover either proofs "nowhere extant" or proofs which exist. Under this head, he first lists those who lack the *opportunity* to find proofs of either kind, saying that "these men's opportunities of knowledge and inquiry are commonly as narrow as their fortunes; and their understandings are but little instructed, when all their whole time and pains is laid out to still the croaking of their own bellies, or the cries of their children."

A man "who drudges on all his life in a laborious trade," Locke goes on, should not be expected to be "more knowing in the variety of things done in the world than a pack-horse, who is driven constantly forwards and backwards in a narrow lane and dirty road, only to market, should be skilled in the geography of the country." Finally, Locke draws a general conclusion about those who, through lack of opportunity to discover proofs, fall into error because of the narrowness of their fortunes, saying that "the greatest part of men, having much to do to get the means of living, are not in a condition to look after those of learned and laborious inquiries." Still, just after having said this, Locke affirms: *"No man* is so wholly taken up with the attendance on the means of living, as to have no spare time at all to think of his soul, and inform himself in matters of religion. Were men as intent upon this as they are on things of lower concernment, there are none so enslaved to the necessities of life who might not find many vacancies that might be husbanded to this advantage of their knowledge."[67]

Now I come to another class of persons whom Locke lists among those who fall into error. They are not poor laborers, who have *no opportunity* to engage in inquiry, but rather rich persons who *lack the will* to engage in it. "Their hot pursuit of pleasure, or constant drudgery in business, engages some men's thoughts elsewhere: laziness and oscitancy in general, or a particular aversion for books, study, and meditation, keep others from any serious thoughts at all; and some out of fear that an impartial inquiry would not favour those opinions which best suit their prejudices, lives, and designs, content themselves, without examination, to take upon trust what they find convenient and in fashion." Locke goes on to say that he does not understand how men "whose plentiful fortunes allow them leisure to improve their understandings,

---

67. *Essay,* Book IV, Chapter XX, Sections 2–3. The emphasis is mine.

can satisfy themselves with a lazy ignorance." But he warns "those who call themselves gentlemen, That, however they may think credit, respect, power, and authority the concomitants of their birth and fortune, yet they will find all these still carried away from them by men of lower condition, who surpass them in knowledge. They who are blind will always be led by those that see, or else fall into the ditch: and he is certainly the most subjected, the most enslaved, who is so in his understanding." So, just as Locke takes occasion earlier in this chapter of the *Essay* to tell the busy laborer that he should find time to think of his soul and to inform himself in matters of religion, he now advises the lazy gentlemen who take care to appear always in neat and splendid clothes but "suffer their minds to appear abroad in a piebald livery of coarse patches and borrowed shreds . . . how unreasonable this is for men that ever think of a future state, and their concernment in it, which no rational man can avoid to do sometimes."[68]

From these statements by Locke I conclude that the laboring poor are not, according to him, the only persons who are incapable of living a fully rational life. I am not prepared to say on the basis of these passages that it is "plain" that he holds that "the labouring class, *beyond all others* [my emphasis], is incapable of living a [fully?] rational life." I do not find Locke holding that the busy, poor laborer's *lack of opportunity* makes him *incapable* of knowing true moral principles, whereas the lazy gentleman's *lack of will does not* make *him incapable* of knowing true moral principles. If both a will to inquire and an opportunity to do so are necessary conditions for being able to know the religious moral truth that is so central in Locke's *Reasonableness of Christianity,* then those who lack the will *and* those who lack the

68. *Ibid.,* Book IV, Chapter XX, Section 6.

opportunity are both incapacitated, so far as I can see; and it becomes difficult to say that the laboring class is incapacitated "beyond all others" on the basis of what Locke says in Book IV, Chapter XX, Sections 2–6, though I take note of McPherson's citation only of Sections 2 and 3 which, unlike 6, do not refer to the error-making, lazy rich.

I come now to a second place where I think McPherson has not accurately represented Locke's thought. McPherson holds that Locke's alleged belief—just considered—that the laboring class, beyond all others, is incapable of living a rational life, is *implied* by Locke's "repeated emphasis on the necessity of the labouring class being brought to obedience by believing in divine rewards and punishments."[69] Here my criticism is connected with Locke's previously quoted statement that no man can avoid thinking of a future state. And the reason why *no* man—not just poor laborers—can avoid doing this, from Locke's point of view, is that he regards the moral law as divine and therefore sanctioned by adequate rewards and punishments. Locke holds this even though he also holds that the moral law is perceivable by reason since, as Sidgwick points out, he "rejects the view that the mere apprehension by the reason of the obligatoriness of certain rules is, or ought to be, a sufficient motive to their performance, apart from the foreseen consequences to the individual of observing or neglecting them."[70] The most striking evidence for this is to be found in the following passage: "That God has given a rule whereby men should govern themselves, I think there is nobody so brutish as to deny. He has a right to do it; we are his creatures: he has goodness and wisdom to direct our actions to that which is best: and he has power to enforce it by rewards and punishments of infinite weight and duration in another life; for nobody can take us out of his hands.

69. McPherson, *op. cit.,* p. 226.
70. Sidgwick, *op. cit.,* p. 176.

This is the only true touchstone of moral rectitude; and, by comparing them to this law, it is that men judge of the most considerable moral good or evil of their actions; that is, whether, as duties or sins, they are like to procure them happiness or misery from the hands of the ALMIGHTY."[71] This passage makes abundantly clear that, according to Locke, *everyone,* and not merely the laboring poor, must be brought to obedience by believing in divine rewards and punishments.

Having differed from McPherson on these matters, I want to emphasize that I do not deny that Locke was aware that the mental powers of men exhibited great differences that he often correlated with social and economic position, as when he says that one does not have to visit "Westminster Hall or the Exchange on the one hand" or the "Alms-houses or Bedlam on the other" to see that some people are better than others at using the evidence of probabilities, carrying an argument in their heads, or determining on which side the strongest proofs lie.[72] And I have also remarked that in the *Reasonableness of Christianity,* he holds that those who can reason well can be taught morality in a less authoritarian way than those who cannot. But I do not think we can say of Locke what McPherson seems to say of him, namely, that because he held that *only* the laboring poor are brought to obedience by divine rewards and punishments, he also held that the laboring class, beyond all others, is incapable of living a fully rational life. This statement is false if only because Locke did *not* hold that *only* the laboring poor are brought to obedience by divine rewards and punishments, but I should also challenge it by asserting that Locke did *not* hold that the laboring class, beyond all others, is incapable of living a fully rational life.

It may be that McPherson is aware that Locke said in his

71. *Essay,* Book II, Chapter XXVIII, Section 8.
72. *Ibid.,* Book IV, Chapter XX, Section 5.

Essay what I have already quoted about divine rewards and punishments as well as the following: "God . . . has in his hand rewards and punishments, and power enough to call to account the proudest offender."[73] Nevertheless, McPherson may believe that this piece of news, so to speak, is *more frequently* published by Locke in an effort to advocate the obedience of the laboring poor than to advocate the obedience of other members of society, and that this greater frequency somehow shows that Locke had the laboring poor in the forefront of his mind when he warned of God's rewards and punishments in the *Reasonableness of Christianity*. However, there are only two passages that McPherson quotes from that work as examples of Locke's "repeated emphasis" on the need to bring the laboring poor to obedience by warning them of divine sanctions,[74] and they are not sufficiently emphatic in singling out the poor to make us forget Locke's unqualified view that *all* persons—even the proudest—may be called to account by the use of divine sanctions. Furthermore, that avid reader of Locke, John Adams, does not, in the following passage, single out the laboring poor as especially in need of divine sanctions when it comes to learning and following the principles of natural law: "One great advantage of the Christian religion is that it brings the great principle of the law of nature and nations, Love your neighbour as yourself, and do to others as you would that others should do to you, to the knowledge, belief and veneration of the whole people. Children, servants, women and men are all professors in the science of public as well as private morality. No other institution for education, no kind of political discipline, could diffuse this kind of necessary information, so universally among all ranks and descriptions of citizens. The duties and rights of the man and the citizen are thus taught, from early

73. *Ibid.*, Book I, Chapter II, Section 6.
74. McPherson, *op. cit.*, pp. 224–226.

infancy to every creature. The sanctions of a future life are thus added to the observance of civil and political as well as domestic and private duties. Prudence, justice, temperance and fortitude, are thus taught to be the means and conditions of future as well as present happiness."[75]

75. *Diary and Autobiography of John Adams*, ed. L. H. Butterfield (Cambridge, Mass., 1962), Volume 3, pp. 240–241.

Self-evident Truth
and the Founding Fathers

For obvious reasons, it is not easy to discover what *all* American revolutionary thinkers held concerning an epistemology of self-evident principles of the kind we have been discussing, and I shall therefore limit my discussion to major figures who gave the matter some thought. But before beginning that discussion I want to emphasize that we must first distinguish between the question whether someone believed that there were self-evident moral principles and the question whether he thought, as Locke and Burlamaqui did, that relatively few people did or could see the self-evidence of those principles. I shall begin this chapter by concentrating on the first question while examining Jefferson's views because of the importance of the Declaration in catapulting the word "self-evident" out of the pages of Locke and into the language of American politics. This means that I shall be concentrating on a period in Jefferson's life when, as it seems to me, he was under the influence of what may be called an intuitionistic or a rationalistic view of morality, according to which we use our intuitive reason in perceiving self-evident truths of natural law.

Self-evidence and Equality in Locke

Before turning to Jefferson's own scrappy and sporadic discussions of the kind of truth the final version of the Declaration called self-evident, it would be well to consider some of the more proximate sources of his thinking on this subject. In one of his few specific statements about the influences on his writing of the Declaration, Jefferson mentions "elementary books of public right, as Aristotle, Cicero, Locke, Sidney, etc."[1] However, even though Aristotle may have been the ultimate source of Locke's doctrine that science begins with self-evident truth because Aristotle insists that the first principles of science must be "immediate,"[2] there is relatively little discussion of that kind of question in Aristotle's *Politics,* which must have been the book by him on public right to which Jefferson refers. Also, I doubt whether Jefferson relied on Cicero's writing on public right for material on either undeniable or self-evident truth, whereas the books on public right by Sidney and Locke *did* contain material on self-evident truth which might well have entered Jefferson's mind while signing the Declaration, though we must remember his

1. *Writings of Thomas Jefferson,* Volume XVI, pp. 118–119.
2. See Aristotle, *Posterior Analytics,* 71 B 20–22, where he says that the premises of demonstrated knowledge must be, among other things, "immediate." See also 72 A 8, "An immediate proposition is one which has no other proposition prior to it," in *The Works of Aristotle* (Oxford, 1928), Volume I. It is worth adding here that although Aristotle thinks of immediate propositions as needing no proof in which they are derived from logically prior propositions by the interposition of *middle* or, as it were, *mediating* terms, he does not call such propositions self-evident. Furthermore, although Aristotle distinguishes between things which are "more knowable and obvious to us" and those "which are more knowable by nature" (*Physics,* 184 A; *Works,* Volume II), he does not, as Aquinas does, speak of some propositions being *self-evident in themselves* by contrast to being *self-evident to us.* I am indebted for this information about Aristotle to Professors Harold Cherniss, Marion Soreth, and Nicholas White.

statement that he "turned to neither book nor pamphlet while writing it."[3]

Like Jefferson, Algernon Sidney was no professional epistemologist, but in his *Discourses Concerning Government* we find an epistemological passage which deserves some notice here. In the course of attacking Sir Robert Filmer's *Patriarcha,* Sidney has occasion to point out that Filmer had tried to smear the principles of liberty by saying that they were espoused by "school divines." In response, Sidney asserts that the Schoolmen were merely espousing a "common notion" or proposition which "all men saw." He even goes so far as to say that the proposition in question was like an axiom of Euclid, from which Euclid proved other propositions "as were less obvious to the understanding." In other

3. Letter to James Madison, August 30, 1823, *Writings,* Volume XV, p. 462. In doubting that Jefferson relied on Cicero, I do not mean to imply that Jefferson was not influenced by the famous passage in Book III, Chapter 22 of *De republica,* where Cicero asserts that there will not be different natural laws at different places or times but that "one eternal and unchangeable law will be valid for all nations and all times." Perhaps Jefferson was. I am rather remarking on Cicero's failure to speak of the *self-evidence* of the law of nature in that work or in *De legibus.* True, Cicero does speak in *De republica* of a violator of the law as "denying his human nature" in the Loeb translation of *"naturam hominis aspernatus"* (which might better be translated as "rejecting his human nature"). But there is no talk about self-evidence in this passage. Furthermore, in his *Tusculan Disputations,* Book I, Chapter XIII, Cicero writes: "But in every inquiry the unanimity of the races of the world must be regarded as a law of nature" (*"omni autem in re consensio omnium gentium lex naturae putanda est"*). Grotius, in *De jure belli ac pacis,* (Book I, Chapter I, Section XII), lists this among *a posteriori* proofs of something's being according to the law of nature. However, he contrasts such proofs invidiously with *a priori* proofs which consist "in demonstrating the necessary agreement or disagreement of anything with a rational and social nature." And, of course, Locke vehemently attacks universal consent as a basis for the assertion that there are innate principles. See his *Essay,* Book I, Chapter I, Section 4. It will also be recalled that Locke in his *Essays on the Law of Nature* also attacked the idea that "the general consent of men" is a basis for accepting principles of natural law. See his views on *"Vox populi vox Dei"* in the passage identified above in Chapter 1, note 25.

words, the axioms were self-evident in the parlance of Locke; and to make matters more interesting, Sidney refers to these axioms as truths which are "undeniable," as Locke did in his *Reasonableness of Christianity*, and this, as we have seen, was the very adjective Jefferson applied in the Rough Draft of the Declaration to truths called "self-evident" in the final version. But when Sidney calls truths "undeniable" he makes clear that he is speaking elliptically and that what he means, in fuller terms, is that they are "denied by none, but such as were degenerated into beasts," which means, of course, those who had lost their *reason*. He also says that they are statements "which none could deny that did not renounce common sense,"[4] a phrase that Jefferson might have been recalling when he wrote Henry Lee that he wished, in the Declaration, "to place before mankind the common sense of the subject."[5]

This brings me to a far more important antecedent of the Declaration's philosophical truths, namely, Locke's *Two Treatises of Government*. In Jefferson's letter of 1823 to Madison, he reports Richard Henry Lee's charge that the Declaration had been "copied from Locke's treatise on government"—undoubtedly the second of Locke's two treatises, for the second was more directly concerned with matters treated in the Declaration. And it was this charge of "copying" that Jefferson dealt with by saying that he had turned to neither book nor pamphlet while writing the Declaration.

4. Algernon Sidney, *Discourses Concerning Government* 3rd ed. (London, 1751), Chapter I, Section II. The first edition appeared in 1698. I have used a reprint published in 1968 by Gregg International Publishers in England. The passages referred to appear on p. 5. Sidney's admirer, John Adams says, after listing what he calls "revolution principles," like "all men by nature are equal," that it is astonishing that writers who call themselves friends of government "should in this age and country be so inconsistent with themselves, so indiscreet, so immodest, as to insinuate a doubt concerning them," *Works*, Volume IV, p. 15.
5. See note 1 above.

Still, we do have Jefferson's word that he was trying to harmonize the sentiments he found in books of public right like Locke's. We know that in 1769 Locke's "On Government" was ordered by him from a London bookseller along with Burlamaqui's *"Le Droit naturel"* and other volumes of interest[6] to students of Jefferson's ideas, and we know that he wrote a correspondent in 1790 that "Locke's little book on government, is perfect as far as it goes."[7]

In the light of this evidence and of certain striking similarities of expression which go under the name of "internal evidence," there is little doubt in my mind that Jefferson had read Locke's *Second Treatise* carefully before writing the Declaration and that he had been influenced by what Locke had said there, in particular by passages in which Locke *freely uses* the concept of self-evident truth. I emphasize the phrase "freely uses" in order to make clear that the *Second Treatise* is not much concerned with the theory of knowledge, with telling us what a self-evident truth is, with the question whether there are or can be self-evident practical principles, or with the question whether morality is or can be a demonstrative science. In my opinion, if Locke had doubts on these questions, they were soft-pedaled in the *Second Treatise*, and he seems as firmly convinced there as Aquinas was in his *Treatise on Law* that there are self-evident practical principles. For example, Locke said in his *Second Treatise* that there is "nothing more evident, than that creatures of the same species and rank promiscuously born to all the same advantages of nature, and the use of the same faculties, *should* [my emphasis] also be equal one amongst another without subordination or subjection, unless the Lord and Master of them all, should by any manifest declaration of his will set one above another, and confer on him by an evident and clear appointment an undoubted

6. Kimball, *Jefferson: The Road to Glory*, p. 210.
7. *Writings*, Volume VIII, p. 31.

right to dominion and sovereignty."[8] When Locke said that there was "nothing more evident," he meant that the proposition was *self-evident,* as may be seen in his discussion "Of the Degrees of Our Knowledge" in the second chapter of Book IV of his *Essay.* There it is clear that he holds that a self-evident truth possesses the greatest amount of evidence that can be supplied for a truth.[9] And for anyone who might doubt that Locke is attributing self-evidence to a *practical* truth in the *Second Treatise,* I have emphasized the word "should" in the quotation. With his usual acumen, Sidgwick noticed this normative word and paraphrased the proposition to which self-evidence is attributed as follows: "God . . . has made men similar in nature and faculties, *therefore* they are *to be* [my emphasis] regarded as mutually independent."[10] Here the gerundive, "to be regarded," is clearly moral.

Another way of formulating Locke's allegedly self-evident principle in the *Second Treatise* is as follows: Because all men have been created equal in the sense of having been given the same nature and the same advantages, they should also be treated as equal in the sense that no one of them should depend on the will of any other man (unless God has by a manifest declaration given one man dominion or authority over others). Now I want to make some comments on

8. *Second Treatise,* Chapter II, Section 4. This passage was virtually quoted in full by James Otis in his famous pamphlet, *The Rights of the British Colonies Asserted and Proved* (1764), reprinted in B. Bailyn, *Pamphlets of the American Revolution: 1750–1776* (Cambridge, Mass., 1965), Volume I (1750–1765), p. 440. On Locke's doubts, see below, p. 178, note 46.

9. See notes 11, 12, and 13 of Chapter 1 of the present work, which identify the places of certain passages relevant to this point after they have been quoted in the text.

10. In my "Original Sin, Natural Law, and Politics" (see above Chapter 1, note 58) I called attention to the moral "should" without giving credit to Sidgwick for having observed it. P. Laslett in his edition of Locke's *Two Treatises* (first published in 1960, Cambridge, Eng.) also calls attention to the "should" without referring to any other comment on it. See the 1970 reprint of Laslett's edition, p. 287, note 11; also Sidgwick's *Outlines of the History of Ethics,* p. 178.

the statement so formulated, and the first point I should like to make about it is purely logical. I have converted Locke's statement into a "because"-statement and in so doing have produced an equivalent which implies its own antecedent, that all men *have been created* equal in the sense of having been given the same nature. It also implies its own consequent, that all men *should be* treated as equal in the sense that no one of them should depend on the will of any other man (unless God has by a manifest declaration given one man dominion or authority over others). And although Locke does not explicitly attribute self-evidence to the antecedent of the "because"-statement, in the sentence which immediately follows the self-evident principle that I have rendered as a "because"-statement, Locke says respectfully that the "judicious Hooker" looks upon the equality of men by nature as evident in itself and beyond all question. I infer from this that Locke agreed with Hooker in attributing self-evidence to the proposition asserting the equality of men by nature.[11]

But what proposition is Locke talking about when he speaks of "this equality of men by nature"? It is, I think, the proposition that God has given all of us the same nature, by which Locke means that we have all been put into the same species or natural kind. But if Locke meant to associate himself with Hooker in asserting the self-evidence of this proposition, the antecedent of his "because"-statement in my rendition of his view, then he would have been saying something which had great influence on Jefferson, as any reader of the Rough Draft and the final version of the Declaration can see when he finds "all men are created equal" among the sa-

11. In A. P. D'Entrèves, *The Medieval Contribution to Political Thought: Thomas Aquinas, Marsilius of Padua, Richard Hooker* (New York, 1959), pp. 125–129, there is a discussion of the relationship between Locke's and Hooker's political theories but, unfortunately for our purposes, no treatment of the concept of self-evidence.

cred and undeniable as well as the self-evident truths. And if one adds to this the fact that Locke believed in the self-evidence of the entire "because"-statement, one can also see his influence on the structure of the Rough Draft of the Declaration, where it is held to be a sacred and undeniable truth that men *derive* certain rights from their equal creation.

When we properly distinguish three propositions held by Locke: *1.* his self-evident "because"-statement; *2.* its implied antecedent, "all men are equal by nature"; and *3.* its implied consequent, "all men should be treated as equal," we may protect Locke against the charge of asserting the trivial statement that because all men are created equal, they should be viewed as equal. When stated without qualification in this way it *seems* to be an instance of the principle that because men are endowed by God with a certain attribute, they should be viewed as having that attribute. But this is an incorrect interpretation of Locke's principle precisely because it *identifies* the attribute of equality expressed in the "because"-clause, or the antecedent, with the attribute of equality which the consequent says that all men should be viewed as having. That is why one must interpret Locke to maintain that "equal" has different *senses* in antecedent and consequent or that men may be said to be equal in different respects. I used the first method when I formulated Locke's principle as follows: "Because all men have been created equal in the sense of having been given the same nature and the same advantages, they should also be treated as equal in the sense that no one of them should depend on the will of any other man. . . ." Once we formulate Locke's principle in this way we see that Locke is *not* asserting anything of the form: "Because men are endowed by God with a certain attribute, they should be viewed as having that attribute." Locke is telling us that because God created men as equal in *one* specified sense (or respect), they should be treated as equal in *another* specified sense (or respect). If one prefers to state the point in another way, one may say that Locke is telling us that because God endowed all men with *one* sort of equality, they should be treated or regarded as possessing *another* sort of equality. He is not asserting that we should view as a spade what God made a spade. Nor is he asserting the truism that equals are equal.

It is extremely important to emphasize the distinction between a truism, or what Locke calls a trifling proposition, and a truth which is instructive. For him, identical propositions, whether they take the general form of "An *A* is an *A*" or the more concrete form of "An oyster is an oyster," are trifling. Identical propositions are for him those "wherein the same term, importing the same idea is affirmed of itself";[12] but he goes on to say that "alike trifling it is to predicate any other part of the definition of the term defined, or to affirm any one of the simple ideas of a complex one of the name of the whole complex idea,"[13] and he thinks that "Every man is an animal or living body" is trifling on this score.[14] This disparagement of trifling propositions had special significance, he thought, for ethics, since he asked: "Let a man abound, as much as the plenty of words which he has will permit, in such propositions as these: 'a law is a law,' and 'obligation is obligation'; 'right is right,' and 'wrong is wrong':—will these and the like ever help him to an acquaintance with ethics, or instruct him or others in the knowledge of morality? Those who know not, nor perhaps ever will know, what is right and what is wrong, nor the measures of them, can with as much assurance make, and infallibly know, the truth of these and all such propositions, as he that is best instructed in morality can do. But what advance do such propositions give in the

12. *Essay,* Book IV, Chapter VIII, Section 3.
13. *Ibid.,* Book IV, Chapter VIII, Section 5.
14. *Ibid.,* Book IV, Chapter VIII, Section 6.

knowledge of anything necessary or useful for their conduct?"[15]

By contrast, there are propositions which are self-evident
but not trifling which serve, as we have seen, as mathematical
axioms. "The whole is bigger than a part" is one, and
"Things equal to the same thing are equal to each other" is
a second truth of this kind. Locke had special views about
the status of such maxims, since he argued that a child can
see that it is self-evident that his body is bigger than his little
finger before he is introduced to the general maxim used by
mathematicians, but this is not of particular importance to
us. What *is* important is the fact that a self-evident truth
could not be instructive or informative if it was trifling.
And because of his insistence upon the distinction between
trifling self-evident propositions and non-trifling ones,
Locke's position would have to be distinguished from that
of theorists of natural law who, like Culverwel, held that a
first principle of morality is "near to a tautology and identity."[16] In short, Locke thought that a first principle of natural law is one whose predicate expressed an idea not contained in its subject, and that is why I think it fair to construe
his principle of equality as I have. Of course, one may argue
with Locke about whether the principle *is* self-evident even
if one accepts his definition of a self-evident proposition as
one that we are forced to accept as soon as we grasp the two
distinct ideas in it, namely, our equality of species and our
obligation not to put each other under subjection, but that is
another matter. Here I am concerned to be as fair as I can to
him and to his American followers.

The same concern to be fair leads me to point out that
Locke did not hold that the statement "all men are created
equal" is incompatible with the existence of age-differences,
height-differences, and other such non-essential differences

15. *Ibid.*, Book IV, Chapter VIII, Section 3.
16. See above, Chapter 1, note 2.

among men. And he cannot be thought to hold that our obligation to treat all men as equal in the sense of mutually independent is incompatible with other obligations or rights to give precedence to those who are greater in age, merit, or excellency of parts.[17] All of these inequalities which, it should be emphasized, do not constitute inequalities of *species* or *nature* may justify inequality in what is owed to one man by another. But such permissible or obligatory inequality of treatment, Locke says, does not conflict with the equal right that every man has to what Locke calls on different occasions his natural freedom, his natural right not to be subjected to the will or authority of another man, his natural independence, or his natural liberty. This equal natural right that all men have in consequence of their equal nature is the affirmative counterpart of the *duty* that all men have *not* to put their fellow-men under dominion, for it will be observed that Locke's self-evident principle in Chapter II of the *Second Treatise* states a duty on the part of all men not to put their fellow-men in a state of subordination or subjection. Let us

17. In Section 54 of the *Second Treatise* he writes: "Though I have said above, Chap. II, *that all men by nature are equal,* I cannot be supposed to understand all sorts of *equality: age* or *virtue* may give men a just precedency; *excellency of parts and merit* may place others above the common level: *birth* may subject some, and *alliance* or *benefits* others, to pay an observance to those to whom nature, gratitude or other respects may have made it due; and yet all this consists with the *equality,* which all men are in, in respect of jurisdiction or dominion one over another, which was the *equality* I there speak of, as proper to the business in hand, being that *equal right* that every man hath, *to his natural freedom,* without being subjected to the will or authority of any other man." See W. F. Dana, "The Declaration of Independence," *Harvard Law Review* XIII (1900): 339, note 1, for a reference to this passage in Locke, which is made in order to clarify Jefferson's use in the Declaration of "equal." C. M. Wiltse, in *The Jeffersonian Tradition in American Democracy* (Chapel Hill, 1935), p. 158, makes the same point about the Declaration without mentioning Section 54 of Locke's *Second Treatise.* Neither Dana nor Wiltse, however, points out that so-called equality before the law is based by Locke on equality of species, and that this doctrine is also employed in the Declaration, as we shall see below.

also bear in mind that "independent" is a negative term, so that what is formulated on Locke's behalf by Sidgwick as "God . . . has made men similar in nature and faculties, therefore they are to be regarded as mutually independent" might also be expressed by saying "God . . . has made men similar in nature and faculties, therefore they are *not* to be regarded as mutually *de*pendent."

Someone might raise the following question here. If the proposition said to be self-evident by Locke is that because all men are created equal, every man has a duty not to put under his dominion another member of his species, why should we regard a logical consequence of that statement, namely, that because all men are created equal, every man has a right to be independent of other members of his species, as self-evident? After all, the latter is *deduced* from the former, and so it might be thought to be a theorem rather than a self-evident axiom. The answer, I venture to say, is that this deduction is carried out by exploiting an equivalence which Locke would have called trifling, namely, the equivalence between "every man has a duty not to put under his dominion another member of his species" and "every man has a right to be independent of other members of his species." So one self-evident proposition may be deduced from another self-evident proposition if the mode of deduction is trifling.

Jefferson, Self-evidence, and Equality

I now wish to compare Locke's views on self-evidence and equality in greater detail with some views expressed in the Declaration of Independence. This is best begun by examining the so-called Rough Draft of it prepared by Jefferson for the Committee of Five, a document ingeniously reconstructed by Julian Boyd,[18] who also shows how it was trans-

18. Julian Boyd, *The Declaration of Independence: The Evolution of the Text as Shown in Facsimiles of Various Drafts by Its Author, Thomas Jefferson* (Princeton, 1945), pp. 19–21.

formed into the document it finally became. After this Rough Draft is altered, perhaps crucially, by putting the word "self-evident" in place of "sacred and undeniable"—a change which some say was made by Jefferson himself before he submitted the Draft to the Committee of Five (John Adams, Franklin, Robert R. Livingston, Roger Sherman, and Jefferson himself)—a highly philosophical passage of the Rough Draft comes to read as follows:

> We hold these truths to be self-evident; that all men are created equal & independent, that from that equal creation they derive rights inherent & inalienable, among which are the preservation of life, & liberty & the pursuit of happiness. . . .

One thing to note about this passage is that whether it is construed as containing the phrase "sacred and undeniable" or the word "self-evident" these terms are applied to two different kinds of truths. The first is illustrated by the proposition "all men are created equal & independent," and the second by one about derivability: "from that equal creation, they derive rights inherent and inalienable. . . ." The second may be converted into a proposition of the form: "Because all men are created equal, they have rights inherent & inalienable . . . ," since it seems to me that when Jefferson says that men *derive* certain rights from their equal creation, he means that equal creation is the ground or foundation of these rights. And once we convert his statement of derivation into a "because"-statement, we can more clearly see the links between what Locke says in the *Second Treatise* and what Jefferson says in the Declaration. We can see that Jefferson's assertion in the Rough Draft of the undeniability of "all men are created equal" is the counterpart of Locke's remark that the "judicious Hooker" believed in the self-evidence of "this *equality* of Men by Nature." And we can also see that Jefferson's belief in the undeniability of the proposition I have rendered as: "Because all men are created equal, they have rights inherent and inalienable . . ." is the counterpart of Locke's belief in the self-evidence of the proposition I have earlier rendered as: "Because all men have been created equal in the sense of having been given the same nature and the same advantages, they should also be treated as equal in the sense that no one of them should depend on the will of any other man (unless God has by a manifest declaration given one man dominion over others)." It is true that the consequent of Locke's "because"-statement differs from the consequent of Jefferson's by virtue of referring only to the right of liberty, but that difference should not be allowed to obscure the two points of similarity which I wish to underscore in this chapter. The first point is that Locke (on the assumption that he agreed with Hooker) and Jefferson both believed in the undeniability of the equality of men by nature, provided this is interpreted as Locke interprets it, namely, as an equality of species which is compatible with the various differences that Locke treats in Section 54 of his *Second Treatise*. And the second point is that both Locke and Jefferson believed in the undeniability of principles which asserted that certain moral rights were *derived from* this natural equality or equality of species.

We are now in a better position to evaluate certain criticisms of the statement that all men are created equal. *The Scots Magazine* of August 1776 reprinted the Declaration and attached two anonymous critical footnotes to it, one to the word "equal." Concerning the statement that all men are created equal, the hostile critic asks whether they are alleged to be equal in size, strength, understanding, figure, moral accomplishments, or civil accomplishments. "Every ploughman," the critic says in answer to his own question, "knows that they are not created equal in any of these." But then, after granting that all men are "equally created," the critic denies that this is "to the purpose." Indeed, he goes further and says that the fact that all men are equally created is no reason why the Americans should rebel against the people of Great Britain, who are fellow creatures of the Americans.[19] This allows us to observe that the critic failed to see that Jefferson, following Locke, thought that "created equal" meant "created as members of the same species," and that like Locke, Jefferson certainly did not mean to imply that all men are equal in size, strength, understanding, figure, moral accomplishments, or civil accomplishments.[20] Furthermore, if Congress had adopted the Rough Draft, containing as it did Jefferson's statement that the right to preserve one's life, the right to preserve one's liberty, and the right to pursue happiness are *derived* from equal creation, Jefferson's intent would have been harder to lampoon. Needless to say, if Jefferson could have added footnotes to Locke, such lampooning would have been made still harder. I say this because it would, or should, have been evident from the Rough Draft that if "equal creation" was used in a sense from which the right to liberty was derived, it could hardly have been meant to include equality in size. And certainly another British critic, John Lind, would not have been able to have inferred from the Rough Draft with apparent ease that "all men are created equal" implied that "a child, at the moment of his birth, has the same quantity of *natural* power as the parent, the

19. *The Scots Magazine*, XXXVIII (August 1776): 433. This note is reproduced in R. Ginsberg, ed., *A Casebook on the Declaration of Independence* (New York, 1967), pp. 6–7.

20. That Jefferson's views on this point were shared by other revolutionaries may be seen by consulting several passages in the works of signers. Although all were written after 1776, they may be regarded as retrospective clarifications of what John Adams and James Wilson had meant by "created equal" when they subscribed to the Declaration. See especially Adams, *Works*, Volume I, p. 462; Volume VI, pp. 285–286 and pp. 453–454; Volume X, pp. 52–53. See *The Works of James Wilson*, ed. R. G. McCloskey (Cambridge, Mass., 1967), Volume I, pp. 240–241.

same quantity of *political* power as the magistrate."[21] I realize, of course, that a tough political antagonist might not have been deterred by the use of even the Rough Draft's language and would have been able to lampoon that as well. But I argue merely that statements in the Rough Draft were closer to Jefferson's philosophical intent and less susceptible to tendentious misinterpretation, especially of what he meant by "created equal."

In a chapter which is primarily devoted to showing that Jefferson and other founding fathers were as rationalistic in their view of morality as Locke was, I shall not comment in detail on the rights mentioned in the Rough Draft or in later versions of the Declaration. But in defending the idea that their view of morality was as rationalistic as that of Locke, I shall divide my argument into two parts, one in which I focus on the use of the phrase "sacred and undeniable" in the Rough Draft and another in which I focus on the use of "self-evident" in the final version. I do this because there is some reason to believe that the phrase "undeniable truth" was used in the philosophical literature of the time to cover a broader class of truths than that covered by "self-evident" since theorems deduced from self-evident truth, which is to say, demonstrated, were also called undeniable. Therefore, on the assumption that "undeniable" was wider than "self-evident" in extension, a serious philosophical change was made when the Rough Draft was altered because Jefferson was now put in the position of asserting that he could know truths by intuition which, perhaps, he regarded as merely

21. John Lind, *An Answer to the Declaration of the American Congress* (London, 1776), p. 120. The last part of this work of 132 pages, entitled "Short Review of the Declaration," contains a very brief criticism in its earliest pages of the more philosophical parts of the Declaration. The bulk of the book is devoted to answering, point by point, the more factual parts of the Declaration. This "Short Review" is reprinted in Ginsberg, *op. cit.,* pp. 9–17.

demonstrable. However, if Jefferson was being cautious in the Rough Draft and inclined not to commit himself as to whether his undeniable truths were self-evident or demonstrable, the fact is that even if he thought they were demonstrable rather than self-evident, he would have had to believe that some *other* truths were self-evident. In that case, he would still have been committed to moral rationalism of the Lockean variety. On the other hand, if we focus on the final version, in which "self-evident" is used, and if we construe that word as Locke construed it, then it is even more certain that Jefferson was a moral rationalist.[22] For the present, I shall be content to argue that the use of either "sacred and undeniable" or "self-evident" would have made Jefferson a moral rationalist, but later on I shall argue that Jefferson would have been better off if he had let "sacred and undeniable" stand—on the assumption that he himself made the change, an assumption about which experts[23] seem to be in disagreement—or if he had resisted the person, probably Franklin, who proposed the change to "self-evident." All of

22. See Supplementary Notes, Moral Rationalism . . . , p. 273.
23. Carl Becker says on one page of his *Declaration of Independence* (New York, 1922), p. 142, note 1, that "it is not clear that this change was made by Jefferson. The handwriting of 'self-evident' resembles Franklin's." But on another page (p. 198) Becker writes: "When Jefferson submitted the draft to Adams the only correction which he had made was to write 'self-evident' in place of 'sacred & undeniable' . . . I suspect that he erased '& independent' because, having introduced 'self-evident,' he did not like the sound of the two phrases both closing with 'dent.' " Julian Boyd presents on p. 22 of his *Declaration of Independence* a very interesting discussion in which he seems to favor the view that Jefferson himself made the change. Concerning the removal of "& independent" from "all men are created equal & independent," an assertion made in the Rough Draft, I opine that whoever removed it realized that once the final version asserted that it was self-evident that the Creator endowed all men with the right to *liberty*, it was superfluous to say that he created them *independent*. For to have the right to liberty is to be independent, i.e. not under the dominion of other men.

this will become clearer, I hope, when I deal with Burlamaqui's effort to *derive* the principles of natural law in a manner which Jefferson might well have approved.

I should add that colonists other than Jefferson explicitly
adopted a Lockean, rationalistic view, according to which
some truths are self-evident and others demonstrated. As we
have seen, the very passage on equality in Locke's work that
I have been analyzing and linking with the Declaration was
quoted favorably by James Otis in his famous pamphlet of
1765, *The Rights of the British Colonies Asserted and
Proved*.[24] And Alexander Hamilton was even more explicit
in his appeal to the epistemology of self-evidence, not only
in his pre-Revolutionary writing but also in his contributions
to the *Federalist Papers*.

Hamilton and Self-evidence

In 1774 and 1775, Hamilton engaged in a controversy with
the pseudonymous "A. W. Farmer" in which Hamilton wrote
one pamphlet called (for short) *A Full Vindication of the
Measures of the Congress* and another briefly entitled *The
Farmer Refuted*.[25] Both of them contain passages that show
Hamilton's attachment to doctrines of the kind I have been
discussing. At one place he writes: "That Americans are inti-
tled to freedom is incontestible upon every rational principle. All men have one common original: they participate in

24. *Pamphlets of the American Revolution: 1750–1776*, ed. B. Bailyn, p. 440.
   For other examples of the rationalistic use of "self-evident" and allied ex-
   pressions by signers of the Declaration, see *The Papers of Benjamin Frank-
   lin*, ed. L. W. Labaree (New Haven, 1959), Volume I, p. 59; *The Works of
   James Wilson*, Volume I, p. 223; *Works of John Adams*, Volume X, p. 85.
   One of the most Lockean statements may be found in *Diary and Auto-
   biography of John Adams*, ed. L. H. Butterfield (Cambridge, Mass., 1962),
   Volume I, p. 32.
25. *The Papers of Alexander Hamilton*, ed. H. C. Syrett (New York, 1961),
   Volume I, pp. 45–165.

one common nature, and consequently have one common right.''[26] Hamilton's reference to incontestability upon "every rational principle" is further support for what I have in mind, and his brief sentence about all men having one common original, one common nature, and consequently one common right is virtually a summary of Locke's self-evident principle in Section 4 of the *Second Treatise*—the *common right* of Hamilton being what Locke called in Section 54 of the *Second Treatise* "that *equal Right* that every man hath, *to his Natural Freedom.*" In keeping with the rhetoric of "self-evidence" and allied terms, Hamilton says that "we may pronounce it a matter of undeniable certainty, that the pretensions of Parliament are contradictory to the law of nature."[27] And in *The Farmer Refuted,* he condescendingly advises his adversary: "Apply yourself, without delay, to the study of the law of nature. I would recommend to your perusal, Grotius, Puffendorf, Locke, Montesquieu, and Burlamaqui. I might mention other excellent writers on this subject; but if you attend, diligently, to these you will not require any others."[28] To this Hamilton adds an attack on the pseudonymous Farmer as one who subscribes to principles like those of Hobbes. Hobbes is then dismissed as an atheist who held that morality derived from the introduction of civil society and therefore that all virtue is artificial rather than natural. After a short disquisition on natural law in which he leans on Blackstone, Hamilton concludes with a typical intuitionistic

26. *A Full Vindication, ibid.,* p. 47. The spelling is Hamilton's.
27. *Ibid.*
28. *Ibid.,* p. 86. Well before Hamilton wrote this, James Otis had defended the proposition that Colonial rights were inherent and indefeasible by saying that it is "self-evident . . . to everyone in the least versed in the laws of nature and nations, or but moderately skilled in the common law," *A Vindication of the British Colonies* (1765), Bailyn, *Pamphlets,* Volume I, p. 562. This shows the influence of the idea that not everyone could perceive self-evidence. Moreover, Otis's passage was directed against Martin Howard's statement (Bailyn, p. 535) that he would "shun the walk of metaphysics in [his] inquiry," that is, the appeal to natural rights.

flourish: "To deny these principles will be not less absurd, than to deny the plainest axioms: I shall not, therefore, attempt any further illustration of them."[29] And although Hamilton opposes the Farmer by appealing to natural law as well as by appealing to the British Constitution and to colonial charters, there is an interesting passage in which, after noting that New York has no charter, Hamilton says that New York might "plead the common principles of colonization" on the ground that New York should not be prevented from enjoying the most important privileges of the other colonies. But Hamilton does not stop there: he goes on to employ a figure that is familiar to students of the history of natural law and natural rights: "There is no need, however, of this plea: The sacred rights of mankind are not to be rummaged for, among old parchments, or musty records. They are written, as with a sun beam [*sic*], in the whole *volume* of human nature, by the hand of the divinity itself; and can never be erased or obscured by mortal power."[30]

29. *Ibid.*, pp. 88–89.
30. *Ibid.*, pp. 121–122. See Stourzh, *Alexander Hamilton and the Idea of Republican Government* (Stanford, Calif., 1970), for an interesting discussion of certain elements of Hamilton's thought. It is interesting to find that when Cicero in his *Tusculan Disputations*, Book I, Chapter XIII, is discussing the basis for belief in the existence of the gods and comes to the conclusion that what is unanimously accepted by the races of the world must be regarded as a law of nature and that belief in the existence of the gods is established in the same way, he begins the chapter on this by saying (in the Loeb Library translation by J. E. King) that if he were "to investigate old records and rummage out (*eruere*) of them the instances given by Greek writers," he could show us that the existence of the gods was accepted even by barbarous men. It is also interesting to find Jefferson reporting in his *Autobiography* that while preparing his *Summary View of the Rights of British America* (1774), he and his friends "rummaged over" John Rushworth's *Historical Collections* "for the revolutionary precedents and forms of the Puritans of that day" (*Writings*, Volume I, p. 9). There is a plain suggestion that this rummaging was for rhetorical purposes since Jefferson goes on to say that after finding some useful passages in Rushworth, "we cooked up a resolution, somewhat modernizing their [the Puritans'] phrases" (*ibid.*). In the *Summary View*, Jefferson

Without stopping here to examine certain non-epistemological aspects of Hamilton's thoughts on natural law, I wish to observe that his reference to God's writing the sacred rights of mankind into the volume of human nature by means of something like a sunbeam is not unrelated to Locke's notion that self-evident propositions express knowledge which is "irresistible, and, like bright sunshine, forces itself immediately to be perceived, as soon as ever the mind turns its view that way,"[31] not to speak of the notions of other celebrators of the light of nature. However, the reader of the first chapter of *this* volume will recall that when discussing Locke's views I pointed out how he made deliberate use of that part of his figure which allowed him to deny that any person whatever could see this light. Not only was it necessary, said Locke, for the mind to turn its view toward the light, but the mind had to have the power of sight, it had to open its eye, and so on, to see self-evident truth.[32] These figurative Lockean requirements for the perception of self-evident truth were, as I have shown, intimately connected with Locke's idea that "there are only few who, neither corrupted by vice nor carelessly indifferent, make a proper use of that light [of nature]"[33] and with his forceful rejection of the principle that the voice of the people is the voice of God.[34] And Hamilton, as one might expect, was also a partisan of self-evident principles who attempted to close loopholes through which his opponents might try to escape in their efforts to dispute his claims on *political* issues.

This attempt is most conspicuous in Federalist Number

rested a good part of his argument on natural rights, even though he also appealed to legal precedents. (See Chapter 3, note 65 below.)

31. See Chapter 1, notes 12 and 13 and the related parts of the text.
32. See Chapter 1, note 23 and the related parts of the text.
33. See Chapter 1, note 24 and the passage cited there.
34. See Chapter 1, note 25 and the passage cited there. Hamilton also rejected the principle that the voice of the people is the voice of God. See *The Papers of Alexander Hamilton,* Volume IV, p. 200.

31, where Hamilton brings out very big epistemological guns in order to defend the "necessity of a general power of taxation in the government of the union."[35] It should be underscored that the main proposition at stake in Federalist Numbers 30 and 31 is not an axiom of natural law, and that it is not, therefore, a moral principle in our contemporary sense of the word "moral." It is rather a political principle. Yet, so eager is Hamilton to bludgeon the opponents of a strong national union that he begins Federalist Number 31 with a little essay on first principles or primary truths which is worth our attention because it shows that some partisans of the doctrine of self-evident truth tried to win substantive political arguments by appealing to epistemology.

Hamilton begins Federalist Number 31 with the familiar philosophical statement that in disquisitions of every kind there are certain primary truths or first principles "upon which all subsequent reasonings must depend."[36] Then, in what will be recognized as a familiar move, Hamilton asserts that first principles "contain an internal evidence, which antecedent to all reflection or combination commands the assent of the mind."[37] But, next, we find Hamilton hedging in a manner with which we have also become familiar, for he says: "Where it produces not this effect, it must proceed either from some defect or disorder in the organs of perception, or from the influence of some strong interest, or passion, or prejudice."[38] And after illustrating the notion of self-

---

35. *The Federalist*, ed. J. E. Cooke (Middletown, Conn., 1961), p. 195. In discussing Hamilton's views in *The Federalist* I go beyond the temporal boundaries I generally observe in this study because such a discussion helps me delineate the political uses to which the epistemology of natural law could be and was put.

36. See Supplementary Notes, The Ambiguity of "Depend . . . ," p. 276.

37. *The Federalist*, pp. 193–194. By "antecedent to all reflection or combination" Hamilton means antecedent to all discursive reasoning or deduction in Locke's sense.

38. *Ibid.*, p. 194. This kind of hedging we have observed in Locke and Burlamaqui. It is also to be found, for example, in Cumberland's *De*

evident truth by citing mathematical principles like "The whole is greater than any part," Hamilton asserts that both ethics and politics contain similar "maxims." When he comes to illustrate the maxims of ethics and politics, he presents the following list: "that there cannot be an effect without a cause; that the means ought to be proportioned to the end; that every power ought to be commensurate with its object; that there ought to be no limitation of a power destined to effect a purpose, which is itself incapable of limitation."[39]

After listing his allegedly self-evident maxims of ethics and politics, Hamilton notes that there are other truths in ethics and politics which, even though they are not self-evident, are so directly inferred from self-evident axioms "and so obvious in themselves, and so agreeable to the natural and

---

legibus naturae (1672). In Chapter I, he says that the laws of nature are necessarily suggested to the minds of men, and that they are understood and remembered by men "whilst the faculties of their minds continue unhurt," trans. Maxwell (London, 1727), p. 39. The same idea that reason may fail to perceive moral truth because of the influence of passion, bias, ignorance, or madness may be found in Adams, Works, Volume III, p. 435 and in Wilson, Works, Volume I, p. 223.

39. Ibid., p. 194. For a similar appeal to self-evidence, see Madison in Federalist Number 44, J. E. Cooke's ed., pp. 304–305. One wonders why Hamilton's first maxim is said to be ethical or political. One also wonders whether it is deliberately formulated by Hamilton in this way, even though he might have known that the principle of universal causation had been stated by Hume, for example, as follows: "Every object, which begins to exist, must owe its existence to a cause"—a proposition which, Hume asserted, was neither intuitively nor demonstratively certain. Hume had also written as follows in criticism of those who had, in effect, formulated the principle of causation as Hamilton had: "They are still more frivolous, who say, that every effect must have a cause, because 'tis imply'd in the very idea of effect. Every effect necessarily pre-supposes a cause; effect being a relative term, of which cause is the correlative. But this does not prove, that every being must be preceded by a cause; no more than it follows, because every husband must have a wife, that therefore every man must be marry'd. The true state of the question is, whether every object, which begins to exist, must owe its existence to a cause; and this I assert neither to be intuitively nor demonstratively certain," David Hume, A Treatise of Human Nature, ed. L. A. Selby-Bigge (Oxford, 1888), p. 82.

unsophisticated dictates of common sense, that they challenge the assent of a sound and unbiased mind, with a degree of force and conviction almost equally irresistable [sic]."⁴⁰ Here, Hamilton's idea is to introduce a few more truths—those that are theorems of ethics and politics—into the class of propositions that he wants to set upon a pedestal. To be sure, they are on a lower pedestal because they are almost as irresistible—Locke's word, it will be recalled—as axioms; but Hamilton the political thinker is very eager to speak with the authority of one who is working in what Locke calls "demonstrative science," and that is why he is determined to regard the theorems of his "sciences" as virtually self-evident. And there is in Hamilton a great desire to show that anyone who disagrees with him on taxation is disputing a self-evident truth or something close to a self-evident truth. But it is interesting to note that instead of taking the line of Aquinas, which would allow ignorance of essence to be a cause of another man's failure to see self-evidence where the assertor does, Hamilton is more inclined in this work to accuse his opponents of a defect in the organ by which man perceives truths of this kind, or of some strong interest, passion, or prejudice. Interestingly enough, it is just as easy to think of Hamilton's opponent who may be accused of having a defective "organ" or of being dominated by prejudice, interest, or passion, as either a member of the mob or as an over-sophisticated doctrinaire speaking for the few. In either case, Hamilton is not above using epistemology to bully his political opponents.

Whatever class of opponent Hamilton is attacking in the epistemological prologue of Federalist Number 31, that opponent is testily accused of being far less tractable in accepting the alleged truths—whether axioms or theorems—of ethics

40. *The Federalist,* p. 194.

and politics than he is in accepting those of geometry. Hamilton's explanation is that geometry is so removed "from those pursuits which stir up and put in motion the unruly passions of the human heart," that mankind without difficulty accepts even the most unnatural and paradoxical theorems—like the infinite divisibility of matter—from geometers, whereas they will balk at religious mysteries which are "not less incomprehensible." I am tempted to say here that the persons who accept the allegedly incomprehensible theorems of geometry do not strike one as making up all "mankind" at large. Hamilton must be speaking here of persons of more education than the average even though he speaks of them condescendingly, saying: "Caution and investigation are a necessary armour against error and imposition. But this untractableness may be carried too far, and may degenerate into obstinacy, perverseness or disingenuity. Though it cannot be pretended that the principles of moral and political knowledge have in general the same degree of certainty with those of the mathematics; yet they have much better claims in this respect, than to judge from the conduct of men in particular situations, we should be disposed to allow them. The obscurity is much oftener in the passions and prejudices of the reasoner than in the subject. Men upon too many occasions do not give their own understandings fair play; but yielding to some untoward bias they entangle themselves in words and confound themselves in subtleties."[41]

On this note Hamilton's epistemological prelude ends, and he begins to use the prelude concretely against political opponents, about whose disagreement with him he asks the following question: "How else could it happen (if we admit the objectors to be sincere in their opposition) that positions so clear as those which manifest the necessity of a general power

41. *Ibid.,* p. 195.

of taxation in the government of the union, should have to encounter any adversaries among men of discernment?"[42] The question is, of course, rhetorical since Hamilton can think of no other way in which opposition to his views of taxation might be explained, except by supposing that his opponents fail to "give their own understandings fair play" because they yield to some "untoward bias." This explanation is related to, but different from Locke's observation that there are few men, who in matters of daily practice or matters easy to know, "surrender themselves to the jurisdiction of reason or follow its lead." Locke was speaking of the *many* who are led astray by passion and who "readily follow the inducements of pleasure or the urges of their base instincts rather than the dictates of reason."[43] But Hamilton, writing more than a hundred years after Locke and in defense of the United States Constitution, defended a view of how more discerning men might fail to use their understandings and to perceive self-evident truth, a view that resembled Locke's. Hamilton, because he was defending a people's Constitution, was more inclined to use the supplementary machinery of the theory of self-evidence against men of discernment who "confound themselves in subtleties" rather than against the many who have the unruly passions of a mob.

Perhaps it would be helpful to examine Hamilton's view of arguments against the necessity of a general power of taxation in order to show how at least one advocate of the doctrine of rationally intuited, self-evident truth used this doctrine to rebut political opponents. Immediately after indicating that only one who yields to untoward bias, entangles

42. *Ibid.* It is clear from this passage that Hamilton was attacking the passions and prejudices of "men of discernment" (unless he was being ironical) rather than the rude or ignorant multitude and therefore that a previously published comment of mine on this part of Federalist Number 31 needs alteration. See my *Science and Sentiment in America* (New York, 1972), p. 316.

43. See Chapter 1, note 23 and the passage identified there.

himself in words, and therefore fails to give his understanding fair play would oppose the necessity of a general power of taxation, Hamilton recapitulates his own argument for this necessity before dealing with opponents. First, he says, a government ought to contain in itself every power requisite to its care and for the execution of the trusts for which it is responsible, being controlled only by a concern for the public good and for the sense of the people. This seems to be an illustration of Hamilton's maxim or primary truth that "every power ought to be commensurate with its object." In short, if the federal government is assigned a goal of a certain kind, it must be granted a power of a certain kind. Secondly, says Hamilton, since the duties of superintending the national defense and securing public peace against both foreign and domestic violence involve providing for casualties and dangers "to which no limits can possibly be assigned," the power of making that provision ought to know no bounds other than those set by the needs of the nation and the resources of the community. This seems to be an instance of the supposedly self-evident maxim "that there ought to be no limitation of a power destined to effect a purpose, which is itself incapable of limitation." Thirdly, he says, since revenue is the "essential engine" by which the means of satisfying the nation's needs must be procured, "the power of providing for that article must necessarily be comprehended in that of providing for those" needs.

Note that so far Hamilton's argument seems to remain within the realm of self-evidence: (1) If you assign a certain end to a government, you ought to assign the government a power through the exercise of which it can attain that end. (2) If the end is illimitable, the power ought to be illimitable. (3) If you give government the power to attain an end, you should empower it to use the only means that will help it attain the end. But then we come to a fourth proposition that Hamilton needs in his argument, a proposition which is not self-evident. He says: "As theory and practice conspire to prove that the power of procuring revenue is unavailing, when exercised over the States in their collective capacities, the Federal government must of necessity be invested with an unqualified power of taxation in the ordinary modes."[44] But it is clear that even if one were to accept Hamilton's first three steps as based on self-evident maxims—however vague these maxims may seem—Hamilton, to arrive at his conclusion, needs a proposition which is not one to which the reason or the understanding must assent as soon as it is comprehended. Hamilton asserts that "the power of procuring revenue is unavailing when exercised over the States in their collective capacities," but this is not a self-evident proposition, such as "The whole is greater than its part." He is in the realm of what Locke would have called opinion and probability, and not in the realm of demonstrative moral *science*. Therefore, since Hamilton cannot seriously attribute self-evidence to this fourth proposition, there would be no *opportunity* for his opponents to demonstrate in connection with *this* step of his argument the kind of bias, passion, and prejudice that would interfere with the perception of self-evidence.

Is there any place in his comments on the view of his opponents where Hamilton shows that they have failed to see self-evidence for such reasons? I confess that I can find only feeble efforts of this kind in the pages of Federalist Number 31, and they come after the Hamiltonian argument that I have just outlined. Hamilton first congratulates himself on the power of his own argument, saying that "the propriety of a general power of taxation in the national government might safely be permitted to rest on the evidence of these propositions." But, lamentably, he seems to say with a sigh, the opponents of the proposed constitution "seem to make their principal and most zealous effort against this part of

44. *Federalist*, p. 196.

the plan," and so he must examine their arguments.[45] Hamilton concentrates on one effort to rebut his own argument but never tries to discredit it by reference to bias or passion, even though it rests on a view which directly challenges the truth of one of his own supposedly self-evident propositions, that is, one of those which is said to "contain an internal evidence, which antecedent to all reflection or combination commands the assent of the mind." Hamilton formulates the challenge as follows: "it is not true, because the exigencies of the Union may not be susceptible of limitation, that its power of laying taxes ought to be unconfined."[46] However, it is remarkable that Hamilton formulates this flat denial of what he himself took to be a self-evident proposition, such as "The whole is greater than its part" or Locke's "Red is not green," without immediately accusing his opponent of lunacy, bias, passion, or prejudice. On the contrary, Hamilton goes on to state his opponent's argument in favor of the flat denial in words which deserve to be reproduced *verbatim*:

> Revenue is as requisite to the purposes of the local administrations as to those of the Union; and the former are at least of equal importance with the latter to the happiness of the people. It is therefore as necessary, that the State Governments should be able to command the means of supplying their wants, as, that the National Government should possess the like faculty, in respect to the wants of the Union. But an indefinite power of taxation in the *latter* might, and probably would in time deprive the former of the means of providing for their own necessities; and would subject them entirely to the mercy of the national Legislature. As the laws of the Union are to become the supreme law of the land; as it is to have power to pass all laws that may be NECESSARY for carrying into execution, the authorities with which it is

45. *Ibid.*
46. *Ibid.*

proposed to vest it; the national government might at any time abolish the taxes imposed for State objects, upon the pretence of an interference with its own. It might alledge a necessity of doing this, in order to give efficacy to the national revenues: And thus all the resources of taxation might by degrees, become the subjects of federal monopoly, to the intire exclusion and destruction of the State Governments.[47]

Whatever the merit of this criticism of a crucial step in Hamilton's argument, it is clear that Hamilton would have a hard time making his critic seem like a man trying to show that two and two do not make four or that red was green. Hence, there is only a comparatively feeble effort on Hamilton's part to paint his opponent as mentally deficient or deranged, an effort to which we come after Hamilton has made the following comment: "This mode of reasoning appears some times to turn upon the supposition of usurpation in the national government; at other times it seems to be designed only as a deduction from the constitutional operation of its intended powers. It is only in the latter light, that it can be admitted to have any pretensions to fairness."[48] Now we are ready for what I call Hamilton's feeble effort to impugn his opponent's mental standing. Immediately after saying what I have just quoted, Hamilton focuses on his opponent's statements about what the national government *might* do in a spirit of usurpation and complains: "The moment we launch into conjectures about the usurpations of the federal Government, we get into an unfathomable abyss, and fairly put ourselves out of the reach of all reasoning. Imagination may range at pleasure till it gets bewildered amidst the labyrinths of an enchanted castle, and knows not on which side to turn to extricate itself from the perplexities into which it has so rashly adventured. Whatever may be the limits or

47. *Ibid.*, pp. 196–197.
48. *Ibid.*, p. 197.

modifications of the powers of the Union, it is easy to imagine an endless train of possible dangers; and by indulging an excess of jealousy and timidity, we may bring ourselves to a state of absolute scepticism and irresolution."[49]

I think it should be plain that there is a good deal of bluster in this passage. Hamilton's reference to his critic's putting himself "out of the reach of all reasoning" because the critic fears that the national government might ride roughshod over the state governments if given an illimitable power to tax, is mere rhetoric riding on the back of "self-evident truth." Surely a man might have the mentioned fears about usurpation without being a madman, and this is why I think that Hamilton's efforts to place his opponent beyond the reach of reasoning are feeble. They do, nevertheless, show that American thinkers have invoked the epistemology of self-evident truth in support of concrete political views. This is not to say that Hamilton's political views were indefensible, that *no* argument could be constructed in support of them. It is rather to say that such an argument would not be demonstrative in nature, that it would not move from self-evident truths to theorems in imitation of pure mathematics as conceived by Locke. Before concluding the discussion of Hamilton's epistemological views on this subject, however, I should point out that he was quite preoccupied with them and that they do not appear only in Federalist Number 31. They also appear in Number 23, where Hamilton says that the powers to raise armies, build and equip fleets, to prescribe rules for the government of both, to direct their operations, and to provide for their support are powers which ought to exist without limitation because, Hamilton insists, it is impossible to foresee or define the extent and variety of national exigencies or the means necessary to satisfy them. So once again we are treated to a little lecture in the theory of knowledge:

49. *Ibid.,* p. 197.

"This is one of those truths, which to a correct and unprejudiced mind, carries its own evidence along with it; and may be obscured, but cannot be made plainer by argument or reasoning. It rests upon axioms as simple as they are universal. The *means* ought to be proportioned to the *end;* the persons, from whose agency the attainment of any *end* is expected, ought to possess the *means* by which it is to be attained."[50]

Interestingly enough, however, when Hamilton uses his so-called truths that carry their own evidence while discussing common defense, he is willing to make remarks which to some extent soften his dogmatic appeal to self-evidence. He asserts, characteristically, that whether the federal government *should* be entrusted with the care of the common defense "is a question in the first instance open to discussion." But, he insists, the moment it is decided that it should, it will follow that the government ought to be given the powers requisite to the complete execution of its trust.[51] However, these requisite powers, as in the case of taxation, are powers over the individual citizens of America and not powers over the States in their collective capacities. Moreover, when Hamilton defends his view that the federal government should have *these* unlimited powers in the case of defense, he takes the occasion to say that "experiment" has demonstrated that the practice, under the Articles of Confederation, of allowing Congress to make requisitions only on the *States* for these purposes, was based on an expectation that was "ill founded and illusory." "It was presumed," he says, "that a sense of their true interests, and a regard to the dictates of good faith, would be found sufficient pledges for the punctual performance of the duty of the members to the Federal Head."[52] This remark seems to imply that *if* the States

50. *Ibid.,* p. 147.
51. *Ibid.*
52. *Ibid.,* p. 148.

had behaved differently, the Federal Head would have accomplished its goal by a means other than one which Hamilton said was logically *necessitated*. Obviously, Hamilton believed that it was *logically* possible for the States to have behaved differently. But if it was logically possible for the States to have behaved differently, then one could imagine the federal government being entrusted with the care of the common defense and carrying out its trust, not in the manner which Hamilton regards as logically necessitated by the nature of the trust, but by the method contemplated under the Articles of Confederation. In short, the Hamiltonian necessity which he expresses in an allegedly self-evident truth is not a logical necessity, and the truth is not self-evident. In the end, Hamilton must resort to the proposition that a failure to give the national government the right to go directly to the people—and not to the States—is "improvidently to trust the great interests of the nation to hands, which are disabled from managing them with vigour and success."[53] But improvidence, of course, is not irrationality.

The idea behind both Federalist Number 31 and Number 23 is to do away with a need on the part of the national government to accomplish some of its goals by way of the States, and to allow it to go directly to the people, whether to collect certain taxes or to raise an army. And for this idea one might provide an argument based on experience or prudence. It is better, other things being equal, not to have to work through intermediaries like the States when the national government may have to do many different things quickly in a time of danger. This, however, is not "one of those truths, which to a correct and unprejudiced mind, carries its own evidence along with it." It is based on the observation of human political behavior rather than on an immediate perception of the agreements or disagreements of ideas alone. Whether Hamil-

53. *Ibid.,* p. 149.

ton failed to see this because he was hypnotized by the Lockean model of demonstrative science, or whether he deliberately tried to inflate the certainty of what he had to say in a rhetorical effort to convince his political opponents, I do not know. In either case, it is clear that the doctrine of self-evident truth had an influence on the day-to-day political language of the eighteenth century and through that, I dare say, on the political behavior of the same period.

A Concluding Word

In this chapter I have tried, among other things, to reinforce the view that Locke's moral rationalism played a crucial part in the Declaration of Independence, especially in the revealing Rough Draft of it. Jefferson held there, in agreement with Locke, or Hooker, or both of them, that it may be discovered by reason that all men are created equal in the sense of having been given the same nature and advantages. He also held under the influence of Locke that it may be discovered by reason that because men are created equal in this sense, they all have certain inherent rights. And concerning Alexander Hamilton's thought I have tried to show not only that he appealed to Locke's theory of self-evidence in his defense of natural law against the Farmer in 1774 and 1775 but that in the *Federalist Papers* he was so carried away by Locke's model of demonstrative science that he tried to show that only a biased, prejudiced, passionate man could fail to agree with his supposedly self-evident political belief that the federal government ought to collect taxes from individuals as opposed to States.

In short, the rationalistic intuitionism of Locke was a powerful influence on two of the most important Colonial thinkers who, in spite of their many differences, held that there are truths in ethics and politics which have all the certainty of mathematical axioms and which would be denied, in the words of Algernon Sidney, by "none, but such as were degenerated into beasts" or, in Hamilton's more temperate language, by those who were so "untractable" as to "degenerate into obstinacy, perverseness, or disingenuity." This onslaught against those who might depart from a debatable epistemology of morals and politics also had the support of Locke, who went so far as to say that a man who violates the self-evident law of nature, that is, the rule of reason, shows himself to have become "degenerate, and declares himself to quit the principles of human nature, and to be a noxious creature,"[54] a beast of prey. The frequent use of the word "degenerate" shows that the man who violates and hence by implication is so irrational as to deny the rational laws of nature loses the essential qualities given by God to all men. He sinks to a lower kind in the scale of nature and may therefore be treated as we would treat a wild beast. Small wonder, then, that Thomas Paine called the English king the "Royal Brute," thereby making him fair game for those who thought they knew a self-evident truth when they saw one.

Small wonder, too, that John Stuart Mill might have worried, as we saw at the end of the preceding chapter, about the political consequences of accepting the kind of rationalistic intuitionism to which Hamilton was certainly wedded in the *Federalist Papers*. However, it is important to bear in mind that when Hamilton exploited what I have called the jokers in the epistemology of self-evidence—notions like that of an unbiased, unprejudiced mind—he was not using them in an effort to bully Burlamaqui's "stupid wretches" so much as men of discernment, as Hamilton calls them, who degenerate into obstinacy, perverseness, or disingenuity when they deny what Hamilton regards as undeniable. This shows, I think, that the theory of self-evident truth was a politically versatile instrument, but it also shows, perhaps, how arrogant Hamil-

54. *Second Treatise*, Section 10.

ton was. For he could administer the same kind of treatment to his fellow-statesmen that they might administer to the "stupid wretches" mentioned by Burlamaqui and the credulous people whom Locke wished to protect from the dictators of principles. About Jefferson's view on this question, I shall have more to say in the next chapter. Naturally, it was complicated, as Jefferson's views always were when he was pulled in one direction by his respect for reason and in another by his sentiments regarding the people.

· 3 ·

Reason, Moral Sense,
and the People

Although the main concern of this study is the philosophy of the Revolution as expressed in the Declaration of Independence and in other documents of eighteenth-century America, and although I have argued that Locke's rationalistic doctrine of self-evident principles was accepted by Jefferson when he was writing the Declaration, I cannot, in my discussion of the Revolutionaries' theory of moral knowledge, avoid considering the impact of what is called the doctrine of moral sense on American thought in the revolutionary period. Because we find references to the moral sense in the writings of Jefferson, John Adams, and James Wilson,[1] we

1. Many of Jefferson's references to the moral sense will be discussed later in this chapter, as will those of James Wilson. Adams refers to the moral sense less frequently, but after Jefferson wrote to him in 1816 that he believed "that the moral sense is as much a part of our constitution as that of feeling, seeing, or hearing," Adams replied: "I agree perfectly with you, that 'the Moral Sense is as much a part of our constitution as that of feeling,' and in all that you say, upon this subject," *The Adams-Jefferson Letters,* ed. L. J. Cappon (Chapel Hill, 1959), Volume II, pp. 492 and 494. In a letter to John Taylor in 1814, Adams writes: "Being men, they have all what Dr. Rush calls a *moral faculty;* Dr. Hutcheson a *moral sense;* and

are obliged to ask whether the predominant epistemology of revolutionary morals ever ceased to be that of Lockean rationalism and whether it was ever replaced by the doctrine of moral sense.

It is hard to identify this doctrine with precision because different versions of it were adopted by its many advocates in the eighteenth century. Yet all those who adopted it had at least this much in common: they believed that when we engage in moral assessment we exercise a moral faculty which is different from reason or the understanding because that moral faculty resembles the normal five senses in certain respects. Appealing to such a faculty distinguished advocates of the moral sense from philosophers who subscribed to moral rationalism. According to the former, we are supposed to *sense* that a certain kind of action, such as telling the truth, is right, whereas lying is wrong; according to the latter we are supposed to see this by the use of reason—the same reason that is employed in mathematics. Advocates of the doctrine of moral sense also held that we use that faculty rather than Locke's reason while evaluating ultimate ends of human conduct. As we keep trying to answer those who keep asking us why we do certain things, we must finally cite a goal or an end which is approved of by the exercise of our moral sense and not by our reason. Why do we walk? For exercise. Why do we seek exercise? For our health. Why do we seek health? To attain happiness. Why do we wish to be happy? At some point such as this we must, theorists of the moral sense said,

the Bible and the generality of the world, *a conscience,*" *Works,* Volume VI, p. 449. Earlier, in his *Novanglus* of 1774, Adams had expressed the same view, *Works,* Volume IV, p. 14. It is interesting to discover, therefore, that in 1756 Adams was reading Hutcheson's *Short Introduction to Moral Philosophy,* the translation of a work written by Hutcheson in Latin under the title *Philosophiae Moralis Institutio Compendiaria.* A translation had first appeared in 1747, the original in 1742. See *Diary and Autobiography of John Adams,* Volume I, p. 2.

stop offering further goals to be attained by the use of certain means and must flatly say that our moral sense immediately sees the worth of happiness and that of any other ultimate end to which we may have been driven in the course of such moral questioning.

The emergence of the doctrine of moral sense in the eighteenth century precipitated a controversy in which the main participants "were Shaftesbury, Hutcheson, Hume and Adam Smith on the side of sense or feeling, and Samuel Clarke, Wollaston, Balguy, Richard Price and Reid on the side of reason or knowledge,"[2] and the controversy engaged the attention of many educated Americans. Colonists who read philosophy and law often mentioned the moral sense, and signers of the Declaration such as Witherspoon, Jefferson, and James Wilson hoped to resolve the issues that divided the British moralists whom they read while seeking moral support for their own political positions. We must keep in mind, however, that it was one thing to acknowledge the *existence* of the moral sense, which some writers identified with conscience, and another to accept the technical *doctrine* of moral sense according to which it was the faculty that had the final say in morals. Even Locke admitted that moral principles could be supported in some degree by appealing to conscience, while insisting that reason was *the preferred* way of establishing moral principles. He also maintained that men could to some extent support their belief in such principles by appealing to utility or to the Gospel, but, as we have observed, Locke, like Pufendorf,[3] regarded logical demonstra-

2. D. D. Raphael, *The Moral Sense* (Oxford, 1947), p. 2. Raphael remarks in a footnote to Reid's name that he must be classed with the rationalists in spite of narrowing the gap in the controversy by reinterpreting the moral sense theory. He discusses Reid's views in Chapter V of his work.

3. Pufendorf writes that "although by the wisdom of the Creator the natural law has been so adapted to the nature of man, that its observance is always connected with the profit and advantage of men, and therefore also

tion from self-evident principles as the way in which a philosopher would show them to be true. And it was this insistence on seeking final support from reason so conceived that made Locke's rationalism unacceptable to the most radical advocates of the doctrine of moral sense.

In this chapter I shall try to do a number of things. I mention them in a preliminary way so that the reader may distinguish certain intersecting threads of my argument. I shall begin by expounding a relatively pure form of the doctrine of moral sense, defended by Francis Hutcheson in his earlier work.[4] When we understand this version of the doctrine, we can more clearly see the contrast between the doctrine of moral sense and the moral rationalism of Locke. We can also see more easily how someone like Burlamaqui—whose views I shall also examine—could combine elements of the doctrine of moral sense and moral rationalism in a sort of hybrid doctrine that Jefferson seems to have accepted when he was drafting the Declaration. Burlamaqui believed in the existence of the moral sense but, unlike Hutcheson, denied that it, all by itself, could firmly establish general moral principles; and, in my opinion, Jefferson followed Burlamaqui in holding that the moral sense *indicates* or *intimates* certain moral principles but that it was the task of Lockean reason to verify or establish those principles. However, Jefferson's

---

this general love tends to man's greatest good, yet, in giving a reason for this fact, one does not refer to the advantage accruing therefrom, but to the common nature of all men. For instance, if a reason must be given why a man should not injure another, you do not say, because it is to his advantage, although it may, indeed, be most advantageous, but because the other person also is a man, that is, an animal related by nature, whom it is a crime to injure," *De jure naturae et gentium*, Book II, Chapter III, Section 18 (Oldfather translation). Sidgwick cites this same passage, *Outlines of the History of Ethics*, p. 178, note 2, while maintaining that "Locke's relation to utilitarianism is exactly characterised by some phrases of Pufendorf."

4. See Supplementary Notes, Moral Sense and Reason . . . , p. 277.

statements on these matters are complex and require considerable explication which I shall present in detail below.[5]

So much for my preview of some of the main expository threads of this chapter. I now want to add a foreword about a thread which is more political in character. Many advocates of the doctrine of moral sense praised it for enlarging the class of persons who could form reliable moral judgments because, according to the doctrine, it does not take a Pufendorf to see that a certain kind of action is right or wrong. For example, James Wilson gave credit to the doctrine of moral sense for explaining why a ploughman is as good as a Pufendorf at making moral judgments. However, when we carefully examine what Wilson says on this subject, we see that for him only a pure, undebauched, undepraved moral sense could lead one to correct moral principles, and this makes us wonder about the vaunted democratic implications of the doctrine of moral sense.

Hutcheson's Early Doctrine of Moral Sense

The early Hutcheson held that the moral sense is completely different from and independent of reason. Regarding the moral sense as in certain respects analogous to the normal five senses, Hutcheson thought of it as a faculty which is exercised without being influenced by the will. In other words, when we respond favorably or unfavorably to moral actions, our will cannot prevent us from having the moral sensations we have. The action impinges on us, and we are caused directly to approve or disapprove. In addition, the early Hutcheson held that no form of reason intervenes between the perception of a feature of an action—e.g., its being heroic—and

---

5. I no longer hold views on the subject which I put forth in my *Science and Sentiment in America* (New York, 1972), pp. 68–70. There I exaggerated the extent to which some of Jefferson's references to the moral sense signified an abandonment of moral rationalism.

the immediate moral sensation that it is good or right. Our approval of a heroic act would not depend on our rationally intuiting the truth of the proposition "All heroic actions are good or right or ought to be praised" in the way that Locke says we intuit the truth of "The whole is greater than a part." Nor does anything like Locke's deductive reason intervene. Moreover, Hutcheson does not think that we use that form of reason which we today call empirical science when we attribute *immediate* goodness because, obviously, Hutcheson does not believe that when a person's moral sense *immediately* approves of someone else's heroic action, the first person *infers* anything on the basis of an empirical generalization that such actions tend to bring about the advantage of the person himself or of the public. And when the first person himself contemplates performing a heroic action, he does not engage in any similar reasoning before performing the action of which his own moral sense approves, even though Hutcheson says that while we are intending the good of others we "undesignedly promote our own greatest private good." According to the early Hutcheson, "We are not to imagine, that this *moral sense,* more than the other senses, supposes any *innate ideas, knowledge,* or *practical proposition:* We mean by it only a *determination of our minds to receive amiable or disagreeable ideas of actions, when they occur to our observation, antecedent to any opinions of advantage or loss to redound to ourselves from them;* even as we are pleas'd with a *regular form,* or an *harmonious composition,* without having any knowledge of *mathematics,* or seeing any *advantage* in that form, or composition, different from the immediate pleasure."[6]

It would appear that Bernard Peach[7] is correct in speaking

6. *Inquiry Concerning Moral Good and Evil,* Section I, Part VII. This *Inquiry* is the second of two treatises printed in *An Inquiry into the Original of Beauty and Virtue,* 2nd ed. (London, 1726).
7. See Bernard Peach, Introduction to Hutcheson's *Illustrations on the Moral*

of the noncognitive nature of the sensing which is done in the exercise of the moral sense as described above, even though Hutcheson often speaks of the moral sense as *discerning* things. It would also appear that even though moral sensing was noncognitive for the early Hutcheson, it could entitle us to assert a moral *proposition* about, say, an heroic action. In other words, Hutcheson's allegedly noncognitive moral sensing allegedly entitles us to assert moral propositions that we can claim to *know*. In his early writings this claim to knowledge seems to be established immediately by the sensing, but later, presumably after absorbing the influence of Butler and the Stoics, Hutcheson acknowledged the need for some kind of correction of the moral sensations by reason before we could claim to have moral knowledge about an action.

Although Hutcheson does not make it altogether clear that a moral proposition about an action involves characterizing the action as, say, an act of heroism or an act of stealing, it is obvious that he must view moral propositions in this way. The moral sense responds to the action *as an action of a certain kind,* and this in itself suggests that the moral sense is at least partly cognitive. For if the moral sense, before it judges the action to be good, bad, right, or wrong, must view the action as possessed of a certain attribute, such as being a heroic act or an act of stealing, then the moral sense cannot react to the act without knowing or thinking *something.* Furthermore, when the moral sense responds unfavorably to an act which is known or thought to be an act of stealing, it must be responding unfavorably to that act *because* it is an act of stealing.[8] And this suggests that the moral sense is capable

---

Sense (Cambridge, Mass., 1971), p. 20. Also see W. T. Blackstone, *Francis Hutcheson and Contemporary Ethical Theory* (Athens, Georgia, 1965), Chapter V.

8. See Hutcheson, *Inquiry,* Section I, Part II, where he writes: "as soon as any action is represented to us as flowing from *love, humanity, gratitude,*

of assessing a moral proposition such as "No one should steal" since it is hard to see how the moral sense could arrive at the conclusion that an act was wrong *because* it was an act of stealing without issuing a favorable verdict on the general proposition that all acts of stealing are wrong or on the proposition that no one should steal.

It is only by viewing Hutcheson's moral sense in this enlarged way that we can see how it could even be a competitor of Locke's intuitionism. For it must be remembered that Locke's notion of self-evidence, when it was used in ethics, was applied to *general* moral principles about what men should or should not do. And when Hutcheson's view is regarded as a competitor of Locke's in this sphere, we must think of Hutcheson as saying that the moral sense *immediately* perceives *the truth* that all men should honor their engagements or that no man should harm another, whereas Locke holds that rational intuition immediately perceives such truth. Nevertheless, the moral sense as conceived by Hutcheson must not be confused with Locke's intuitive reason, even though both of these faculties are said by their advocates to be exercised immediately. Locke explicitly avows that we use our rational intuition to see immediately that a certain *proposition* is true, whereas Hutcheson holds that we use our moral sense to see immediately that an action of a certain kind is good, bad, right, or wrong. Yet, once followers of Hutcheson say that his moral sense must pass judgment on moral propositions, they are put in an awkward position because of his insistence that the moral sense does not "suppose" a "practical proposition."

---

compassion, a *study* of the good of others, and a *delight* in their happiness, although it were in the most distant part of the world, or in some past age, we feel joy within us, admire the lovely action, and praise its author. And on the contrary, every action represented as flowing from *hatred, delight* in the misery of others, or *ingratitude,* raises abhorrence and aversion."

It is extremely important to recall that the "immediacy" of a primary truth as construed by Aristotle meant that it was not deducible by the interposition of middle terms from logically prior premises—and this was closely related to Locke's view of the immediacy of his self-evident principles. By contrast, the immediacy of the operations of the moral sense was more like the direct apprehension that certain theorists of sense-perception speak of, whether they are realists who say we see the physical object directly, or representationalists, who speak of seeing a sense-datum directly. The moral sense was thought to be like eyesight, but it was sharply distinguished from intuitive reason, even though philosophers like Locke spoke of the intuitive reason as "seeing" or "perceiving" *truths*. We must bear in mind, of course, that throughout the whole tradition of rationalism philosophers who believe in immediate and self-evident truth have been forced, for want of other ways in which to make themselves understood, to use—only analogically, they would say—terms that refer to such sensory faculties as ordinary vision while referring to theoretical vision. And for this reason dictionaries are forced to report that words like "discern" in English, as well as its cognates in French and Latin, have both a sensory and an intellectual connotation. Nevertheless, while Locke thought of his rational intuition as seeing truth and perceiving agreements and disagreements of ideas, the early Hutcheson wished to strip his moral sense of all such rationalistic elements.

The extent of Hutcheson's opposition to Locke's moral rationalism is underscored when we observe his unwillingness to accept Gilbert Burnet's view that the seeings of the moral sense should be checked by, and their rightness derived from, the deliverances of reason in the form of self-evident truths. During a correspondence in the year 1725, Burnet tried to persuade Hutcheson to adopt this view but failed. Burnet tried to get Hutcheson to agree that one needed to appeal to self-evident truth to show that the moral sense was *right* in regarding benevolence as the ultimate end of human behavior. According to Burnet, the conjunction of the statements, "It is best that all should be happy" and "Benevolence is the properest and fittest means to procure the happiness of the species," logically implies that benevolence should be the ultimate end of one's behavior and that the moral sense was *right* in seeing it as such. Yet, as I have said, Hutcheson never budged from his view that such a rationalistic proof of the rightness of the moral sense was not necessary to complete his theory.[9]

Hutcheson not only spurned Burnet's rationalistic addition to his system, but unlike most expositors of the doctrine of natural law, he played down the role of self-evident truth even in that happy hunting ground of rationalism. Thus he wrote even in his *Short Introduction to Moral Philosophy*, which was a late work: "The *Law of nature* as it denotes a large collection of precepts, is commonly divided into the *primary* and *secondary;* . . . This division is of no use as some explain it, that the primary consists of self-evident propositions, and the secondary of such as require reasoning . . . The only useful sense of this distinction is, when such precepts as are absolutely necessary to any tolerable social state are called the *primary;* and such as are not of necessity, but tend to some considerable improvement or ornament of life, are called *secondary*."[10] This passage should make clear that unlike Locke, who thought that it was intuitive reason which should *really* establish the fundamental precepts of natural law, even though a test of their social utility might also be made, Hutcheson seems willing and even eager to by-pass

9. See *The Correspondence between Gilbert Burnet and Francis Hutcheson,* an appendix to Peach's previously cited edition of Hutcheson's *Illustrations on the Moral Sense.*

10. Francis Hutcheson, *A Short Introduction to Moral Philosophy in Three Parts, Containing the Elements of Ethics and the Law of Nature,* p. 94. I have used the English translation published in Dublin in 1787.

the rationalistic use of intuitive reason on the precepts as well as the use of discursive reason in deducing secondary precepts of natural law. The only kind of reason he seems willing to use in moral contexts is one which would establish *empirically* that primary precepts are absolutely necessary to any tolerable social state and that the secondary precepts tend to some considerable improvement or ornament of social life. But *this* reason is not Locke's intuition or deduction; it is rather the kind of reason that tells us whether one thing is in fact a means to an end. It is what Locke would have used, as he says in the *Reasonableness of Christianity,* to establish the "convenience" of the precepts of morality, their tendency to promote man's happiness.[11]

Burlamaqui on Reason and the Moral Sense

Hutcheson's diffidence about appealing to self-evident and deductively derived principles of natural law is, I think, enough to show that *his* epistemology of natural law was not that of Jefferson in *the Declaration.* Rather, as I have already indicated, it was a view like Burlamaqui's which permitted Jefferson to believe in the moral sense and reason, and to regard reason as so much more reliable as to refer to truths of reason alone in the Declaration. So let me now turn to Burlamaqui, who wrote his textbook late enough for the publisher of the first English translation of his *Principes du droit naturel* in 1748 to subtitle it: "In which the true systems of morality and civil government are established; and the different sentiments of Grotius, Hobbes, Pufendorf, Barbeyrac, Locke, Clarke, and Hutchinson [*sic*] occasionally considered." Burlamaqui was the beneficiary of two distinct intellectual traditions within the history of moral philosophy, rationalism and

11. Hutcheson asks at one point: "What is *Reason* but *that sagacity we have in prosecuting any end?*", *Inquiry Concerning Moral Good and Evil,* Section III, Part XV. See Raphael, *op. cit.,* p. 29.

the doctrine of moral sense; and he tried to reconcile them in a way that may illuminate the views of certain Americans, notably those of Jefferson.

Burlamaqui entitles Chapter III of Part II of his *Principes du droit naturel,* first published in Geneva in 1747, as follows: "Of the means, by which we discern (*discernons*) what is just and unjust, or what is dictated by natural law; namely, 1. moral instinct, and 2. reason."[12] What Burlamaqui has to say on this subject is of special interest because he had read not only all of the standard treatises on natural law by Continental jurists like Grotius and Pufendorf but also the works of British philosophers like Locke, Clarke, and Hutcheson. One commentator on Burlamaqui holds that *"il n'est pas impossible"* that Burlamaqui's addition of moral instinct was inspired by his reading of Hutcheson, but the commentator underestimates the connection between the two thinkers. For Burlamaqui, in explaining what he means by "moral instinct," says: "Moral instinct I call that natural bent or inclination, which prompts us to approve of certain things as good and commendable, and to condemn others as bad and blameable, independent of reflection. Or if any one has a mind to distinguish this instinct by the name of moral sense, as Mr. Hutchinson [*sic*] has done, I shall then say, that it is a faculty of the mind, which instantly discerns, in certain cases, moral good and evil, by a kind of sensation and taste, independent of reason and reflection."[13] I should add that Richard Price would have jumped on Burlamaqui's use of the verb "discern" (*discerne*), as he did on Hutcheson's use of it, because, as we shall see later, Price explicitly denies that the senses *discern*. The fact remains, however, that the translator of

12. *The Principles of Natural Law*, Part II, Chapter III.
13. *Ibid.*, Part II, Chapter III, Section I. "Hutchinson" is Burlamaqui's own spelling, repeated by the English translator. The commentator is B. Gagnebin in *Burlamaqui et le droit naturel* (Genève, 1944), pp. 109–110.

Hutcheson's Latin refers to nature's implantation of that "most divine of all our senses, that *Conscience* by which we *discern* [my emphasis] what is graceful, becoming, beautiful and honourable in the affections of the soul, in our conduct of life, our words and actions,"[14] and this is in accord with what Hutcheson writes in his text about the moral sense. Burlamaqui may have realized that someone might complain in the manner of Price about letting a sense "discern," for Burlamaqui speaks of "this emotion of the heart, which prompts us, *almost without any reasoning or inquiry* [my emphasis], to love some actions, and to detest others."[15] The use of the phrase "almost without" suggests that there is, for Burlamaqui, *something* rational about the moral sense. "Without any *great thought or reasoning* [my emphasis]," Burlamaqui also says, as he illustrates the exercise of the moral instinct, "a child, or untutored peasant, is sensible that ingratitude is a vice, and exclaims against perfidy, as a black and unjust action, which highly shocks him, and is absolutely repugnant to his nature."[16]

Burlamaqui goes on to say that if anyone should ask him where this *"mouvement du cœur"* comes from, he can only answer that "it is therefore a kind of instinct, like several others, which nature has given us, in order to determine us with more expedition and vigour, where reflection would be too slow. . . . The pressing and indispensable wants of man

14. *Short Introduction to Moral Philosophy*, p. 14. The text of Hutcheson justifies the translator's use of "discern," since the corresponding Latin passage reads: *"insitus est omnium divinissimus ille sensus, decorum, pulchrum, et honestum, in animi ipsius motibus, consiliis, dictis, factisque cernens."* Note *"cernens"* and also the fact that the translator has inserted the word "conscience" into this passage. However, the insertion is in accord with Hutcheson's own identification throughout his writings of the moral sense and the conscience. And the Latin verb *"cerno"* may refer to something done with the senses as well as with the intellect.
15. *Principles of Natural Law*, Part II, Chapter III, Section III.
16. *Ibid.*, Part II, Chapter III, Section II.

required that he should be directed by way of sense, which is always quicker and readier, than that of reason."[17] Indeed, the instinct that attaches us to life and our desire for happiness—"the primum mobile of all our actions"—are also given to us for our benefit because of the slowness of reason. And this is in accord with what Hutcheson says on the subject, namely: "Notwithstanding the mighty *reason* we boast of above other animals, its processes are too slow, too full of doubt and hesitation, to serve us in every exigency, either for our own preservation, without the *external senses,* or to direct our actions for the *good* of the *whole,* without this *moral sense.*"[18]

So, according to Burlamaqui, God has given us a moral sense because of our need for a speedier route to moral rectitude and for a device that may be used either by children who have not reached the age of reason or by adults who do not usually engage in any great thought or reasoning. And it is in this context that we find a question and statement by Burlamaqui to which I have referred in an earlier chapter: "For what numbers of people would never trouble their heads with reflecting? What multitudes there are of stupid wretches, who lead a mere animal life, and are scarce able to distinguish three or four ideas, in order to form what is called ratiocination? It was therefore our particular advantage, that the Creator should give us a discernment of good and evil, with a love for the one, and an aversion for the other, by means of a quick and lively kind of faculty, which has no necessity to wait for the speculations of the mind."[19]

Nevertheless, says Burlamaqui, God did not stop after implanting in us this moral instinct or moral sense, which is "the first means of discerning moral good and evil." He also thought it proper that "the same light, which serves to direct

17. *Ibid.,* Part II, Chapter III, Section III.
18. *Inquiry Concerning Moral Good and Evil,* Section VII, Part III.
19. *Principles of Natural Law,* Part II, Chapter III, Section IV.

us in every thing else, that is reason, should come to our assistance, in order to enable us the better to discern [*démêler*] and comprehend the true rules of conduct."[20] It appears, then, that Burlamaqui moved in a direction not unlike that in which Gilbert Burnet urged Hutcheson to move. That is to say, Burlamaqui held that reason verifies what the moral sense first brings to our attention. In the same spirit, Witherspoon had said that conscience "intimates . . . duty, previous to all reasoning,"[21] and Burlamaqui said that reason was better able than the moral sense to discern [*démêler*] the true rules of conduct. Reason, *"le flambeau de l'Ame,"* also serves, says Burlamaqui, "to illustrate, to prove, to extend, and apply what our natural sense"—and here I turn again to Burlamaqui's French because of the importance of the verbs used in describing what the moral sense does—*"indiquoit déjà touchant le juste & l'injuste"* (already indicated concerning justice and injustice). For example, reason, far from weakening (*affoiblir*) paternal tenderness, strengthens it by making us see how appropriate it is to the relationship between father and son, and how it redounds to the advantage of the whole family.[22] At this point Burlamaqui goes so far as to say that the light of reason has several advantages over the moral sense. The former, for one thing, serves to verify (*vérifier*) the latter by showing *"la justesse du goût"* (the propriety of taste), which is reminiscent of what Gilbert Burnet had said in his correspondence with Hutcheson. Reason

20. *Ibid.*, Part II, Chapter III, Section VIII.
21. *Lectures on Moral Philosophy* (Philadelphia, 1822), p. 39. These lectures had been delivered as early as 1772. See the Introduction to V. L. Collins's edition of the *Lectures* (Princeton, 1912), p. xxii. Witherspoon also tried to steer between the rationalists and the advocates of the moral sense. He writes: "Dr. Clarke, and some others, make *understanding* or *reason* the immediate principle of virtue. Shaftesbury, Hutcheson, and others, make *affection* the principle of it. Perhaps neither the one nor the other is wholly right. Probably both are necessary," *ibid.*, Philadelphia ed., pp. 15–16.
22. *Principles of Natural Law,* Part II, Chapter III, Section VIII.

shows us that the moral sense is neither blind nor arbitrary but directed by principles, and in this respect reason performs a similar service in the case of a sense such as sight. It helps us, for example, to judge with greater certainty the distance or shape of an object after having compared, measured, and examined it at leisure; and this leads us to a more accurate judgment than we should have made if we had relied solely on our first glimpse of the object. Reason also helps us avoid the prejudice that might be created by the influence of opinion and custom on our sentiments. "It is reason's province to rectify this erroneous judgment, and to counterbalance this effect of education, by setting before us the true principles, on which we ought to judge of things."[23]

Another advantage that reason has over moral sense is its capacity to develop principles and to extract their consequences with attention to varying circumstances, times, and places.[24] And a third advantage mentioned by Burlamaqui is reason's capacity to cover more cases than moral sense or instinct, which can cover only a small number of simple cases that require quick determination.[25] Summing up his conception of the relationship between moral sense and reason, Burlamaqui says: "Such are the two faculties, with which God has invested us, in order to enable us to discern between good and evil. These faculties happily joined, and subordinate one to the other, concur to the same effect. One gives the first notice, the other verifies and proves it." So, for Burlamaqui, the moral sense is only the subordinate faculty which *"donne la première indication"* (gives the first indication), whereas *"l'autre vérifie & prouve"* (the other verifies and

---

23. *Ibid.*, Part II, Chapter III, Section IX. B. F. Wright, Jr., in his *American Interpretations of Natural Law* (Cambridge, Mass., 1931), notes that Burlamaqui held that man may "discover" the natural law "through the use of his reason and his moral sense" (p. 7) but fails to mention Burlamaqui's belief in the logical priority of reason.
24. *Ibid.*, Part II, Chapter III, Section X.
25. *Ibid.*, Part II, Chapter III, Section XI.

proves). By means of (1) the moral sense, which gives us the first notice of, or directs us to, the good and the right and (2) the reason, which verifies or shows that what we *take to be* good and right is *really* good and right, we come to *know* the good and the right, or *"ce qui est la même chose, à connoître quelle est la Volunté de Dieu"* (what is the same thing, to know the Will of God) with regard to our moral conduct.[26]

Burlamaqui, it should be remarked, did not confine reason to what Locke called intuitive and discursive reason but also included under it what Locke sometimes called judgment or opinion. "Reason," Burlamaqui says, "I call the faculty of comparing ideas, of investigating the mutual relations of things, and thence inferring just consequences";[27] and I suggest that whereas comparing ideas and inferring just consequences might correspond respectively to Locke's intuitive and deductive reason, the activity of investigating the mutual relations of things seems to cover what we today would be more likely to call empirical science. It, rather than intuitive reason, is what Burlamaqui may have in mind when he speaks of our using our reason to improve our first impressions concerning the distance or shape of a given *object*. On the other hand, when Burlamaqui writes that the moral sense feels, gives us notice of, acquaints us with, discerns, or intimates *principles* which reason verifies or corrects, he is best understood as identifying reason with intuitive reason. Like the conscience of Pufendorf, Burlamaqui's moral sense introduces us to "maxims" or "precepts" which are then certified by reason.

Jefferson, Moral Sense, and Reason

Having presented the outlines of Burlamaqui's moral philosophy, I want to emphasize two conspicuous components of

26. *Ibid.*, Part II, Chapter III, Section XI.
27. *Ibid.*, Part II, Chapter III, Section VIII.

it before analyzing certain colonial American views on the same question. The first and more general one is that both moral sense and reason have roles in his system, but the second, which is more specific and more important, is that the moral sense is *logically subordinate* to intuitive reason. Now we may ask whether Jefferson assigned roles to both moral sense and intuitive reason, and whether he too regarded the former as subordinate to the latter. I should answer both questions in the affirmative with regard to Jefferson's thought while he was writing the Declaration, but the period after the Declaration is another matter and requires more elaborate discussion.

One reason for believing that both intuitive reason and the moral sense are assigned roles in the earlier period is that Jefferson in 1774, in his *Summary View of the Rights of British America,* asserts that "not only the principles of common sense, but the common feelings of human nature must be surrendered up, before his majesty's subjects here can be persuaded to believe that they hold their political existence at the will of a British parliament."[28] Here Jefferson appeals to reason, as expressed in the *principles of common sense,* and to the moral sense, as expressed in the *common feelings of human nature.* But since Jefferson asserted that both moral sense and reason had declared themselves on the wrongness of British domination of the Colonies only two years before he wrote the Declaration—where he defended a similar moral position by appealing to undeniable or self-evident truths of reason—he showed that he held in the Declaration that the moral sense was *subordinate* to reason simply because he dispensed with an appeal to moral sense in the Declaration. Dispensing with such an appeal did not mean that he denied the *existence* of a moral sense. Rather, the fact that he used only the language of undeniable or self-evident rational truth

28. *Papers of Thomas Jefferson,* ed. J. P. Boyd (Princeton, 1950–   ), Volume I, p. 126.

suggests that he wanted to use only his strongest guns in the Declaration. And his strongest guns were truths which could be certified by intuitive reason, which could in turn *verify* and lend support to the moral sense, which only *intimated*— to use the signer Witherspoon's word—that the principles of natural law were true. The common feelings of human nature, being expressed by the subordinate faculty of the moral sense, did not *need* to be referred to in the Declaration once the voice of the superior faculty of reason had spoken.

In his *Notes on Virginia,* written in 1781, Jefferson deals with reason and the moral sense but in a context which does not permit any firm conclusion about his views on the advantages of one over the other so far as moral judgment is concerned. Speaking of the black writer Ignatius Sancho, Jefferson says that "his letters do more honor to the heart than the head," and that "his subjects should often have led him to a process of sober reasoning; yet we find him always substituting sentiment for demonstration."[29] And expressing what he calls an as yet unestablished "suspicion" about blacks in general, Jefferson maintains that they are "in reason much inferior [to whites], as I think one could scarcely be found capable of tracing and comprehending the investigations of Euclid."[30] Jefferson adds that "whether further observation will or will not verify the conjecture, that nature has been less bountiful to them in the endowments of the head, I believe that in those of the heart she will be found to have done them justice."[31] Such remarks imply that in 1781 reason was

29. See Supplementary Notes, Jefferson on Ignatius Sancho, p. 279.
30. *Writings,* Volume II, p. 194. By contrast, Franklin had written as follows in 1763 after visiting a school in Philadelphia: "I was on the whole much pleas'd, and from what I saw, have conceiv'd a higher opinion of the natural capacities of the black race, than I had ever before entertained. Their apprehension seems as quick, their memory as strong, and their docility in every respect equal to that of white children," *The Papers of Benjamin Franklin,* Volume X, p. 396.
31. *Writings,* Volume II, p. 199.

still a faculty which Jefferson respected and that for him deficiency in rational power was a serious deficiency even in those who were full of moral feeling.[32]

In 1793 he also speaks of reason and the moral sense without ranking them. In discussing the principles of natural law, he writes: "For the reality of these principles I appeal to the true fountains of evidence, the head and heart of every rational and honest man. It is there nature has written her moral laws, and where every man may read them for himself." And in the same paper he writes: "Questions of natural right are triable by their conformity with the moral sense and reason of man."[33] In 1788, Jefferson wrote as follows to Richard Price upon receipt of the third edition of Price's highly rationalistic work, *A Review of the Principal Questions in Morals.*

> I thank you for the volume you were so kind as to send me some time ago. Everything you write is precious, and this volume is on the most precious of all our concerns. We may well admit morality to be the child of the understanding rather than of the senses, when we observe that it becomes dearer to us as the latter weaken, and as the former grows stronger by time and experience, till the hour arrives in which all other objects lose all their value.[34]

Although Jefferson mentions no title, it would appear that he was speaking about the third edition of Price's *Review,* since the book appeared in 1787 and Jefferson's letter was sent from Paris on February 7, 1788. What, then, are we to say about the fact that the very first section of Price's book contains a sharp criticism of Hutcheson's view that right and wrong are perceived by the *moral sense* and that Price insists that it is a very different power called the *understanding* by

32. See Supplementary Notes, Jefferson, Scientific Inquiry . . . , p. 281.
33. Jefferson, *Writings,* Volume III, pp. 228–229 and 235.
34. *Ibid.,* Volume VI, p. 424.

which we perceive the distinctions of right and wrong? How could Jefferson, who, as we shall soon see, called the moral sense the "true foundation of morality" in 1786 and 1787, turn around in 1788 and "admit morality to be the child of the understanding rather than of the senses," when Price says the following in Section II of Chapter I of his *Review?*

> In a word, it appears that *sense* and *understanding* are faculties of the soul totally different: The one being conversant only about *particulars;* the other about *universals:* The one not *discerning,* but *suffering;* the other not *suffering,* but *discerning;* and signifying the soul's *Power* of surveying and examining all things, in order to judge of them; which *Power,* perhaps, can hardly be better defined, than by calling it, in *Plato's* language, the power in the soul to which belongs . . . the apprehension of TRUTH.

It might be said in reply that Jefferson was offering polite and perfunctory praise to a great friend of the young nation, for Dr. Price had clearly shown such friendship when he published his *Observations on the Nature of Civil Liberty, the Principles of Government, and the Justice and Policy of the War with America* (1776). Indeed, the praise Jefferson gives to Price's work is so different from what Jefferson says about "the head" and science in letters to Mrs. Cosway in 1786 and Peter Carr in 1787—to which I shall soon come— that some readers may find it hard to regard the letter to Price as indicating much about Jefferson's views on morality in 1787.

So far, then, I have offered evidence, which is as strong as the documents available to me can reveal, that Jefferson believed in reason's logical superiority to moral sense while he was working on the Declaration. I have mentioned passages written in 1782 and others in 1793 in which both faculties are said, without being ranked, to be fountains of moral evidence, but this is compatible with the theory of reason's superiority. And whatever Jefferson's motives were for writing the letter to Price, it too is compatible with that theory. But now I come to three letters which reveal views that do not so clearly show a confident belief in the subordination of the moral sense to reason. First, I quote the important and long letter to Peter Carr of 1787, in which Jefferson offers his nephew his views on the subject of moral philosophy; then I quote some remarks from another well-known letter to Mrs. Cosway of 1786; and finally I quote part of a letter Jefferson wrote to James Fishback in 1809.

The much-quoted part of the letter to Peter Carr reads as follows:

> Moral philosophy. I think it lost time to attend lectures in this branch. He who made us would have been a pitiful bungler if he had made the rules of our moral conduct a matter of science. For one man of science, there are thousands who are not. What would have become of them? Man was destined for society. His morality therefore was to be formed to this object. He was endowed with a sense of right and wrong merely relative to this. This sense is as much a part of his nature as the sense of hearing, seeing, feeling; it is the true foundation of morality, and not the το χαλον [*sic*] truth, &c., as fanciful writers have imagined. The moral sense, or conscience, is as much a part of man as his leg or arm. It is given to all human beings in a stronger or weaker degree, as force of members is given them in a greater or less degree. It may be strengthened by exercise, as may any particular limb of the body. This sense is submitted indeed in some degree to the guidance of reason; but it is a small stock which is required for this: even a less one than what we call Common sense. State a moral case to a ploughman and a professor. The former will decide it as well, and often better than the latter, because he has not been led astray by artificial rules. In this branch therefore read

good books because they will encourage as well as direct
your feelings. The writings of Sterne particularly form
the best course of morality that ever was written. Besides
these read the books mentioned in the inclosed paper;
and above all things lose no occasion of exercising your
dispositions to be grateful, to be generous, to be chari-
table, to be humane, to be true, just, firm, orderly, cour-
agious &c. Consider every act of this kind as an exercise
which will strengthen your moral faculties, and increase
your worth.[35]

The letter to Mrs. Cosway—a dialogue between the Head
and the Heart—contains the following words: "Morals were
too essential to the happiness of man, to be risked on the uncertain combinations of the head. She [nature] laid their
foundation, therefore, in sentiment, not in science. That
[sentiment] she gave to all, as necessary to all; this [science]
to a few only, as sufficing with a few."[36] This statement is not
unlike Jefferson's declaration to Peter Carr a year later. The
moral sense is what the ploughman uses, the reason is what
the professor uses, and, of course, there are more ploughmen
than professors. Only a small stock of reason (science) guides
the moral sense (sentiment), according to the letter to Carr,
but using reason may lead to artificiality, which is the counterpart of "the uncertain combinations of the head" in the
letter to Mrs. Cosway. In a related vein, Jefferson wrote to
James Fishback: "The practice of morality being necessary
for the well-being of society, he [the Creator] has taken care
to impress its precepts so indelibly on our hearts that they
shall not be effaced by the subtleties of our brain."[37]

I begin my analysis of these letters—especially Jefferson's

35. *Papers of Thomas Jefferson*, Volume 12, pp. 14–15. As Nicholas White has
    pointed out to me, the Greek expression should contain a *kappa* instead of
    a *chi*. See *Writings*, Volume VI, p. 257. Accents are omitted in the *Papers*
    and the *Writings*.
36. *Writings*, Volume V, p. 443.
37. *Ibid.*, Volume XII, p. 315.

letters to Carr and Cosway—by observing that they may well be compatible with a continued acceptance of what I have called Lockean rationalism in morality. I call special attention to Jefferson's statement that the moral sense or conscience, even though he calls it the true *foundation* of morality, is submitted to the *guidance* of reason. By contrast to Jefferson, Hutcheson held that reason, conceived as empirical science, could be used in showing what means would accomplish ends approved by the moral sense, but for him, reason did not *guide* the moral sense to its immediate approvals and disapprovals. *Guiding* the moral sense is more reminiscent of the process advocated by Gilbert Burnet when he tried to get Hutcheson to acknowledge the necessity of appealing to rational principles. True, Jefferson minimizes the number of rational principles required for such guidance, but when Burnet tried to persuade Hutcheson, even he did not ask Hutcheson to accept more than two self-evident truths as premises in a demonstrative argument which allegedly deduced the rightness of the perceptions of Hutcheson's moral sense. And, of course, Aquinas thought that all rational precepts of natural law flowed from *one*.[38]

Insofar, then, as intuitive reason is said by Jefferson to *guide* the moral sense, he seems, in his letter to Peter Carr, to subscribe to a view like Burlamaqui's. True, we do not find Burlamaqui speaking of the moral sense or conscience as the *true foundation of morality* when he describes it as the faculty which gives us the *first notice* of the principles, the *intimations* or *indications* of them which reason is to verify and correct. But the word "foundation" was not the clearest of philosophical words in that period, just as it is not the clearest of words in contemporary philosophy, and a good argument may be made for the idea that a faculty which God gave to all of us and which we all use instinctively from earli-

38. *Summa Theologica,* First Part of the Second Part, Question XCIV, Second Article.

est childhood was viewed as more fundamental than even the more sophisticated faculties we use in *establishing* moral principles. If Jefferson had meant that the moral sense or the conscience was the faculty through which we get the first glimmerings of moral precepts, then he would not have been veering from Burlamaqui or even from Locke and Pufendorf, who affirmed that man had such a conscience. With this in mind, many of Jefferson's statements in praise of the moral sense might well be accommodated by a reader who maintained that Jefferson remained a Lockean rational moralist for at least some time after the Declaration and, as such, continued to believe in the superior power of reason or science to arrive at moral truth, even though he believed in the existence of the moral sense.

But how, a reader may ask, can this attribution of rationalism be squared with Jefferson's writing to Peter Carr that God "would have been a pitiful bungler if he had made the rules of our moral conduct a matter of science. For one man of science, there are thousands who are not. What would have become of them?" In my opinion, Jefferson meant in this passage that God would have been a pitiful bungler if he had made the rules of our moral conduct a matter of science *alone*. Moreover, Jefferson's remark that there *are* men of science— however few—leaves open at least the possibility that those men of science establish moral rules through the use of intuitive reason. But Jefferson went further. When he says in the same letter that the moral sense should be submitted in some degree to the guidance of reason, he acknowledges the kind of superiority of reason that Burlamaqui and Locke had both asserted. True, Jefferson adds that the stock of rational principles which are necessary for guiding the moral sense is a small one. But this does not destroy the implication that the bulk of mankind should cheerfully accept whatever amount of supervision only a man of "elevated understanding"—to use Locke's term—can give. Therefore, I cannot see how

Jefferson could avoid agreeing with Burlamaqui that men of reason possess a faculty which is logically superior to the moral sense if that faculty must *guide* moral sense.[39] Jefferson's letter to Mrs. Cosway may be interpreted similarly. When he asserted there that nature—the counterpart of God in the letter to Carr—gave sentiment to all, but science only to a few "as sufficing with a few," he granted that the few have powers which the many do not have.

The reader may now ask about Jefferson's disparaging references to men of science and to professors, to their being likely to be led astray by artificial rules and the "uncertain combinations of the head." How shall we deal with such apparently anti-rationalistic remarks? By answering that Jefferson was merely repeating his fear that the fabric of society would be destroyed if moral precepts could be arrived at *only* by intuitive reason. This fear is evident in his letter to Fishback, where Jefferson explains that the Creator has written his precepts so indelibly on our hearts because he did not wish to let the very existence of society depend on what man could achieve by his brain alone, a brain that might have effaced these precepts if they were not deeply rooted in instinct, the moral sense, or conscience. I repeat, however, that this does not show that Jefferson had surrendered his belief that some men could discover self-evident moral truths nor his belief that such truths would amplify, verify, and correct the deliverances of the unaided moral sense or conscience. What it shows is a fear that the fortunes of social cohesiveness

39. Much as I should like to accept the support of C. M. Wiltse in his *Jeffersonian Tradition in American Democracy* when he quotes Jefferson as writing to Peter Carr in the letter I have been using that "your own reason is the only oracle given you by heaven" (p. 68), I am bound to point out that Jefferson makes this remark while discussing religion rather than morals. True, it is strange to find Jefferson writing such a sentence just after he has written his paean to the moral sense, but if Jefferson were thinking in this context of the manner in which we establish religious belief, we can draw no inferences from it about his views on the epistemology of morals.

could not be entrusted to the very few, who might be able to arrive at the rational principles asserted in the Declaration but who might also make mistakes that could destroy that cohesiveness. God gave all of us a moral sense, Jefferson held, as insurance against the vicissitudes of intuitive reason, but Jefferson did not deny the power of some men to use intuitive reason in discovering the laws of morality. This, however, was not very far from the views of Pufendorf, who, though he staunchly advocated the primacy of intuitive reason in discovering the principles of natural law, insisted that we are imbued from childhood by society with a consciousness of some of the maxims that we later see rationally, and that this early instillment of these maxims makes it certain that "they can never again be destroyed, no matter how the impious man, in order to still the twinges of conscience, may endeavor to blot out the consciousness of those precepts."[40] Jefferson's concern that the subtleties of the brain and the uncertain combinations of the head might efface the precepts of conscience or the moral sense was the counterpart of Pufendorf's fear of what impious men might do while trying to still the twinges of conscience. So both of them thanked God for providing mankind with some kind of moral ballast in the form of moral sense or conscience.

What I have attributed to Jefferson so far I have attributed to him mainly as a figure of the eighteenth century. His view that both reason and the moral sense are avenues to moral truth and that reason is logically superior because it guides the moral sense cannot easily be regarded as a view that he held throughout his life, though a case *may* be made for regarding it as such—a case which I am not inclined to make for a number of reasons. Very few of Jefferson's comments on morality, which appear chiefly in letters rather than in treatises or essays upon which he lavished reflection, allow

40. Pufendorf, *De officio hominis et civis*, trans. F. G. Moore (New York, 1927), Book I, Chapter III, Section 12.

confident exegesis of the kind that one can offer when one is dealing with a more systematic writer on moral philosophy. In fact, I am prepared to admit that even what I have said so far may be questioned by scholars inclined to shift emphases upon which I have relied in my interpretation. But when one presses on into letters written by Jefferson later in life, one finds oneself grasping at straws and trying to bind them into consistent but fragile bundles that may not hold together for very long. Besides, my main interest is in Jefferson the Revolutionary thinker, and for that reason I do not feel obliged to make extensive forays into the nineteenth century except when they may illuminate the ideas of the younger Jefferson. One cannot help feeling that during the years when the ideas of canonical moral philosophers and jurists were still vividly before his mind, Jefferson held views in moral philosophy that are easier to expound just because they were the views of other and greater thinkers which he did not alter very much. But as he grew older and as new influences, new thoughts, and new problems crowded in on him, he gives the impression of a beleaguered sage, a philosopher-president who really has no deep or original ideas in moral philosophy but who, to his credit, tries very hard to produce some—often in response to inquiring correspondents. For this reason I am happy to stay for the most part within the temporal boundaries imposed by this book and to avoid excessive speculation on what Jefferson thought during the twenty-six years of life in the nineteenth century granted to him.

My reason, as I have indicated, for not conducting extensive forays into Jefferson's later moral philosophy is that once we leave the Jefferson who appeals to both the moral sense and reason in supporting the principles of natural law, it becomes more difficult to say just where he stood on some of the fundamental questions of moral philosophy. In particular, it becomes more difficult to represent him as holding that the

moral sense is subordinate to reason. For one thing, he becomes so eloquent about the virtues of the moral sense that
one wonders whether he has abandoned Burlamaqui's idea
that intuitive reason can verify the precepts which the Creator had impressed indelibly on our hearts so that they could
not "be effaced by the subtleties of the brain." After this remark to Fishback in 1809, Jefferson began to sound like
Locke in the *Reasonableness of Christianity,* especially when
he announced to Fishback that "We all agree in the obligation of the moral precepts of Jesus, and nowhere will they be
found delivered in greater purity than in his discourses."[41]
This thought lay behind the *Jefferson Bible,* in which Jefferson tries to extract the morality of Jesus, stripped of the
mystifications of philosophers and theologians; and so one
cannot help thinking that Locke's earlier retreat to the
Gospel after failing to produce his demonstrative science of
morality may have prefigured Jefferson's search for a scrip-
tural heart-morality in the Gospel.[42] The similarity extends
even to Locke's concern that dairy-maids be provided with a
revealed morality, the counterpart of Jefferson's desire that
ploughmen get theirs directly from Jesus or from Laurence
Sterne. Indeed, in 1814, Jefferson continues to argue in a
letter to Thomas Law[43] that it was necessary for the Creator
to make "the moral principle so much a part of our constitution as that no errors of reasoning or of speculation might
lead us astray from its observance in practice"; that by "the
moral principle" he means the moral sense or instinct, the
"brightest gem with which the human character is studded"
and the absence of which is "more degrading than the most
hideous of the bodily deformities."

Had Jefferson said no more than this we might suppose
that he was returning to something like the early Hutche-

41. *Writings,* Volume XII, p. 315.
42. See Wiltse, *op. cit.,* pp. 45–56.
43. *Writings,* Volume XIV, pp. 138–144.

son's views. But in the same letter to Law in which Jefferson
extolled the moral sense with no clear reference to a supporting role for intuitive reason, he acknowledged that if a man
were to lack a moral sense, we could try to educate him by
appealing "to reason and calculations." However, this reason
and these calculations are not intuitive and discursive reason,
as they were for Locke. They are to be used in presenting the
man who lacks a moral sense, or who has an inferior one,
with motives to do good and to avoid evil. We may point out
to him that he will gain the love of his fellow-men if he does
good, or their hatred and rejection if he does evil, reminding
him that their society is necessary to his happiness and even
his existence. We may show him "by sound calculation that
honesty promotes interest in the long run," and we may also
call his attention to future rewards and punishments in an
afterlife. And when Jefferson tries to deal with critics who
attack the existence of a moral sense on the ground that a
virtuous act in one country may be a vicious one in another,
Jefferson denies that this argues against the existence of a
moral sense and asserts that it shows that the moral sense can
operate in different ways under different circumstances,
much as Aquinas might have said that the rational natural
law could be applied differently in different circumstances.
In this connection, Jefferson also says that "nature has constituted *utility* to man, the standard and test of virtue" and
therefore that a kind of act which is "useful, and consequently
virtuous in one country" may be "vicious in another differently circumstanced."[44]

Needless to say, the reference to utility as the standard and
test of virtue has been seized upon by commentators who see
it as evidence for Jefferson's utilitarianism. But even if they
were right—as I doubt that they are—Jefferson would have
to be viewed as a utilitarian who was also an intuitionist. For
one thing, he says that *nature* has constituted utility the

44. *Ibid.*

standard and test of virtue, and therefore one wonders whether the principle of utility itself is viewed by Jefferson as an intuitively perceived principle of natural law. For another, he shows his continuing attachment to self-evident moral truths as late as 1823, when he repeated his belief in the self-evidence of the proposition that the earth belongs in usufruct to the living and that one generation cannot bind another.[45]

For all of these reasons, the student of Jefferson's moral thought in the last years of his life will find it very hard to pin a clear label on him. Moral sense, utility, revelation, intuitive reason—all of these are offered by him at one time or another as avenues to moral truth, but no one of them is clearly given the sort of preference that intuitive reason was given by Locke, utility by Bentham, and the moral sense by Hutcheson. Under the circumstances I gladly defer to scholars who think that they can extract a clear moral theory which was consistently held by the Sage of Monticello from his earliest years to his death.[46]

On the other hand, the temporal boundaries of this book do not prevent me from dealing with other eighteenth-century American politicians who spoke more systematically than Jefferson did about the relationship between reason and sense in morals, in particular with James Wilson. But before dealing with Wilson's views I am obliged—as usual—to say something about British and Continental antecedents of his thought.

The People and the Moral Sense

Turning to the supposed social and political implications of man's having a moral sense, I should point out that it was

45. *Ibid.*, Volume XV, p. 470.
46. Adrienne Koch, who recognizes that Jefferson's moral philosophy underwent change, tries to depict the development of his thinking in Part I of her *Philosophy of Thomas Jefferson.*

widely believed in the eighteenth century that if the only method of establishing moral precepts was that described by Locke in his rationalistic moods or that described by Samuel Clarke, then "the bulk of mankind," as Lord Kames said while using a phrase we have met in Locke's *Reasonableness of Christianity*,[47] would be unable to arrive at moral truth. For most men were not moral Euclids, either through failure to use their intuitive reason in arriving at moral axioms or to exercise their powers of discursive reason in order to arrive at moral theorems. As a matter of fact, we have already seen that Locke himself shared something of this concern. When he was not berating the populace for being too stupid or too biased to intuit the first principles of morality or to deduce its theorems, he seems to have worried about where they would find moral guidance—perhaps after he realized that he had, in setting up his ideal of a demonstrative science of morality, constructed a goal which even *he* could not attain. This was the Locke who expressed his satisfaction with the Gospel as a sufficient source of moral truth because he doubted that day-laborers, tradesmen, spinsters, and dairy-maids could become perfect in his science of deductive ethics.[48] And it was also the Locke who once wrote in a commonplace book: "A ploughman that cannot read, is not so ignorant but he has a conscience, and knows in those few cases which concern his own actions, what is right and what is wrong. Let him sincerely obey this light of nature, it is the transcript of the moral law in the Gospel; and this, even though there be errors in it, will lead him into all the truths in the Gospel that are necessary for him to know."[49]

The notion that ploughmen, dairy-maids, and other such persons can make moral judgments without the benefit of mathematical morality, Scripture, or any other comparatively

47. See Chapter 1, note 29 above, and the passage cited there.
48. *Works,* Volume VII, p. 146.
49. See Lord King, *The Life of John Locke* (London, 1830), Volume 2, p. 78.

sophisticated method was not new in the history of Western thought. It may be traced at least as far back as Paul's statement: "For when the Gentiles, which have not the law, do by nature the things contained in the law, these, having not the law, are a law unto themselves: Which shew the work of the law written in their hearts, their conscience also bearing witness, and *their* thoughts the meanwhile accusing or else excusing one another."[50] Paul's view of heart-law prompted rationalists like Pufendorf and Locke to speak of conscience, but conscience was later identified with the moral sense and thereby elevated by philosophical critics of Locke and Clarke into a more technical concept.[51] The doctrine of moral sense attributed a power of perception to persons who lacked many of the ideas contained in Locke's self-evident principles as well as the capacity to use God-given intuitive and deductive reason. It also attributed that power to savages who lacked the heart-law revealed in the Scriptures. It was therefore a godsend to ploughmen, to the uneducated, and to those who had not the law in Paul's sense.

With concern for such persons, Lord Kames writes as follows after summarizing part of Samuel Clarke's rationalistic and intuitionistic ethics: "If this demonstration, as it is called, be the only or chief foundation of morals, unlucky it is, that a doctrine of such importance should have so long been hid from mankind. And now that the important discovery is made, it is not however likely to do great service; considering how little the bulk of mankind are able to enter into abstruse reasoning, and how little influence such reasoning generally has when apprehended." Then, after complaining that Clarke makes the common error of moral philosophers

---

50. Romans II, 14–15.
51. Witherspoon commented as follows on Hutcheson's views of the moral sense: "This *moral sense* is precisely the same thing with what, in Scripture and common language we call *conscience*. It is the law which our Maker has written upon our hearts; and both intimates and enforces duty, previous to all reasoning," *Lectures on Moral Philosophy*, p. 24.

in substituting reason for sentiment, Kames continues to speak up implicitly for ploughmen and other such people when he writes that even if "our duty could be made plain to us by an abstract chain of reasoning, yet we have good ground to conclude, that the Author of nature has not left our actions to be directed by so weak a principle as reason: and a weak principle it must be to the bulk of mankind, who have little capacity to enter into abstract reasoning; whatever effect it may have upon the learned and contemplative."[52] In a related vein, Francis Hutcheson sought to call attention to certain virtues of his own version of the doctrine of moral sense, according to which moral reactions are based on a benevolent "instinct, antecedent to all reason from interest," by pointing out that "an honest *farmer* will tell you, that he studies the *preservation* and *happiness* of his children, and loves them without any design of good to himself."[53] Kames's concern for the bulk of mankind and Hutcheson's admiration of the honest farmer were connected with the idea that the development of British moral philosophy from rationalistic intuitionism to the doctrine of moral sense was a step in the direction of democracy. Farmers, ploughmen, and, indeed, the bulk of mankind were thought to be better at using the moral sense than intuitive reason. Therefore, the moral judgments of the lowly would, in the view of those who looked at philosophical theories as political weapons, count for as much as the judgments of those "elevated understandings" who could do ethics in a deductive manner. We have also seen that some ethical rationalists required those who were able to arrive at "really" self-evident truths to be virtuous, learned, rational, or unbiased—to mention

52. Kames, *Essays on the Principles of Morality and Religion*, 3rd ed. (Edinburgh, 1779), pp. 104–105; 106–107.
53. *An Inquiry Concerning Moral Good and Evil*, Section II, Part IX. It might be noted that Hutcheson here uses the verb "studies" to mean the same as "aims at." See Scott, *Francis Hutcheson*, p. 186, on Hutcheson's effort to "democraticize" Shaftesbury's philosophy.

only some of the requirements for moral judgeships that we have found in the literature. Consequently, many persons who arrived at moral truths which were unpalatable to those rationalists who set up these requirements might be dismissed as unvirtuous, ignorant, irrational, prejudiced, or in the grip of passion.

The question to which we now begin to address ourselves is whether advocates of the doctrine of moral sense were able to avoid setting up corresponding qualifications and hence able to make their theory much more democratic than the moral rationalism they were trying to escape. Because Hutcheson's early version of the doctrine of moral sense seemed not to require the use of anything that could be called reason while making immediate judgments, Hutcheson held that ploughmen were at least as able as professors to make such moral judgments and that an aristocratic bias in the doctrine of moral rationalism would be diminished or eliminated if a sense rather than reason were *the* moral faculty. Yet even Burlamaqui, who allowed the moral sense to be tinged with *some* element of rationality, however small, was concerned to answer critics of his belief in the existence of a moral sense who complained that there are men in *civilized* countries who seem to be devoid of all shame, humanity, and justice. In trying to defend the existence of a moral sense against such critics, Burlamaqui replied that "we must take care to distinguish between the natural state of man, and the depravation, into which he may fall by abuse, and in consequence of irregularity and debauch."[54] But once the moral sense has to be exercised by moral judges who are not in a depraved or debauched state, those who abandoned rational intuitionism because of its élitism and who fled to the doctrine of moral sense because of its supposedly democratic qualities, might wonder whether they had left the frying pan for the fire.

54. *Principles of Natural Law,* Part II, Chapter III, Section VI.

James Wilson and the Undepraved Moral Sense

One of the more innocent travelers along that path may well
have been James Wilson, who appears to have felt the same
concern that Kames and Jefferson felt for ploughmen and
the bulk of mankind. For Wilson says: "If the rules of virtue
were left to be discovered by reasoning, even by demonstrative reasoning, unhappy would be the condition of the far
greater part of men, who have not the means of cultivating
the power of reasoning to any high degree."[55] Gilbert Chinard was one of the first to point out that Wilson was a great
admirer of Burlamaqui,[56] who actively influenced the American jurist's views in the latter's important pamphlet, *Considerations on the Nature and Extent of the Legislative Authority of the British Parliament* (1774). But the influence of
Burlamaqui is also evident in Wilson's *Lectures on Law,*
especially those delivered in 1790–91, only a few years after
Jefferson was writing his letters to Cosway and Carr in praise
of the moral sense.

I must say quickly that Wilson is not the clearest of thinkers on ethics and natural law, and although we have more of
his systematic philosophical writing to go on than we have in
the case of Jefferson, we cannot always be sure of his position
on a number of fundamental questions of moral philosophy.[57]
Nevertheless, he does address himself to the question which
is our main concern in this section because at some places—
though not in all—he regards the moral sense as a faculty
which is noncognitive and which is exercised in *feeling* that
the performance of a certain kind of action is a duty, or that

55. *Works,* Volume I, p. 136.
56. See *The Commonplace Book of Thomas Jefferson: A Repertory of His
    Ideas on Government,* ed. G. Chinard (Baltimore, 1926), Introduction by
    the editor, pp. 39–44.
57. See A. Beitzinger, "The Philosophy of Law of Four American Founding
    Fathers," *American Journal of Jurisprudence,* 21 (1976): 14–15.

it is right. In fact, at one place in his account of the moral sense, he shows the extent of his reliance upon the early Hutcheson by taking a whole passage from that author (without attributing it to him). The passage reads: "If there is no moral sense, which makes benevolence appear beautiful; if all approbation be from the interest of the approver; 'What's Hecuba to us, or we to Hecuba?' " To this Wilson attaches a footnote reading *"Hamlet,"* thereby departing in at least one respect from Hutcheson, who had attached a footnote reading *"Tragedy of Hamlet."*[58] Believing, then, that there is a moral sense which is that of the early Hutcheson and hence is noncognitive, Wilson replies to those who deny its existence or authority, or who arraign the certainty and uniformity of its decisions, that the authoritative moral sense is not that of an individual who exemplifies human nature "in her most rude or depraved forms. 'The good experienced man,' says Aristotle, 'is the last measure of all things.' To ascertain

---

58. With regard to Wilson's appropriation of the words of others without giving them credit, I should point out that in my *Science and Sentiment in America* (pp. 65–67), I call attention to a striking similarity between a passage in Wilson and one in Hume—a passage which clearly suggests that Wilson agreed with Hume in regarding the approval of ultimate ends as noncognitive in nature. I also point out that Wilson never mentions the similarity between his own remark and that of Hume. Mr. Beitzinger (*op. cit.*, p. 15, n. 37) says that Wilson paraphrased the passage in question from a direct quotation of it in Thomas Reid's *Essays on the Active Powers of Man* (Essay V, Chapter VII) and that Wilson did not read the passage in Hume's first Appendix to his *Enquiry Concerning the Principles of Morals*. The only evidence Mr. Beitzinger appears to give for his contention that Wilson read Hume's remark only *as quoted by Reid* is the fact that the passage *is* quoted by Reid and that there is other evidence of Wilson's having been influenced by Reid in the same chapter of Wilson's *Lectures on Law*, "Of the Law of Nature," *Works*, Volume I, Chapter III. Nevertheless, it is noteworthy that Reid attributes the quoted words to Hume, whereas Wilson does not mention Hume in the chapter. Indeed, Wilson does not mention *Reid* in the chapter! I wonder whether the passage that Wilson lifted from Hutcheson came directly from the latter's *Inquiry Concerning Moral Good and Evil*, Section I, Part II, or whether Wilson found it quoted elsewhere.

moral principles, we appeal not to the common sense of savages, but of men in their most perfect state."[59]

Now the story becomes complicated. How, we may ask, does Aristotle enter the story? First we must observe that Wilson is not quoting Aristotle directly but, characteristically, takes Aristotle's translated words from Hutcheson's *System of Moral Philosophy*, published posthumously in 1755, nine years after its author's death. Hutcheson writes there: "Aristotle well observes, that 'many points in *morals*, when applied to individual cases, cannot be exactly determined; but good men know them by a sort of sensation: *the good experienced man is thus the last measure of all things.*' "[60] But although in the passage quoted by Hutcheson, Aristotle is certainly not referring to the determination of moral *principles* like his principle of the mean but rather to the problem of determining whether *in an individual case* a man is *in fact* deviating from the mean, Wilson blithely regards Aristotle as formulating in this passage a criterion for the determination of general *moral principles*. For immediately after quoting Aristotle, Wilson writes: "To ascertain moral principles, we appeal not to the common [or moral] sense of savages, but of men in their most perfect state."[61]

Given Wilson's familiarity with Burlamaqui's *Principles of Natural Law,* as indicated throughout Wilson's chapter on natural law, and especially in the passage which immediately precedes the reference to Aristotle, it seems clear that Wilson was trying to meet the same sort of arguments that Burlamaqui tried to meet in *his* effort to defend the existence of the moral sense in an undepraved, natural man as the indicator—at least—of moral principles. But when Wilson refers to Aristotle's good experienced man—whether correctly or not—he

59. *Works,* Volume I, p. 139.
60. Hutcheson, *System of Moral Philosophy,* Book II, Chapter I, Section V (p. 237).
61. Wilson, *op. cit.,* Volume I, p. 139.

more blatantly reminds us of something we have seen in our examination of moral rationalism. First of all, this reference is reminiscent of Locke's exclusion of certain people as unable to see the natural law because they have been brought up in vice. Secondly, it resembles Locke's view in being subject to the charge of circularity. After all, we are sent to the moral sense in order to discover what is *good,* but we are also warned that not just any individual's moral sense can be trusted to detect what is good. So, we ask, to whose moral sense *shall* we appeal? Answer: to that of a *good* experienced man. But at this point we have a right to ask: How shall we find out who is a good man? And if we are sent to the good moral sense once again, we shall have a perfect right to complain that we are being given what is known in the vernacular as a run-around, and in logic as a circular definition. Finally, if we are told that there is no circle involved because the word "good" in the phrase "good experienced man" is not to be defined by reference to what is sensed by the moral sense of a good man, we have a right to ask how it *is* defined. If it is said to be undefinable or definable only by pointing to particular individuals, then we may well complain that the supposedly democratic move of the theorists of moral sense is not as democratic as it was cracked up to be. Of course, there seems to be a move in the direction of increasing the class of reputable moral judges by virtue of dropping the requirement that they use the reason of moral rationalists. However, as soon as the moral sense is characterized as it is by Wilson—in the wake of Burlamaqui and Hutcheson—we may well come to think that we have not been brought as far from moral élitism as we might have supposed.[62]

Indeed, the idea of Burlamaqui that moral principles are *indicated* by a perfect, undebauched, undepraved moral sense, when coupled with his idea that these principles must

62. See Supplementary Notes, Hutcheson's Appeal . . . , p. 282.

then be verified by reason of the kind celebrated by Locke, results in a demand that a given person's moral sensings be *doubly* screened before they are to be trusted as guides to conduct. In order to get into the court of reason, so to speak, such sensings had to be those of a superior moral sense; and once inside that court they had to be scrutinized and verified by persons who had to pass muster before other stringent criteria. The net effect, therefore, of adopting a view like that of Burlamaqui was to limit even more severely the number of persons in a position to tell a true moral principle from a false one, and therefore to make us wonder how many persons in revolutionary America could be trusted to know the truth of the principles that supposedly justified the Revolution.

Jefferson, the People, and the Epistemology of Morals

In these first three chapters I have said a good deal about the epistemology which lay behind what John Adams called the "revolution principles" expressed in the Declaration of Independence. I have expounded the elements of Locke's moral rationalism, and I have shown how they influenced the Jefferson of the Declaration. I have called attention to certain possible consequences of that epistemology of natural law by pointing out that the seer of self-evident moral principles had to be learned, virtuous, dispassionate, and unbiased, and that such a seer of moral principles could, under certain circumstances, claim to be a dictator of principles, whereas Locke had regarded the theory of self-evident principles as a vast improvement over the doctrine of innate principles precisely because it could not be used as a tool of political dictators. Yet no sooner was the rationalistic theory of self-evident principles challenged by Wilson's version of the doctrine of moral sense, which seemed to give all moral

power, as it were, to the people, than it too showed a similar capacity to be used by dictators. The doctrine of moral
sense also sets up job-specifications for moral judgeships
which might easily exclude some of the people from casting
their moral ballots and even their electoral ballots.

Nevertheless, philosophical minds can seriously differ on
one crucial matter even when they are forced into the seemingly paradoxical position of resting the rights of all the people on moral principles that only some of the people can
know without instruction by the few. They can either be
optimistic about the capacity of the people to rise to the lev-
els demanded by their theories of moral knowledge or they
can be less than optimistic, and I think it fair to place Jefferson among the optimists. To see how optimistic he was, we
need only contrast some of his statements with some of the
statements made by his mentor Locke, who announced that
"there are only few who, neither corrupted by vice nor carelessly indifferent, make a proper use of [the] light" of reason
in discovering the law of nature,[63] and who also said that, in
discovering that law, "not the majority of the people should
be consulted but those who are more rational and perceptive
than the rest."[64] Jefferson might have been logically forced
to adopt a position like Locke's if pressed hard enough to explain his statement in 1793 that the head and heart of a
rational man are the fountains of evidence for the principles
of natural law. On the other hand, one finds him declaring
in 1774: "The great principles of right and wrong are legible
to every reader: to pursue them requires not the aid of many
counsellors."[65] And where he is discussing the education of
"the great mass of the people" in his *Notes on Virginia* he is
confident that "the first elements of morality . . . may be

63. See Chapter I above, note 24.
64. See Chapter I above, note 23.
65. *A Summary View of the Rights of British America* (1774), *Papers of
    Thomas Jefferson*, Volume I, p. 134.

instilled into their minds; such as, when further developed as their judgments advance in strength, may teach them how to work out their own greatest happiness, by showing them that it does not depend on the condition of life in which chance has placed them."[66] The tone of this reference to "the condition of life in which chance has placed them" is very different from Locke's reference to what he seems to have regarded as the inevitable shortcomings of those who happened to be day-laborers, tradesmen, spinsters, or dairy-maids and who would therefore be obliged to listen to plain commands without asking questions. True, Jefferson believed that those he called men of science were intellectually superior to others and that those who were really equipped to see the Lockean self-evidence of his truths in the Declaration may have made up a comparatively small number in spite of the rhetorical suggestion that the signers were speaking for *all* Americans in 1776. But it is clear from Jefferson's "Bill for the More General Diffusion of Knowledge" that he hoped to prevent tyranny by illuminating "as far as practicable, the minds of the people at large" and that he wished those "whom nature hath endowed with genius and virtue" to be educated to become guardians of public liberty at public expense "without regard to wealth, birth or other accidental condition or circumstance."[67] He seems to have believed that certain people who might not at a certain moment be able to know the natural law could be educated to know it in all of its ramifications while others, less gifted, could be trained to see the truth of at least its elementary principles. Furthermore, when Jefferson spoke rhapsodically about the moral sense he was also optimistic about who could serve as a moral judge. He believed, as we have seen, that God gave man a moral sense partly to swell the class of reputable moral judges so that it would include the ploughman of Jefferson. But Jefferson,

66. *Writings,* Volume II, pp. 204–205.
67. *Papers,* Volume 2, pp. 526–527.

recognizing, as we have also seen, that some people have stronger moral senses than others, held that these senses could be strengthened by exercise and that a ploughman who happened to have a weak moral sense could be taught how to exercise it and thereby elevate himself to a moral judgeship.

I do not wish to suggest by these remarks that Jefferson thought very deeply about the *criterion* for what I have called moral judgeships, but there is little doubt that he believed that many people could be educated to preside, so to speak, in the lower courts of natural law and that many *gifted* people could be educated to preside in the higher courts. This was the democratic optimism of Jefferson as expressed in the epistemology of morals and the philosophy of education. He held, it is true, that in his system of education "the best geniuses will be raked from the *rubbish* annually,"[68] but when he said that the minds of the people must and therefore could be improved to a certain degree because the people are the only safe depositories of government,[69] he was certainly departing from the spirit of Locke's denunciation of the maxim, "Vox populi vox Dei."[70]

Still, Jefferson's reference to "rubbish" must be reckoned with, and we must bear in mind that one Jefferson scholar has written: "For all his faith in the people and their ultimate possibilities and achievements he had no love for what

---

68. *Notes on Virginia, Writings,* Volume II, p. 203, my emphasis.

69. *Ibid.,* p. 207. Although Jefferson believed that the people were the only safe depositories of government, he thought that they could not, so to speak, go it alone without leadership. This is evident when he writes in 1776 against the direct election of senators: "I have ever observed that a choice by the people themselves is not generally distinguished for its wisdom," *Papers of Thomas Jefferson,* Volume I, p. 503.

70. See above, Chapter 1, note 25. This is a convenient place at which to remark that John Adams, not always known as a tribune of the populace, subscribed to that maxim. See *Works,* Volume IV, p. 404. On the other hand, we have seen (Chapter 2 above, note 34) that Alexander Hamilton flatly denied the maxim, saying that "the people are turbulent and changing; they seldom judge or determine right."

he called 'the rabble.' His early education made him an aristocrat, and an aristocrat of the intellect he remained to the end of his days."[71] An aristocrat of the intellect he was and did remain, but this was compatible with his thinking that education would produce distinguished minds from among those not born to power or wealth.[72] These minds, he thought, would serve the whole people and guard their liberties by knowing relevant moral principles and historical facts. There was, I agree, some condescension in Jefferson's attitude toward the people, especially when he spoke of them as his children.[73] But Jefferson was a parent, it must always be remembered, who freely left those children to self-government while others, he said, were afraid to trust them without nurses.[74] And while he was a man of the Enlightenment who would have resented on some occasions the imperative: "Do not argue but believe," Jefferson would not have hesi-

71. Gilbert Chinard, *The Literary Bible of Thomas Jefferson*, p. 1.
72. Although Jefferson is often seen as more optimistic in this regard than John Adams, it is worth citing a few passages in which Adams expressed the view that education could and should be provided to all ranks of society, with the idea that some of the people would rise to great heights as a consequence of this aid. This idea was connected with Adams's Burlamaquian view that God, who does nothing in vain, gave man an understanding which he has a duty to perfect. See in this connection, Adams, *Works*, Volume I, p. 195; Volume III, p. 457; Volume IV, p. 259.
73. In his *Self-evident Truths* (Bloomington, Indiana, 1974), p. 122, Paul Conkin has written of Jefferson's condescension toward the common people, taking this to be indicated in the following passage in Query XVIII in the *Notes on Virginia*: ". . . can the liberties of a nation be thought secure when we have removed their only firm basis, a conviction in the minds of the people that these liberties are of the gift of God? That they are not to be violated but with his wrath." William Peden, an editor of the *Notes*, tells us that Jefferson in his original manuscript had at this point also written but later deleted the following words: "when they can not imagine a single argument in their [the liberties'] support which their own daily practice does not bely?", *Notes on the State of Virginia* (Chapel Hill, 1955), p. 292.
74. *Writings*, Volume XIV, p. 489. Letter to Dupont de Nemours, April 24, 1816.

tated to approve of Beccaria's exclamation: "How great are
the obligations due from mankind to that philosopher, who
from the obscurity of his closet, had the courage to scatter
amongst the multitude, the seeds of useful truth, so long un-
fruitful!"[75]

75. *An Essay on Crimes and Punishments*, trans. ed. (London, 1775), pp. 2–3.
I quote this passage merely as an example of the Enlightenment's view
that philosophers should scatter seeds of truth amongst the multitude.
However, because the passage follows Beccaria's introduction of his famous
phrase, "the greatest happiness of the greatest number," W. R. Scott specu-
lates that Beccaria was specifically referring to Francis Hutcheson as the
originator of the famous slogan. See Scott's *Francis Hutcheson*, p. 273.

· 4 ·

The Laws of Nature
and of Nature's God

In the first three chapters of this work I have concentrated not only on the contents but also on certain antecedents of a theory of knowledge adopted by many American revolutionaries who accepted Locke's rationalistic theory of self-evident truth. In doing so, I have tried to uncover the older epistemological foundations upon which our founding fathers built their own philosophical houses since they were men of affairs who read famous philosophers but who did not contribute anything original to the theory of moral knowledge.[1] Had they been given to writing extended works in epistemology or ethics, there would be less need to expound what Locke, Burlamaqui, or Hutcheson had said in order to reveal what Jefferson meant or did not mean by "undeniable" or "self-evident" truths, and what Aquinas meant by related expressions.

My need to go back to earlier views will be equally great in

1. Perhaps with undue modesty, Jefferson wrote to Richard Price in 1789, "Is there anything good on the subject of the Socinian doctrine, levelled to a mind not habituated to abstract reasoning?", *Papers,* Volume XV, p. 272.

the next part of this book, where I shall begin with the idea
of natural law. Like the idea of self-evident truth, this idea
also has its roots in antiquity. But, fortunately, it will not be
necessary to trace the American colonists' ideas on this subject all the way back to Plato, Aristotle, or the Stoics because
American thinkers were primarily influenced by modern
theorists of natural law who had transformed ancient ideas of
natural law before bequeathing them to American colonists.
This does not mean that it will not be useful to refer to pre-
modern writers, both ancient and medieval, but it does mean
that we shall be concentrating on the more proximate illum-
inators of American thinking whose candles may have been
lit by the candles of others. Historians of ideas who wish to
give good marks to thinkers who "started it all" would take
the reader further back in time, but such a trip is as unnecessary as it is impossible to accomplish in this limited study.
We need not revisit Heraclitus to understand what Jefferson
and his co-signers meant by "the laws of Nature and of Nature's God."

Although not all of the thinkers whom we have discussed
and shall discuss drew an explicit distinction between metaphysics—the science of being—and epistemology—the theory
of knowledge, many of them said things which we may profitably assign to one of those disciplines rather than to the
other. The statement that some of the "revolution principles,"
as John Adams called them, are self-evident is an epistemological statement because it tells us how these principles are
allegedly *known*, but when the revolutionaries claimed that
these same principles were principles of natural law, they
characterized them metaphysically in a sense which will become clearer, I hope, as this study progresses. In addition,
when the revolutionaries called these principles laws of Nature's *God*,[2] they spoke of them theologically, and therefore

2. Among the many Colonial references to God as the source of natural law,
   see especially those made by James Otis in his *Rights of the British Colo-*

it is difficult to understand the revolutionaries without taking into account the theology they accepted. For them, the
God who created Nature—the universe or totality of all
things—*a fortiori* created man's specific nature or essence.
The God-ordained laws of man's nature laid certain moral
duties upon man which in turn implied certain of his rights.
Therefore, the God of theology, and the nature or essence of
man, a staple of metaphysics, are crucial entities in the theory
of natural law. And the path that led from God to man's
essence, to man's ends, to man's duties, and to man's rights
will be my concern in the remainder of this book, where I
shall analyze that path which led the revolutionaries from
theology to metaphysics to ethics.

It will be convenient to begin that analysis with a discussion of the laws of nature as understood by many revolutionaries, a discussion I shall launch by dealing with two questions that might be invited by my remark that the laws of
nature laid *duties* on man. The first question it raises might
occur to any careful reader of the Declaration of Independence, namely: How can a law of nature express a *duty* when,
according to the first paragraph of the Declaration of Independence, laws of nature are said to *entitle* one people to a
separate and equal station among the powers of the earth?
To say that a law of nature entitles a people to something
suggests that the law asserts that the people have a rightful
claim or a right to that thing. In short, if the laws of nature
are thought to express *duties,* how can they be regarded as
asserting rights? A reader of other writings by Jefferson will
know that even before drafting the Declaration he referred
in his pamphlet, *A Summary View of the Rights of British
America* (1774), to "a free people, claiming their rights as

---

nies *Asserted and Proved* (1764) and his *Vindication of the British Colonies*
(1765), reprinted in Bailyn's *Pamphlets,* Volume I, pp. 438–440; p. 559.

derived from the laws of nature."[3] Those who reply that the answer to this question is obvious I shall ask to wait until we consider the subtleties of what Hobbes had to say on this subject.

The second question that might be invited by the remark that some laws of nature laid moral duties upon man is: How can a law of nature, which supposedly *de*scribes the world, *pre*scribe anything? This might be asked by a reader of philosophical works of the nineteenth and twentieth centuries.

I shall deal with the first question first.

Natural Law and Natural Right

There is an old tradition according to which natural law should be distinguished from natural right. In *Essays on the Law of Nature* Locke holds that "right [*jus*] is grounded in the fact that we have the free use of a thing, whereas law [*lex*] is what enjoins or forbids the doing of a thing."[4] And this distinction is also present in the writings of Francisco Suarez, who says that, strictly speaking, "only that is law [*lex*] which imposes an obligation of some sort," whereas "according to the . . . strict acceptation of *ius* [right], this name is properly wont to be bestowed upon a certain moral power which every man has, either over his own property or with respect to that which is due him."[5]

As von Leyden, the editor of Locke's *Essays on the Law of Nature,* points out, a similar view is to be found in Hobbes's *Leviathan.* But if one examines Hobbes's text, one finds a statement more complex than Locke's, namely, that "RIGHT consisteth in liberty to do, or to forbeare; Whereas LAW,

---

3. *Papers of Thomas Jefferson,* Volume I, p. 134.
4. *Essays on the Law of Nature,* p. 111.
5. *De legibus, ac deo legislatore,* trans. G. L. Williams et al. (1612; reprint ed., Oxford, 1944), Book I, Chapter I, Section 7, and Chapter II, Section 5.

determineth, and bindeth to one of them: so that Law, and Right, differ as much, as Obligation, and Liberty; which in one and the same matter are inconsistent."[6] This is crucially different from Locke's statement because Locke limits a right to that which is grounded in the fact that we have the free *use* of a thing, whereas Hobbes tells us in more general terms that right is a liberty to *do* or to *refrain from doing* something. Hobbes's definition of a right is such that if I am said to have a certain right with regard to a certain action, I have a right to perform that action *and* a right not to perform it, which is tantamount to regarding "One has a right to do that" as elliptical for "One has a right to do that *and* one has a right to refrain from doing that." A reader of Hobbes's definition of "Right" might complain that Hobbes says that it consists "in the liberty to do, *or* to forbeare," whereas in my explication I have used the word "and"; but this objection can be met as follows. If I tell you that you are at liberty to perform *or* to forbear from performing the act of raising your arm, I do not mean that you have only one liberty, namely that of raising your arm *or* that of refraining from raising it. I am telling you that you are free to raise your arm *and* that you are free to refrain from raising it and hence that you have, so to speak, *two* liberties, that is, that you may raise your arm *and* you may refrain from raising it, even though the performance and the refrainment are mutually exclusive since you cannot at the same time perform *and* refrain from performing the action. It should be clearer now why Hobbes adds that law and right, like obligation and liberty, "in one and the same matter are inconsistent." For Hobbes, having a right with regard to a certain action is expressed in a logical conjunction asserting the liberty to perform *and* the liberty to refrain from performing the action, whereas having an

6. *Leviathan,* ed. A. R. Waller (Cambridge, Eng., 1935), pp. 86–87. See also Hobbes, *Dialogue between a Philosopher and a Student of the Common Laws of England,* ed. J. Cropsey (Chicago, 1971), p. 73.

obligation with regard to the same action must be expressed in just one nonconjunctive sentence like "One must perform the action" or "One must refrain from performing the action."

Hobbes's way of drawing the distinction between natural law and natural right runs directly counter to the temptation to say that having a duty to perform a certain action implies a right to perform that same action. This follows from his definition of "right" and his contention that in asserting a duty, one must either say simply that one has a duty to perform X or say simply that one has a duty to refrain from performing X. To see this, let us assume that it has been asserted that one has a duty to perform X. Now let us recall the Hobbesian assertion of a *right*, namely, "One may perform X and one may refrain from performing X." Clearly, the simple Hobbesian assertion of a duty does *not* imply the conjunctive Hobbesian assertion of a right because "One has a duty to perform X" certainly does not imply "One may refrain from performing X," a conjunct of the assertion of a right. Therefore, Hobbes's statement of duty does not imply the corresponding conjunctive statement of right since it would have to imply *both* Hobbesian conjuncts for that to be the case. Moreover, since "One has a duty to perform X" not only does not imply the truth of "One has a right to refrain from performing X" but implies its falsity, Hobbes holds that obligation and liberty, that is, duty and right, "in one and the same matter are inconsistent."

What is one to say about this view which departs from the views of Jefferson and that other philosophical signer, Dr. Witherspoon, who wrote: "whatever men are in *duty* obliged to do, that they have a *claim* to," meaning a right to do?[7] The nub of the problem is this. If we say "He has a right to do

7. *Lectures on Moral Philosophy* (Philadelphia, 1822), p. 69. The idea that natural rights may be derived from natural laws of duty may also be found in Hamilton. See his *Papers,* Volume I, pp. 87–88.

X," *do* we mean to say something which is more fully expressed by "He has a right to do X *and* he has a right to refrain from doing X," as if the first statement were elliptical for the longer one? Couldn't we merely say that the man has a right to do X and stop right there, without being required to add that he also has a right to refrain from doing X? Clearly, if we reversed the picture and began by saying that the man had a right to *refrain* from murdering someone, we would not feel forced to add that he had a right to murder that person as well. In ordinary language it would seem that statements of the forms "He had a right to do X" and "He had a right to refrain from doing X" are both complete and distinct, and that only by forcing us to link them in a conjunction of the kind to which he is committed does Hobbes succeed in foiling our inclination to think that the statement that we have a duty to do X implies that we have a right to do X. What I have called our inclination seems to have been the inclination of Jefferson and Witherspoon, for in no other way, I shall argue later, can we understand how Jefferson supported his belief in some of the statements about rights which he wrote in the Declaration. They are statements about rights to do X that he deduces from statements that *explicitly* assert *duties* to do X. But if he had adopted Hobbes's view of the inconsistency between right and law, he would not have been able to accomplish this deduction or derivation. I might add that the idea that a duty to do something implies the right to *do the same thing* is not only explicitly present in the minor moralist Witherspoon's writing; it is also to be found in the writing of the much-cited Pufendorf,[8] who also recognized that if we must do something, then we may do it.

---

8. *Elementorum Jurisprudentiae Universalis*, trans. W. A. Oldfather (Oxford, 1931), Book I, Definition XIV, Section 1. Pufendorf says that a man has the moral power, meaning the right, to do what is enjoined (*praecipiatur*) by the laws.

Of course, the converse is not true. It does not follow from the statement that we *may* do something or *have a right to* do it, that we *must* do it or *have a duty to* do it. Yet the fact that duties imply corresponding rights raises the interesting question whether, if a right is implied by a corresponding duty, we are obliged to make that implication explicit. This is part of a more general problem in the philosophy of language. It is the problem whether, if you know that you may assert the logically stronger of two propositions, you should always assert the stronger. For example, if you know that there are *exactly* three persons in a room, can you not say, under certain circumstances, merely that there are *at least* three—which is logically less, or weaker, than what you think you *could* say? I think that under certain circumstances one is entitled to say less than what one knows about a certain matter; and as I shall argue later, I think the author of the Declaration of Independence did exactly that when he asserted certain rights which were implied by certain duties about which he remained silent.

In the light of this, it is extremely interesting to find an eighteenth-century British commentator on Locke's *Second Treatise,* Thomas Elrington, protesting Locke's tendency to speak of rights to do certain things when he could and should have spoken of duties to do them. Elrington says concerning Section 10 of the *Second Treatise,* where Locke speaks of a man's right in a state of nature to punish a criminal and to seek reparation for the injury: "He not only *may* do so, but it is his *duty* to join in punishing the offender and obtaining reparation for the injury. Throughout the whole of this treatise of Locke's, the attentive reader will perceive that his zeal for liberty has very frequently led him to speak of men's *duties* as *rights* which they might exercise or renounce at pleasure.—There are few distinctions less attended to, and yet perhaps few more important than that between those rights which can be renounced at pleasure and those which cannot. Of the latter sort, it is obvious, are all those which are connected with duties."[9] And a half century before Elrington made this point, Burlamaqui had remarked that some rights "have a natural connection with our duties, and are given to man only as means to perform them. To renounce this sort of rights would be therefore renouncing our duty, which is never allowed." For example, Burlamaqui continues, a father cannot renounce the right he has over his children, whereas a creditor may forgive a debt which is due him.[10] And, as we shall see later, because a duty to do something implies a right to do it, American revolutionaries were often willing to assert rights when they could have asserted corresponding duties—perhaps for reasons like those that Elrington had attributed to Locke. Furthermore, the revolutionaries called those rights *unalienable* for reasons similar to those which led Elrington and Burlamaqui to say that they could not be renounced: they were implied by corresponding *duties* of those who held the rights.

Two Kinds of Natural Laws

It will be recalled that I began to discuss the phrase "laws of nature" in an attempt to deal with *two* questions that might be prompted by the statement that the laws of nature asserted moral duties rather than moral rights. Having answered the first, I now come to the second question, which I described as likely to be raised by a reader of certain works of the nineteenth and twentieth centuries. Such a reader might be puzzled by the application of the phrase "laws of nature" to a moral principle. The origin of his puzzlement would be

9. Thomas Elrington, in his annotated edition of Locke's *Second Treatise* (Dublin, 1798), note to the passage in which Locke writes that another person *may* join with the injured party and assist him in seeking reparation. See Laslett's edition of Locke (1970), p. 291, note.

10. J. J. Burlamaqui, *Principles of Natural Law*, Part I, Chapter VII, Section VIII.

the tendency to characterize laws of nature as "descriptive" and hence illustrated by, say, Boyle's law of gases, or Galileo's law of freely falling bodies, or Newton's law of universal gravitation, no one of which would be called moral by a contemporary reader because they supposedly tell us of the way in which things *do* behave, whereas some at least of the laws of nature asserted by jurists do not tell us how things *do* behave but rather how men *should* behave.

Before trying to explain why the expression "laws of nature" was applied to *both* kinds of statements, it is only fair to point out that earlier philosophers showed awareness of the problem that troubles certain contemporaries. For example, Bishop Berkeley in a discourse delivered in 1712, wrote: "we ought to distinguish between a twofold signification of the terms *law of nature;* which words do either denote a rule or precept for the direction of the voluntary actions of reasonable agents, and in that sense they imply a duty; or else they are used to signify any general rule which we observe to obtain in the works of nature, independent of the wills of men; in which sense no duty is implied."[11] And in the first book of Richard Hooker's *Laws of Ecclesiastical Polity,* published in 1593, one will also find a distinction like Berkeley's between two *kinds* of laws of nature, a distinction that helps illuminate not only the language of Locke but also that of the American colonists.

Hooker begins his discussion of law in general by saying that all things that exist have some power to operate in a man-

11. *The Works of Berkeley,* ed. A. C. Fraser (Oxford, 1871), Volume III, p. 127. This passage appears in Berkeley's *Passive Obedience,* subtitled *The Christian Doctrine of Not Resisting the Supreme Power, Proved and Vindicated.* Berkeley's clear statement of the distinction shows that it was understood close to two centuries before the appearance of, for example, Karl Pearson's *The Grammar of Science* in 1892. However, in Chapter III, Sections 5 and 6, respectively entitled "The Two Senses of the Words 'Natural Law'" and "Confusion between the Two Senses of Natural Law," Pearson makes some useful general remarks as well as some specific comments on the views of the Stoics and those of Richard Hooker.

ner that is neither violent nor casual, that nothing ever begins to exercise this power "without some fore-conceived end" toward which it operates, and that this end will not be obtained unless the mode of operation is appropriate.[12] In other words, not everything will bring about this end, and therefore Hooker offers a definition of law which reads as follows: "That which doth assign unto each thing the kind, that which doth moderate the force and power, that which doth appoint the form and measure, of working, the same we term a Law."[13] Hooker maintains that a law states some kind of *regularity* which governs the working of a kind of thing toward its fore-conceived end. In effect, then, Hooker regards a law as having the following form: "Everything of kind *A* works to achieve an end of kind *B* in manner *C*." A law, Hooker goes on to say, has as its author a superior, to whom the governed things are subject. This, Hooker holds, is true of all laws that govern *things created by God*, but since God himself works toward an end according to law, Hooker must deny that what he calls the law of God's *internal* workings has a superior author since God has no superior. "The law eternal" which concerns God's internal workings—"the Generation of the Son" and "the Proceeding of the Spirit"—are beyond the compass of Hooker's concern here,[14] but he is very much concerned with that part of "the law eternal" according to which other things operate. Hooker tells us that the part of the eternal law which does not concern God's *internal* workings is called by different names de-

---

12. *Of the Laws of Ecclesiastical Polity*, Book I, Chapter II, Section 1. The first four books of this work appeared in 1593. In his edition of Locke's *Essays on the Law of Nature*, von Leyden calls attention to the closeness between what Locke says in Essay I of the work and what Hooker says on natural law in the passages I am about to expound, even to the point of Locke's using the same paraphrase of Aquinas as one used by Hooker, p. 116, note 3.

13. *Ibid.*

14. *Ibid.*, Book I, Chapter II, Section 2.

pending on the different kinds of things which are subject to it. Thus nature's law orders "natural agents"; the celestial or heavenly law is that which angels clearly behold and observe without swerving; the law of reason is that which binds "creatures reasonable in this world, and with which reason they may most plainly perceive themselves bound"; the divine law is what binds the same individuals but is known to them only by special revelation from God; and the human law is what men extract from the law of reason or divine law and make positive law because they gather it to be probably "expedient."[15]

It will have been observed that Hooker distinguishes between "natural agents" and "creatures reasonable in this world," and that the former are said to be governed by the law of nature, whereas the latter are said to be governed by the law of reason. He is aware, however, that sometimes the phrase "the law of nature" is applied to *all* created things. And so this prompts him to say that "those things are termed most properly natural agents, which keep the law of their kind unwittingly," for example, the heavens and elements of the world. Planets "can do no otherwise than they do," and they are to be distinguished from "creatures reasonable" or "intellectual natures" called *"voluntary* agents." For this reason, it will be expedient, he goes on to say, to "sever the law of nature observed" by natural agents like planets from that which is observed by voluntary agents.[16] What this shows is a

---

15. *Ibid.*, Book I, Chapter III, Section 1.
16. *Ibid.*, Book I, Chapter III, Section 2. It should be noted that Aquinas asserts, as translated by Pegis, *Basic Writings*, Volume II, p. 743, that "Law is a rule and measure of acts, whereby man is induced to act or is restrained from acting; for *lex* [law] is derived from *ligare* [to bind], because it binds one to act," *Summa Theologica*, First Part of the Second Part, Question 90, First Article. Suarez comments on this in his *De legibus, ac deo legislatore*, Book I, Chapter I, Section 1, where he says a number of interesting things. To discuss them here would take me too far afield, but I cannot resist remarking that Suarez criticizes Aquinas's definition. Suarez contends that it is too broad because it is applicable to creatures other

terminological variation of which Hooker is quite aware. There is a broader sense of "natural agents" which includes both planets and men, but then there is a narrower sense which applies only to planets and other things which keep the law of their kind unwittingly. Analogously, therefore, there is a broader sense of "natural law" which governs things in the broadly conceived class of natural agents and a narrower sense which governs things in the more narrowly conceived class. But what must be remembered is that Hooker applies the word "law" univocally in both cases: a law concerning planets governs created things which seek a God-ordained end in a God-ordained manner just as a law concerning men governs created things which seek a God-ordained end in a God-ordained manner. The difference between the two kinds of laws is that one kind is followed unwittingly, whereas the other is followed by creatures who may use their reason to see that they are bound by the law. Moreover, when Hooker refers to *the* law of nature in the singular, he usually has in mind the set of all the different manners of working, or laws, which God has decreed for the different kinds of agents he has created, whether they be agents that act "unwittingly" or "voluntary agents." According to Hooker, God dictates the laws of motion of heavenly bodies insofar as he dictates the manner in which a heavenly body should seek a goal he has set for it. And he also dictates the manner in which voluntary agents should seek their goals, but—and this is crucial—voluntary agents may depart from the laws decreed for them by God.

It is true, of course, says Hooker, that there are occasional departures of "non-intellectual" agents from the course of behavior decreed for them by God. But these departures are

---

than men, "since everything has its own rule and measure, in accordance with which it operates and is induced to act or is restrained therefrom."

brought about by "divine malediction, laid for the sin of man upon these creatures which God had made for the use of man";[17] and in spite of these "swervings" it is obvious, Hooker holds, that nonintellectual natural agents observe their laws quite constantly. By contrast, man resembles God in manner of working because he is made in the image of God. Therefore, whatever we do as men, we "do wittingly and freely." We are not tied as nonintellectual natural agents are, and therefore we are not constrained to do what we do. "Choice there is not," Hooker declares, "unless the thing which we take be so in our power that we might have refused and left it." On the other hand, "if fire consume the stubble, it chooseth not so to do, because the nature thereof is such that it can do no other."[18] Once men are said to have the power of choice, we begin to see why Hooker held that a law of nature may be a precept for the direction of the voluntary actions of reasonable agents—a law asserting a duty. We are now in a position to understand why Hooker thought that men often violate the law of nature and thereby differ from nonintellectual agents, who are always or almost always "obedient" to the law to which they are subject. The explanation of the possibility of violation is that there is in the will of man "naturally that freedom, whereby it is apt to take or refuse any particular object whatsoever being presented to it," and that man may exercise that freedom in action even in the face of reason's conclusion that he should act otherwise.

This almost completes my discussion of Hooker's *Ecclesiastical Polity* on the laws of nature, offered mainly to show how he tried to differentiate laws of natural science and moral laws while placing them in one genus. I want to em-

17. Hooker, *op. cit.*, Book I, Chapter III, Section 3. This "truth," Hooker adds, is a revealed one and therefore above the reach of merely natural capacity and understanding.
18. *Ibid.*, Book I, Chapter VII, Section 2.

phasize that all laws of nature are conceived by Hooker as laws decreed by God and that they all describe the operations whereby created things of different kinds exercise their powers. But as Hooker runs over the scale of being starting with what he calls "*mere* natural agents," like rocks, up through man—I omit his discussion of plants, animals, and angels— Hooker finds that men, who are voluntary and intellectual creatures, are ordered by God to operate in a manner which they can understand because they have reason, and in a manner from which they can depart because they have free will. Having reason, men have the power to see the truth of the propositions which express duties and also to see that they express what God has decreed as modes of operation appropriate to their kind. Thus the law of nature as applied to men is the law of reason in a triple sense: it is decreed by God, who is a rational being; it is *applicable* to men, who are rational beings, and it is *knowable* by them through the use of their reason.[19]

Hooker's view, which placed the laws of natural science and the laws of morality in one genus, was advocated by someone who believed that *all* of God's creatures worked toward God-ordained ends. Although he acknowledged differences among rocks, plants, fish, fowl, and beasts, saying that some of these subhumans do not work "altogether unwittingly" because fish, fowl, and beasts have some weak degree of understanding, and even holding that beasts, though they are "otherwise behind men, may notwithstanding in actions of sense and fancy go beyond" men,[20] Hooker nevertheless "severed" two species of natural laws, those moral laws which governed humans and those nonmoral laws which governed rocks, plants, fish, fowl, and beasts. In this respect, he shared many Christian theorists' view of the moral species of natural

19. *Ibid.*, Book I, Chapter VIII, Section 4. See R. B. Perry, *Puritanism and Democracy* (New York, 1944), p. 162.
20. *Ibid.*, Book I, Chapter VI, Section 2.

law and rejected the idea that it applied to beasts, an idea sometimes identified with the Justinian Code.[21]

Hooker's effort to differentiate between laws of nature that govern human beings and laws of nature that govern other beings while keeping both species in one teleologically viewed genus was not shared by thinkers who denied that the planets were moved by final causes. And it was mainly through their influence that a law of *physics* continued to be called a natural law but in a sense different from that in which a moral law was called a natural law. Yet Jefferson's *moral* laws of nature and of nature's God were still viewed at the end of the eighteenth century very much as Hooker had viewed them. They were thought to be decreed by God; they were regarded as precepts for the direction of the voluntary actions of reasonable agents; and some of them were thought to be discoverable by intuitive reason. That is why Jefferson called moral laws "Laws of Nature and of Nature's God."

Before concluding this section, I want to comment on the idea, advanced by Carl Becker, Edward S. Corwin, and other writers, that Newton's *Principia* encouraged thinkers of the seventeenth and eighteenth centuries to regard both moral laws of nature and the laws of mechanics as rational truths in the same category as "$2 + 2 = 4$." I find this hard to believe on the basis of the evidence presented by Corwin. He argues that "the vast preponderance of deduction over observation in Newton's discoveries" and Newton's demonstration that the force which brings an apple to earth is the same as that which holds planets in their orbits stirred Newton's contemporaries to think that the universe "was pervaded with the same reason which shines in man and which is accessible in all its parts to exploration by man." And this, as I understand

21. *"Jus naturale est, quod natura omnia animalia docuit,"* Institutes, Book I, Title 2. Cicero, however, said that we do not speak of justice, equity, or goodness in the case of horses and lions, *De officiis,* Book I, Chapter XVI. Grotius agreed, *De jure belli ac pacis,* Book I, Chapter I, Section XI.

Corwin, encouraged adherents of the doctrine of moral natural law to regard their task as similar to that of Newton.
They concluded, Corwin appears to say, that Newton had
lent support to Grotius's idea that the principles of natural
law were like "$2 + 2 = 4$" and that therefore both mechanics
and morals were mathematical sciences which began with self-
evident axioms and which terminated in deduced theorems.[22]

One of the difficulties in this view is that Locke himself
doubted that so-called natural "philosophy" could ever become a "science" in Locke's sense precisely because it could
not present truths that would be perceived by intuitive reason, axioms from which theorems would be deduced by discursive reason. Yet, by contrast, we have seen that Locke
thought that this *could be* accomplished in morals, even
though he failed to accomplish it himself. In other words,
one of the most devoted admirers of Newton did not adopt
the view that Corwin regards as so common in the seventeenth and eighteenth centuries. Locke distinguished episte-
mologically between a law of nature that laid a duty on man
and a law of nature like the law of gravitation. He did *not*
think that one could see *by intuition* that all bodies attract
each other directly as the product of their masses and in-
versely as the square of the distance between them, whereas
he often said that a moral law of nature could be seen in
that way. So if it be true—and I doubt that it is—that "with
Newton's achievement at their back men turned confidently
to the formulation of the inherently just and reasonable rules
of social and political relationship,"[23] such confident men did
not understand the achievement at their back. If they believed that Newton's *physical principles* were like the principles of natural law as the latter were viewed in Locke's epis-

22. E. S. Corwin, *The "Higher Law" Background of American Constitutional
    Law* (Ithaca, New York, 1955), pp. 58–59. This work originally appeared
    in the *Harvard Law Review* XLII (1928–1929).
23. *Ibid.*, p. 59; Locke, *Elements of Natural Philosophy, Works*, Volume III,
    p. 304.

temology or in Grotius's, they might have done so under the misapprehension that Newton's physical axioms, because they *contained* mathematical expressions, were self-evident mathematical truths in Locke's sense. Such a misapprehension *might* have led to the idea that theorists of natural law were engaged in an enterprise like Newton's, but, as I have said, Corwin does not support this point with convincing evidence.

Instead, Corwin relies on the supposed authority of Carl Becker who in turn rests his case on what I think is a misinterpretation of Colin Maclaurin's *Account of Sir Isaac Newton's Philosophical Discoveries* (1748). Becker correctly perceives that Maclaurin viewed Newton's achievement as laying a sure foundation for natural religion and moral philosophy by leading us to knowledge of the author and governor of the universe, but I think Becker misunderstands Maclaurin's point when the latter speaks of the philosopher being "excited and animated to correspond with the general harmony of Nature."[24] If one reads just beyond that passage in Maclaurin, one finds that all that he is saying is that we must avoid "false schemes of natural philosophy" which *may* "lead to atheism," so that when he speaks of being excited and animated to "correspond" with the general harmony of nature, he is *not* giving an argument for the doctrine of natural law and rights as defended, for example by Locke or Jefferson. He means by "correspond with" something like "giving a true account of."[25] Therefore, when Becker, while speaking of Locke, refers to Maclaurin's excitement and animation about corresponding with the general harmony of nature as if it supported Locke's doctrine that "morality, religion, and politics ought to conform to God's will *as revealed in the essential nature of man,*"[26] Becker is simply mistaken. Mac-

24. Becker, *Declaration of Independence,* pp. 49–52.
25. Maclaurin, *An Account of Sir Isaac Newton's Philosophical Discoveries* (London, 1748), pp. 4–10.
26. Becker, *op. cit.,* p. 57. The emphasis is mine.

laurin is *not* trying to give direct support to the doctrine that we may determine man's duties by discovering, as Grotius says, what "is or is not in conformity with rational nature," meaning man's nature or essence. He is merely praising those who study the phenomena of Nature with a capital "N" in order to describe it truly. This is a far cry from supporting Aquinas's, Locke's, and Grotius's notion that we can find man's duties by studying *man's* nature or essence. It is not surprising, therefore, to find Maclaurin dismissing philosophers who "indulged themselves too much in abstruse fruitless disquisitions concerning the hidden essences of things." If Newton did encourage theorists of natural law, it was not by encouraging them to use their intuition or to penetrate man's essence in search of his duties. It was rather by buttressing the argument from design, which allegedly showed that there is a God who is author and governor of the universe and who therefore issues moral decrees. In the next section I shall try to show how Burlamaqui appealed to a God of this kind in defense of a doctrine that many revolutionaries accepted.

God's Will and Natural Law

So far we have seen that a freely violable moral law which expresses a duty is, according to Hooker, a law established by God which orders *men* to behave in a certain way. And we have also seen how a philosopher could, by declining to accept Hobbes's definition of "right," hold that a law of nature which expresses a *duty* to perform a certain action *implies* a principle which expresses a *right* to perform the same action. It is now time to use what I have presented both in the epistemological chapters and at the beginning of the present chapter in order to show that when in the Rough Draft Jefferson applied the term "undeniable" to certain philosophical truths he may have represented his intentions more accurately than he did when he later applied the word "self-evident" instead, or when he consented to that change. I shall argue that since the word "undeniable" is broader in scope than "self-evident" because "undeniable" is applicable to axioms *and* theorems, whereas "self-evident" does not apply to theorems, and since Jefferson probably believed that many of his truths were theorems, he should not have made this change nor acquiesced in it from a philosophical view. I know, of course, that there are those who speak with admiration of "this famous and altogether felicitous change,"[27] but I am not thinking now of rhetoric or style but of philosophy and theology since I believe that Jefferson, under the influence of Burlamaqui, appealed to more fundamental truths than those that in the Declaration are finally called "self-evident." Having published on natural law in 1747, Burlamaqui was, as I have already remarked, much closer to Jefferson in time than Hooker, publishing in 1593, or than Locke, publishing in 1690, and hence more likely to be thought of by Jefferson as uttering "the last word" on the matters that concerned the author of the Declaration with regard to natural law as it affected individuals.[28]

Burlamaqui thinks that God is an omnipotent, wise, and beneficent creator of man who has given man a certain nature or constitution and placed him in different "states." Burlamaqui also holds that from man's nature, essence, or constitution and these states, there follow laws of nature which prescribe his duties. The states in which man may be considered and which embrace all his particular relations, according to

---

27. Boyd, *The Declaration of Independence*, p. 22.
28. Vattel, who published his major work after Burlamaqui's, in 1758, was much more concerned with the law of nations than with the law of nature as applied to individuals. This is evident even in the title of his work, *The Law of Nations, or the Principles of Natural Law, Applied to the Conduct and to the Affairs of Nations and of Sovereigns (Le Droit des gens, ou Principes de la loi naturelle, appliqués à la conduite et aux affaires des nations et des souverains).*

Burlamaqui, are three in number. First of all, man is a creature of God, from whom he has received his life, his reason,
and all the advantages he enjoys. Secondly, he is a being composed of body and soul who naturally loves himself and de-
sires his own felicity. And, thirdly, he is a member of a species, all of whose members live with him on earth in society.
Burlamaqui further maintains that paralleling this trio of
states there is a trio of different sorts of duties: duties toward
God, duties toward oneself, and duties toward other human
beings.[29] These duties are inferable by reflection on the *nature* and *states of man,* which indicate the intentions of God
with respect to man. Beginning with the nature of man as an
individual—without attention to man's relationships to others—we can certainly infer, according to Burlamaqui, that
God, "by creating us, proposed our preservation, perfection,
and happiness."[30] Since God gave us *life,* he must have proposed the preservation of our life. Since he gave us *reason,* he
must have proposed for us the perfection of our reason. And
since he created us with a *desire for our own happiness,* he
must have proposed for us the pursuit of that happiness. In
his wisdom and beneficence and power, he would have created us in this way only if he had proposed these as ends for
us to attain. Moreover, having proposed these as ends for
man, God *wills* that man *should* labor for his own preservation and perfection in order to obtain all the happiness of
which he is capable according to his nature and estate.[31] Here
we see the final link in the chain which begins with man's
God-created essence, moves to the ends God proposed for
him, and from *that* to what God wants man to do, namely, to
man's duties. But once we have shown that we have the *duty*

29. Burlamaqui, *Principles of Natural Law,* Part II, Chapter IV, Section VI.
    Burlamaqui cites Cicero's *Tusculan Disputations,* Book I, Chapter 26, as
    distinguishing duties in this tripartite way.
30. Burlamaqui, *op. cit.,* Part II, Chapter IV, Section IX.
31. *Ibid.*

to preserve our lives, it is easy to deduce that we have the *right* to preserve them; once we have shown that we have the *duty* to pursue happiness, it is easy to deduce that we have the *right* to pursue it; and once we have shown that, having been created members of the same species who are equal by nature and therefore mutually independent, we can know, first, that each of us has a *duty* not to dominate the other and, secondly, that each of us has a *right* to preserve this freedom from domination.

In my opinion, Burlamaqui reveals more explicitly than any other writer read by Jefferson the logical substructure upon which Jefferson built when he wrote in the Rough Draft: "We hold these truths to be sacred and undeniable; that all men are created equal & independent, that from that equal creation they derive rights inherent & inalienable, among which are the preservation of life, & liberty & the pursuit of happiness; that to secure these ends, governments are instituted among men." The use of "sacred" is characteristically Burlamaquian because of its religious connotation; the reference to "inherent" rights, like John Adams's equivalent reference to "essential" rights,[32] is reminiscent of Burlamaqui's constant harping on the fact that the laws of nature follow from the essence of man and his states as created by

32. See Adams's reference to "essential" rights in the *Report of a Constitution or Form of Government for the Commonwealth of Massachusetts, Works,* Volume IV, p. 220. John Adams adopts a view very much like Burlamaqui's when he says that self-love is implanted in us by God and hence that we "can annihilate ourselves, as easily as root out this affection"—which shows that for Adams self-love is a part of our essence or nature. Adams also says that, by the laws of nature, self-love is *our duty and our right.* See *Legal Papers of John Adams,* eds. L. K. Wroth and H. B. Zobel (Cambridge, Mass., 1965), Volume III, p. 244. The passage appears in *Adams' Argument for the Defense* in *Rex* v. *Wemms,* one of the Boston Massacre Trials in December 1770. See also Adams's *Dissertation on the Canon and Feudal Law* (1765), in *Works,* Volume III, p. 456, where Adams argues that since God, "who does nothing in vain," has given men understanding and a desire to know, they have a right to knowledge. He would have also said, with Burlamaqui, that they have a duty to seek knowledge.

God; the reference to the "preservation" of life and liberty; and the reference to the pursuit of happiness and to "ends" as the entities to which men have rights—all of these suggest a telescoping of Burlamaqui's argument. And because they suggest this I think that Jefferson was more deliberate in his use of "undeniable" than one might first suppose.

Even if Jefferson and Burlamaqui were both prepared to maintain that the statement "all men are created equal" is not only "undeniable" but "self-evident," it was not easy to regard as self-evident the statement that "from that equal creation they *derive* rights inherent & inalienable, among which are the *preservation* of life, the *preservation* of liberty, and the *pursuit* of happiness"—in spite of Locke's linking of equal creation and the right to *liberty* in a self-evident proposition. That statement of Jefferson's might be called at most undeniable by a cautious arguer precisely because of the steps that Burlamaqui was forced to take in order to get from the essence of man to his duties since it will be recalled that an undeniable statement may be one which is demonstrated rather than self-evident. For example, the proposition that since man was created, that is, given life by God, man had a duty to preserve his life, is one that Burlamaqui tried to *prove* and not one that he regarded as self-evident. And the proof required certain premises which emerge when we state his argument in full.

In showing that since God created man, he is bound to preserve his own life, Burlamaqui proceeds in the following manner. He first asserts that God made life *part of the essence of man*—that being his version of the statement that God created man. He next asserts that God is good, wise, omnipotent, and does nothing in vain. Therefore, Burlamaqui is able to assert that since God made life part of the essence of man, God must have proposed the preservation of life as an end of his creature, man, because God *would* have given man life in vain if God had not proposed man's preservation of

that life as one of man's ends. Burlamaqui's next step is to
assert that since God proposed the preservation of life as an
end of man, God *wills* that man should preserve his life, a
step which is also justified by appealing to God's attributes.
So we can now collect the following supposedly *demonstrated*
propositions: (1) Since God made life part of the essence of
man, God proposed the preservation of life as an end of man,
and (2) Since God proposed the preservation of life as an end
of man, God wills that man should preserve his life. From
them we can infer by elementary logic the proposition: (3)
Since God made life part of the essence of man, God wills
that man should preserve his life. And the next step in this
argument is to the proposition: (4) Since God made life part
of the essence of man, man has a duty to preserve his life. It
is unclear whether (4) follows from (3) by a definition of a
"duty" as that which is willed by God or by asserting a new
premise, namely, that what God wills that man should do,
man has a duty to do. In any case, we are now at a point
where we may assert that since man has been created as an
essentially living being, he has the duty to preserve his life.
And once we take the trifling step from a *duty* to preserve life
to a *right* to preserve life, we have arrived at Jefferson's belief that the right to preserve life is "derived" from the *creation* of man.

Let me now repeat that since Burlamaqui's statement (4)
above has been deduced from premises which are supposedly
self-evident, it becomes undeniable, along with the corresponding statement about the *right* to pursue happiness. And
that is why I think that Jefferson may have used the phrase
"sacred and undeniable" in his Rough Draft. Now I wish to
show that Jefferson's view that equally created men have the
two other rights mentioned in the Rough Draft may be illu-
minated similarly. To show this, it is necessary to construe
the phrase in the Rough Draft which reads, with Jefferson's
characteristically unsettling punctuation, "the preservation

of life, & liberty & the pursuit of happiness," as meaning the same as "the preservation of life, the preservation of liberty, and the pursuit of happiness." And this reading is easily defended. For one thing, it is in accord with the language of Locke, who speaks of the *preservation* of life and the *preservation* of liberty as ends of government in Chapter IX of the *Second Treatise;* and Jefferson in the very next "sacred and undeniable truth" of the Rough Draft refers to "the preservation of life, & liberty & the pursuit of happiness" as ends to be secured by government. For another, there is a plausible grammatical parallelism in the phrase when construed as I construe it: two "preservations" of things, followed by a "pursuit" of a third thing. We have seen how the view in the Rough Draft that every human creature has the right to *preserve* life can be derived by focusing carefully on Burlamaqui's argument and then deriving a Jeffersonian right from a corresponding Burlamaquian duty, so now we may turn to the other rights in the Rough Draft. The right of every human creature to pursue happiness may be derived in the same way that the right to preserve life was derived because Burlamaqui made the desire for happiness part of the created essence of man. To make a long story less long, we state only the conclusion: since God made the *desire* for happiness a part of man's essence, man has a duty and right to *pursue* happiness.

The right to preserve *liberty* introduces an interesting complication when we try to link the author of the Rough Draft and Burlamaqui because it is a right which is deduced from a duty to *others,* whereas the right to preserve life and the right to pursue happiness are deduced from two Burlamaquian duties to *ourselves.* The complication simply involves dividing the notion of being equally created into its two components: (1) being a creature of God and (2) being equal to all others of the same species. A human *creature* is one who has been given the essential attribute of life by God, and from this Jefferson may derive the *self-regarding* duty and right to preserve one's life. A human *creature* of God is also one who has been given the essential desire for happiness, and from this Jefferson may derive the *self-regarding* duty and right to pursue one's happiness. On the other hand, a human creature of God who is *equal* with his fellow creatures therefore has a *duty to others* not to put them under his dominion. And it is from this duty to others which each of us has that Locke derives the God-given right of all of us to liberty.[33] All of this is in keeping with a doctrine of natural law which is based on the created essence of man developed in the manner of Burlamaqui and some of his predecessors. Moreover, it shows that when in the Rough Draft Jefferson spoke of the rights to *preserve* life and to *preserve* liberty he was speaking of rights which were easily incorporated into the system of Burlamaqui, whereas the successors of these rights in the final version—the right *to* or *of* life and the right *to* or *of* liberty—could not be derived by the kind of argument we have been examining. Therefore, in my opinion,

33. See Chapter 2 above, section entitled "Self-evidence and Equality in Locke." In attributing to Jefferson this distinction between duties to oneself and duties to others, and hence a parallel distinction among rights, I am aware that there is one passage, written in 1822, where he writes: "To ourselves, in strict language, we can owe no duties, obligation requiring . . . two parties" (*Writings*, Volume XIV, p. 140). On the other hand, in 1810 he writes that one of our highest duties is self-preservation (*ibid.*, Volume XII, p. 418); in 1803 he praises the ancient moralists for being great in stressing our duties to ourselves though defective "in developing our duties to others" (*ibid.*, Volume X, pp. 381–382); and in 1782, he says that "if we are made in some degree for others, yet, in a greater, are we made for ourselves" and also that it would be ridiculous to suppose "that a man has less rights in himself than one of his neighbors, or indeed all of them put together" (*ibid.*, Volume IV, p. 196). All of which leads one to suppose that as he grew older, Jefferson changed, but that in the days closest to the Declaration he was quite prepared to speak of a duty to ourselves in the manner of Burlamaqui and other writers on natural law. In this connection, see Burlamaqui's explicit rejection of the doctrine that nobody can oblige himself, *Principles of Natural Law*, Part II, Chapter VII, Sections IX–XII.

the change of the Rough Draft in this respect was more serious than most commentators seem to recognize.[34]

I also want to stress Burlamaqui's dependence in his argument on man's essence as *created by God* because I believe
that Jefferson in the Declaration leaned heavily on that aspect of Burlamaqui's view of natural law.[35] If one carefully
attends to Burlamaqui's argument, one sees that he does not
try to extract man's duties merely from man's essence alone
but rather from man's essence as created by God. Strictly
speaking, he does not typically assert something like "It follows from the fact that man is a living being that he has a
duty to preserve his life." He rather asserts, for example,
"Since God *made* life a part of the essence of man, God *wills*
that man should preserve his life." And this approach is fun-
damentally different in a certain respect from what we find
in other theorists of natural law who, although they believed
that God created man and laid duties on him, tried to derive
the *content* of those duties from his essence or nature without
reference to what may be called God's psychology. Burlamaqui argues that since God *gave* us certain essential features,
he must have *imposed* certain duties upon us, and that is
Burlamaqui's way of answering a man who asks why he
should do certain things. Burlamaqui does not wish to an-

34. See Becker, *Declaration of Independence*, p. 199.
35. There is no doubt that Jefferson believed in essences. I say this with full
awareness that at a certain period in his life Jefferson rejected the doctrine
of essence in no uncertain terms by saying: "We must dismiss the Platonists and Plotinists, the Stagyrites, and Gamalielites the Eclectics, the
Gnostics and Scholastics, their essences and emanations, their Logos and
Demiurgos, Æons and Daemons, male and female, with a long train of
etc., etc., etc., or, shall I say at once, of nonsense," Letter to John Adams,
October 13, 1813, *Writings of Thomas Jefferson*, Volume XIII, p. 389. It
should also be noted *a propos* of Jefferson's supposed aversion to abstract
entities that we find him in his *Notes on Virginia* of 1781 believing in the
existence of *faculties*, which he contrasts with material *substances*, and
saying that a faculty "eludes the research of all the senses," whereas a
material substance may be subjected to the anatomical knife, and to
analysis by fire and solvents, *Writings*, Volume II, p. 200.

swer that question bluntly by saying: "Because God willed that you do them." But when he tries to be less blunt, Burlamaqui merely gives a causal explanation of why God *willed* that the man do those things by pointing out that God—who does nothing in vain—willed the creation of man with a certain essence. Consequently, Burlamaqui never really infers the content of the duties from the essence itself but rather from the fact that God *gave* man that essence. Burlamaqui's entire argument remains, therefore, on the level of God's thought and action: *Since God did or thought so-and-so, then he did or thought such-and-such.* So therefore, if we accept the statement that God did make something part of man's essence or that God did create men as equals, and if we also accept the various "since"-statements which purport to tell us how God behaves, we are led by way of a causal chain to the proposition that God did indeed command or prohibit certain actions. But notice that although the person who prompted this explanation asked for a *demonstration* of why he should do or refrain from doing certain things, he is not given any more than an account of how God came to will that he should do or refrain from doing those things. He is not given a *proof* of why certain things should be done or should not be done which God himself might have provided in justification of his own actions. He is not shown by Burlamaqui how the very essence of man entails certain duties but rather that God's *creation* of man with a certain essence caused God to *impose* certain duties on man. And for this reason he is certainly not shown that these *duties* are essential to man. He has been shown that God gave man certain essential attributes and that since it would have been pointless for God to have given man these essential attributes without laying certain duties on him, God laid those duties on him. But since this does not logically imply that the *duties* are essential to man, it also does not imply that the corresponding rights are essential to man or "inherent," as Jefferson called them in the Rough Draft. Of course, Jefferson *thought* they were inherent because he may have reasoned—fallaciously—that since God gave man *life* as part of his essence, God must also have laid on man a duty to preserve his life, a duty which also formed part of his essence or inhered in it.

Natural Law and the Essence of Man

In order to show that the derivation of the principles of natural law that I think Burlamaqui bequeathed to Jefferson was not the only one available to him and his comrades, I want to turn to the version of those theorists who tried to demonstrate substantive moral propositions of the form, "Every man ought to preserve his own life," and who did not view their task as that of explaining how God came to *will* certain things by appealing to other acts of God. In effect, they tried to maintain propositions like "Since life is part of the essence of man, every man has a duty to preserve his life," without resorting to the psychology of God, and they seemed to think that from this proposition they could infer that the duty to preserve life was as essential to man as life was. Grotius and the early Locke seem to hold that man has certain duties because he has a certain essence, and that having this essence implies having essential duties quite independently of the fact that God created it. But even if one were to grant that, for example, the attribute of being a living being was part of the essence of man, the only ground on which one could conclude that the *duty to preserve life* is also part of the essence of man would be by asserting that the duty to preserve life is part of the essence of *life*. But, plainly, the attribute of life does not contain as part of *its* definition or essence the attribute of having a duty to preserve life. The situation is entirely different from that in which it might be argued: "Since it is part of the essence of a whale to be a mammal and it is part of the essence of being a mammal to be an animal, it is part of the essence of being a whale to be an animal." Furthermore, the proposition, "Since life is part of the essence of man, man has a duty to preserve his life," not only fails to show that having a duty to preserve life is part of the essence of man but also turns out to be a very dubious proposition quite apart from that because it seems to depend on the highly debatable premise that man *should* preserve all or part of his essence.

This goes to the heart of the difficulties that have been felt by many philosophers about the doctrine of natural law not only in its Christianized form but also in the form which it takes in Aristotle's *Nicomachean Ethics,* where he holds that "the function of man is the active exercise of the soul's faculties in conformity with rational principle" after coming to the conclusion that man's rationality is what is specific to him, what distinguishes him from all other things.[36] Assuming for argument's sake that man has certain essential attributes, why, we may ask, should man *act to preserve* those attributes? Even in the face of this difficult question, certain theorists of natural law were determined to defend their doctrine without using an argument like Burlamaqui's, which made what they thought was an avoidable appeal to theological beliefs. They wanted to show that there is some sense in which the attribute of having a duty and a right *to do* certain things *follows from the nature of* man in a way that would allow them to persuade a *non-Christian* of the truth of the doctrine of natural law, and therefore they persisted in their effort to give a rational defense of the doctrine of natural law. In this spirit Grotius had held that "the law of nature is a dictate of right reason, which points out that an act, according as it is or

36. Aristotle, *Nicomachean Ethics,* Book I, Chapter VII, 1098 A. I use Rackham's translation in the Loeb edition. It is of some interest to note that Locke, in his *Essays on the Law of Nature,* cites this passage of Aristotle while presenting his first argument for the existence of a law of nature. See Essay I, pp. 112–113 of von Leyden's edition.

is not in conformity with rational nature, has in it a quality of moral baseness or moral necessity; and that, in consequence, such an act is either forbidden or enjoined by the author of nature, God."[37] He emphasized that "the acts in regard to which such a dictate exists are, *in themselves* [my emphasis], either obligatory or not permissible, and so it is understood that necessarily they are enjoined or forbidden by God."[38] Pufendorf stated the point more pithily: "Things forbidden by natural law are not improper because God forbade them, but God forbade them because they were of themselves improper; while in the same way things commanded by the same law are not proper or necessary because they are commanded by God, but they were commanded because they are of themselves proper."[39] And Locke was prompted by ideas like this when he tried to establish morality as a demonstrative science, even though he, like Grotius and Pufendorf, thought that the principles of natural law were decreed by God. Since these thinkers held that God himself decreed only what was a dictate of right reason and therefore proper, they virtually behaved as though they themselves could provide the argument that God would have given for the *truth* of his precepts if he had deigned to do so. Such an argument by God would, of course, not be an introspective explanation in which God said: "I gave man life with the intention of his preserving it; and since I had that intention, I commanded him to preserve it." It would have been a demonstration of *the truth* that man ought to preserve his life and not an autobiographical account of how God had come to command that he do so.

To get a clearer picture of this approach, it is useful to turn to Locke's early *Essays on the Law of Nature,* not pub-

37. *De jure belli ac pacis,* Book I, Chapter I, Section X.
38. *Ibid.*
39. Pufendorf, *De jure naturae et gentium,* Book II, Chapter III, Section 4.

lished until the twentieth century. Locke wrote: "It seems to me to follow just as necessarily from the nature of man that, if he is a man, he is bound to love and worship God and also to fulfil other things appropriate to the rational nature, i.e. to observe the law of nature, as it follows from the nature of a triangle that, if it is a triangle, its three angles are equal to two right angles, although perhaps very many men are so lazy and so thoughtless that for want of attention they are ignorant of both these truths, which are so manifest and certain that nothing can be plainer."[40] The reader will observe that Locke tells us that a certain theorem of geometry contains a predicate which expresses an attribute that "follows from the nature of a triangle" and that this theorem is so manifest and so certain that nothing can be plainer than it. Here Locke regards a geometrical *theorem* as self-evident since he says that nothing could be plainer than it, and he also seems to say that this theorem attributes a property to all triangles which follows from the nature or essence of triangularity. But both of these statements are incompatible with what Locke maintains in the *Essay,* where he explicitly states that this proposition about triangles is *not* self-evident and where he regards essential predications, or those which are the results of definition, like "Every triangle has three sides," as trifling and uninstructive. In the light of Locke's later and greater wisdom on this matter in his *Essay,* it is fair to complain that when Locke says in the *Essays on the Law of Nature* that it follows necessarily from the *nature* of a triangle that its three angles are equal to two right angles, he cannot mean that this attribute of all triangles is part of the *essence* of being a triangle in the sense of being an attribute which is mentioned in its definition.

What else could he have meant? Probably something akin

40. *Essays on the Law of Nature,* pp. 198–201.

to what Scholastics meant when they said that having its angles add up to two right angles is a *proprium* of triangles.[41] Consequently, whereas *being part of the nature or essence* is *relatively* clear because it may be explained as an attribute which must be mentioned in a definition, *following necessarily from the nature or essence* is not. By the time Locke asserts, as he often does in the *Essay*, that statements like "The angles of every triangle add up to two right angles" are *theorems,* and must be deduced from self-evident propositions, he has come to see that they must be proven or demonstrated by means of an argument which will require reference to axioms. Therefore, the attribute of being a triangle certainly does not contain the attribute of having angles which add up to two right angles. One cannot move from "This figure is a triangle" to "The angles of this figure add up to two right angles" without the mediation of the other premises to which one appeals in the proof. That is why it is difficult to know what Locke means when he says in the *Essays on the Law of Nature* that the attribute of having its three angles add up to two right angles follows necessarily from the *nature* or *essence* of a triangle. True, all and only triangles have this property, and one may demonstrate that they do; but that is not enough to justify the claim that the attribute expressed by its predicate follows necessarily from *the nature* of a triangle.

41. A *proprium* is said to be predicated accidentally of the species because it is not the essence, but it is said to follow necessarily from the essence. It is also thought to be convertible with the species in the sense that everything in the species has the *proprium,* and everything which has the *proprium* is a member of the species. In other words, the *proprium,* though not of the essence of the species, is peculiar to it. I might add that the notion is also present in Aristotle, from whom Locke may have gotten it directly. See Aristotle's *Topics,* Book I, Chapter 5, 102 A on "property." I think that "property" or *"proprium"* comes very close to what Locke has in mind particularly because it is logically convertible with the attribute of being a man, since all *and only men* are bound to love and worship God once we forget about angels.

If anyone should disagree with what I have said about Locke's statement about the geometrical truth he uses as an illustration in the *Essays on the Law of Nature,* I doubt whether many would disagree with me when I say something similar about Locke's illustration from the theory of natural law. Even one who believes in God has no good reason for saying that the property of being obliged to love and worship God follows necessarily from *the nature or essence* of man. The property in question is not part of the *nature or essence* of man (as being a living animal is) simply because it need not be mentioned in the definition of man. Furthermore, even though, angels aside, one might hold that all and only human beings should love and worship God, this proposition, unlike the proposition about triangles, was never deduced by Locke from axioms. Indeed, we know that he abandoned the effort to carry out that deduction and repaired to revelation when asked to demonstrate the moral counterparts of his proposition about triangles.

However, before Locke retreated to revelation in his letters to Molyneux and in the *Reasonableness of Christianity,* he said a number of things in the *Essay* which help us understand why he might have later criticized what he had said in his earlier *Essays on the Law of Nature.* As we have seen in an earlier discussion of the *Essay Concerning Human Understanding,* Locke dismissed trifling propositions like "right is right" and "wrong is wrong" as well as propositions which are true merely by virtue of definitions because, he held, they were incapable of conveying any kind of knowledge. But then he added, as he tried to characterize *instructive* as opposed to trifling propositions: "We can know the truth, and so may be certain in propositions, which affirm something of another, which is a necessary consequence of its precise complex idea, but not contained in it: as that the external angle of all triangles is bigger than either of the opposite internal angles. Which relation of the outward angle to either of the opposite internal angles, making no part of the complex idea signified by the name triangle, this is a real truth, and conveys with it instructive real knowledge."[42] Here we see the crucial connection which, according to Locke, must exist between the complex idea which is the subject of a universal proposition and the predicate if we are to avoid asserting a trifling proposition. The predicate must not be *contained* in the subject but it must be a *necessary* consequence of it. Therefore, instructive moral propositions must not resemble "Every triangle has three sides" but rather the proposition that the external angle of every triangle is bigger than either of the opposite internal angles or the proposition that the angles of all triangles add up to two right angles.

I realize that this later doctrine of Locke's resembles his earlier one insofar as he continues to think of the predicate of the geometrical theorem as a *necessary consequence* of the subject, but he no longer speaks of the predicate as following necessarily from *the nature of* the subject, and he no longer treats this geometrical theorem as if it were a self-evident truth by saying that it is so manifest and certain that nothing could be plainer than it. My guess is that his failure to speak about the predicate's following necessarily from *the nature* of the subject—triangle—is the result of his coming to hold that whatever is contained in the nature or essence of the subject is linkable with the subject only in a trifling proposition. There still remains a question, of course, about what Locke meant by the necessary connection between a predicate not contained in a subject and the subject. Some have interpreted this as an anticipation of Kant's notion of a synthetic necessary proposition,[43] and I have already wondered whether Locke might have had in mind the Scholastic notion of a *proprium*. On the other hand, he might have meant that since

42. *Essay*, Book IV, Chapter VIII, Section 8.
43. For example, Locke's editor, A. C. Fraser. See his note to Locke's *Essay*, Book IV, Chapter VIII, Section 8.

geometrical theorems are deducible from self-evident necessary truths, they too must be necessary truths, and I am inclined to think that this is what he did mean unless it can be
shown that he regarded them as necessary quite independently of their being deduced.

In any event, I think that Locke, by ceasing to speak of
man's duties as following necessarily from man's nature or
essence on the ground that speaking in that way would turn
principles of natural law into trifling propositions, effectively
doomed the whole idea of logically extracting man's duties
merely from his essence or nature. In this way he undercut a
version of natural law which was an alternative to that advocated by Burlamaqui. As soon as he acknowledged that an essential predication of ethics was trifling, he distinguished his
view from that of Culverwel, who, as we have seen in Chapter 1, thought that the principles of natural law were virtually tautologous, and from that of Grotius when Grotius
likened the principles of natural law to statements like "Murder is evil," which, for him, were like "Every man is a living
being," that is to say, statements which were true by virtue of
their predicates being contained in their subjects. Unfortunately, Locke failed to heed his own strictures on this subject
when he maintained that the proposition "Where there is no
property, there is no injustice" would be a theorem in the
demonstrative science of morality[44] that he never produced,
since Hume[45] pointed out that this so-called theorem was sim-

44. *Essay*, Book IV, Chapter III, Section 18.
45. *An Enquiry Concerning Human Understanding*, Section XII, Part III, ed.
L. A. Selby-Bigge (Oxford, 1902), p. 163. Also see my *Science and Sentiment
in America*, p. 60. It is of interest to note that Berkeley, in his *Philosophical Commentaries*, wrote "Lockes instances of Demonstration in Morality
are according to his own Rule trifling Propositions." See *The Works of
George Berkeley*, eds. A. A. Luce and T. E. Jessop (London, 1948), Volume
I, p. 84. This was written before Hume published his comment on the
same subject and could not have been known to Hume since it had not
been published in Hume's lifetime. I am grateful to Professor George
Pitcher for locating this passage for me.

ply the result of using definitions of "property" and "injustice" and was therefore not a theorem of morality but what Locke himself should have called a trifling and uninstructive proposition. Given this blunder, given Locke's own statement in one neglected part of the *Essay* that there could be no self-evident practical principles,[46] and given Locke's admission that he had not constructed a demonstrative science of morality, it is not surprising that the American revolutionaries did not turn to him for a straightforward exposition of the doctrine of natural law. In his writings they *could* find a description of what a science of morality might look like, they *could* find elaborate discussions of intuitive knowledge and self-evident truth, and they *could* find the allegedly self-evident truth in the *Second Treatise* that "creatures of the same species . . . should also be equal one amongst another without subordination or subjection"—a declaration which was easily incorporated into Burlamaqui's system when he argued that since God made us fellow members of the same species, he must have imposed upon us a duty to others not to put them under our dominion. But the revolutionaries found much more than a metaphysical and epistemological prolegomenon to a system of natural law in Burlamaqui's textbook. He tried to use the method recommended by Locke and claimed that he had deduced the principles of natural law from the nature and states of man, even though he did not deduce substantive propositions of natural law and therefore did not carry out the same program that Locke, with characteristic honesty, said he could not carry out. But the revolutionaries did not seem to worry about that. They were quite content to follow a man who boldly announced:

We shall therefore lay down two general propositions, as the foundation of the whole system of the law of nature.

46. *Essay*, Book I, Chapter II, Section 4; also my *Science and Sentiment in America*, pp. 20–21.

First Proposition.

Whatever is in the nature and original constitution of man, and appears a necessary consequence of this nature and constitution, certainly indicates the intention or will of God with respect to man, and consequently acquaints us with the law of nature.

Second Proposition.

But, in order to have a complete system of the law of nature, we must not only consider the nature of man, such as it is in itself; it is also necessary to attend to the relations he has to other beings, and to different states thence arising. Otherwise it is evident we should have only an imperfect and defective system.

We may therefore affirm, that the general foundation of the system of natural law is the nature of man, considered under the several circumstances, that attend it, and in which God himself has placed him for particular ends; inasmuch as by this means we may be acquainted with the will of God. In short since man holds from the hand of God himself whatever he possesses, as well with regard to his existence, as to his manner of existing, it is the study of human nature only, that can fully instruct us concerning the views, which God proposed to himself in giving us our being; and consequently with the rules we ought to follow, in order to accomplish the designs of the Creator.[47]

Burlamaqui believed that if we see a trait in the nature of man, we can conclude that God must have *willed* something with respect to man, and that was enough. It was also enough for his American admirers, who were not bent on proving the substance of God's decrees but content with Burlamaqui's explanation of how God had come to issue them. By this I do not wish to suggest that Burlamaqui held that the mere fact that God willed that man do something was

47. *Principles of Natural Law*, Part II, Chapter IV, Section V.

sufficient to prove it obligatory without attention to God's qualities. I have already indicated that God was assumed by Burlamaqui to be not only powerful but also good and wise. That is why we find Burlamaqui arguing that God's supreme power "is not alone and of itself sufficient to establish the right to command, and the obligation of obeying. But if to the idea of the Creator we join . . . the idea of being perfectly wise and sovereignly good, who has no desire of exercising his power, but for the good and advantage of his creatures; then we have every thing necessary to found a legitimate authority."[48] What I mean to emphasize is that once Burlamaqui has assumed or tried to prove that God is perfectly wise and sovereignly good, then, when he shows that God has willed something, that is enough. After that, there is no need, he thinks, for his readers to examine each decree of God and to determine whether its content is true or false. We examine the essence God has given man and the states into which he has put man, infer his intentions with respect to man, and then infer what God was led to decree, using along the way the premise that God, by his nature, can do nothing but good and nothing in vain. In this way, we do not go through the Lockean process of proving the truth of moral theorems as we would prove the truth of geometrical theorems. Students of the history of natural law may well ask whether, because his argument terminates in a statement about what God wills, Burlamaqui is a "voluntarist" or one who thinks that the essence of natural law is God's will rather than his reason.[49] I do not think so, but on the other hand,

48. *Ibid.*, Part I, Chapter IX, Sections VI–VII.
49. See von Leyden's Introduction to Locke's *Essays on the Law of Nature*, pp. 40, 43, and 50–54, for a discussion of the connections between Locke's so-called *voluntarist* theory of natural law, according to which God is the ultimate source of morality, and his search for a purely rational foundation of ethics. Locke's apparent shifting on this subject in his *Essays* is linked by von Leyden with a medieval controversy on the nature of law which is described in O. Gierke, *Political Theories of the Middle Age,*

Burlamaqui cannot be called a rationalist or intellectualist if that means that he tries to prove principles of natural law by reason and without *any* reference to God's will. His position is a mixture of voluntarism and rationalism since he tries to use reason to show that God must have willed certain things because he willed others. Because Burlamaqui uses as a premise the proposition that God is good and wise as well as supremely powerful, he thinks that he has avoided that form of voluntarism according to which law is *merely* the will of a supremely powerful being. It is the will of a good and wise powerful being, but nonetheless his will.

On the basis of this reading of Burlamaqui and my belief that he influenced Jefferson very strongly, I have argued that Jefferson, by applying the phrase "sacred and undeniable" to his main moral truth in the Rough Draft, may have been acknowledging that it was not self-evident but rather deduced from other self-evident truths. In other words, Jefferson's assertion in the Rough Draft that it was *undeniable* that the right to *preserve* life, the right to *preserve* liberty, and the right to *pursue* happiness were *derived* from equal creation had the status it had in Burlamaqui's system. It was the Swiss jurist's conclusion from what he regarded as two self-evident propositions: (1) that since God gave us life as part of our es-

---

trans. F. W. Maitland (Cambridge, Eng., 1951), pp. 172–173, note 256, a controversy over the question whether the essence of law is will or reason, though "in any case God himself appeared as being the ultimate cause of Natural Law." To this note the translator, Maitland, adds another from Gierke's book on Althusius, in which Gierke associates the view that the law of nature was a mere divine command with nominalism, whereas realists held the view that law was a dictate of reason "grounded in the being of God but unalterable even by him." A third or "mediating view" Gierke describes as "inclined to the principles of realism," and he mentions Aquinas and Suarez as its supporters. "It regarded the substance of natural law as a judgment touching what was right, a judgment necessarily flowing from the Divine Being and unalterably determined by that nature of things which is comprised in God; howbeit, the binding force of this law, but only its binding force, was traced to God's Will" (p. 173).

sence, put us into the same species and into society with our
fellow-men, and gave us as part of our essence a desire for
happiness, God proposed at least three ends for us: the preservation of life, the preservation of liberty, and the pursuit of
happiness; and (2) that since God proposed these three ends
for us, he imposed on us three corresponding duties to attain
these ends. From these two statements Burlamaqui inferred
that from God's equal creation of man as a being with a certain nature and in a certain state, man derived the duty to
preserve life, the duty to preserve liberty, and the duty to
pursue happiness. And by what Locke might have called a
trifling step, I suggest that Jefferson deduced his statement in
the Rough Draft that from equal creation man derives his
rights to preserve life and liberty, and to pursue happiness.

When we see all of this, we see more clearly, I hope, the
metaphysics and theology by means of which the revolutionaries thought they derived from equal creation the rights that
we shall examine from a different angle in the next chapter.
But before we turn our attention in that direction, I think it
worth noting to what extent the appeal to the essence or nature of man was indispensable in their argument as well as
the extent to which that concept could be what I have called
an intellectual joker. The point is that philosophers have not
always agreed as to what the essence of man is, and therefore,
since so many arguments in the history of the doctrine of natural law have taken the form of deriving duties and therefore
rights from the essence of man, a different view of his essence could easily lead to a different conception of what duties and rights man has by nature. I believe that one of the
most important divisions within the history of the doctrine
of natural law probably derives from what might be regarded
as an ambiguity in Aristotle's conception of the essence of
man. On the one hand, we find frequent assertions by him
that man is by nature a rational animal, on the other that he
is by nature a political or social animal. And, interestingly

enough, one finds that there are some theorists of natural law, like Locke in his *Essays on the Law of Nature,* who appeal to what may be called the rationalistic strain in Aristotle's conception of man's nature rather than to what, Franco Venturi tells us, was called the socialistic strain by an Italian writer of the Enlightenment.[50] Grotius, Pufendorf, and the Cambridge Platonists—as von Leyden points out[51]—held that sociability is the origin of the law of nature. And what is of even greater interest to us in this connection is that Burlamaqui criticized Pufendorf for "establishing sociability alone, as the foundation of all natural laws."[52] This, Burlamaqui maintains, would not allow us to derive duties to God and ourselves and would therefore, if I am correct, make it impossible to provide a foundation for two of the rights in the Rough Draft, the preservation of life and the pursuit of happiness.

It is therefore of the utmost importance for an argument like that of Burlamaqui and of the American revolutionaries that the essence or nature of man be what they take it to be, and my point in connection with a more general thesis of this book is that the essence of man is so obscure a notion that it could easily be identified by different thinkers in different ways. Thus, if Jefferson had not held, under the influence, as I think, of Burlamaqui, that a desire for happiness is part of the created essence of man, he could not have defended by means of a Burlamaquian argument the various rights he defended. Furthermore, given the obscurity of the notion of essence, other thinkers might easily have "seen" things in the essence of man that might have led by Burlamaquian arguments to duties which would have been most

---

50. Venturi tells us that Appiano Buonafede applied the word "socialist" to Grotius, Pufendorf, and Cumberland because of their view that *sociality* or *sociability* was the basis of natural law, *Italy and the Enlightenment: Studies in a Cosmopolitan Century,* trans. S. Corsi (London, 1972), p. 59.

51. *Op. cit.,* p. 53.

52. Burlamaqui, *Principles of Natural Law,* Part II, Chapter IV, Section XIX.

objectionable from the revolutionaries' point of view. There-fore, the revolutionaries' reliance upon the concept of essence is, in a certain respect, the metaphysical counterpart of their reliance on self-evident truth. It would take very little effort to turn the concept of essence or nature to uses that the revo-lutionaries would have abhorred. After all, Aristotle believed that some men were slaves by their nature or essence, and he was one of the most inveterate employers of the concept of essence in the history of philosophy—some would say its in-ventor. And we have seen that whatever worries Jefferson might have had about treating blacks equally with whites seem to have been based on worries about whether they pos-sessed enough rational power to warrant inclusion in the spe-cies *man*, that is to say, whether blacks and whites shared the same essence.

· 5 ·

The Nature of Rights

So far I have said a fair amount about rights but have not tried to define the concept of a right as it was understood by the revolutionaries, nor have I discussed some of the characteristics of certain rights, like the unalienability of which the Declaration speaks. I have also spent comparatively little time discussing some of the particular rights mentioned in the literature of the Revolution. However, the reader has seen that a right was understood to be some kind of power and that expressions like "You have the right to do so-and-so," "You may do so-and-so," and "You have the liberty to do so-and-so" meant roughly the same thing to eighteenth-century moralists and revolutionaries. On the other hand, the expression, "You have the power to do so-and-so," though it was used on occasion as an equivalent of the expressions just listed, created a problem for the revolutionaries because they were very much concerned to distinguish the right to do something from the *"mere physical power"* to do something. They thought that a right was a physical power but that it was a special kind of physical power, whose *differentia,* as

Aristotelian logicians would say, had to be mentioned in the definition of a right. Therefore, my first task in this chapter will be to clarify the Revolutionary conception of a right with special attention to the relationship between a right and a physical power. After that, I shall turn to one of the most important *kinds* of rights for the revolutionaries, namely, *unalienable rights,* in order to discuss not only the meaning of the word "unalienable" but also to consider certain rights which were often said by the revolutionists to be unalienable, for example, the right to preserve life, the right to preserve liberty, the right to pursue happiness, and the right to judgment or belief, as it was sometimes called. In the course of this discussion I shall deal with a number of questions concerning such rights, for example, with questions raised by certain critics who wondered why the revolutionaries, after saying that the right to life is unalienable in the beginning of the Declaration, *pledge* to each other their lives at the end of the document. Another kind of right I shall consider is the so-called *adventitious right;* and by the time I have done so, it will be easier to understand why the adventitious and alienable right to property in goods and estates was not listed by the signers of the Declaration as one of their sacred trinity of rights.

Rights, Powers, and John Adams

The question to which I first address myself is: How did Jefferson and his fellow-revolutionaries understand the noun "rights" as used in the Declaration and in other kindred documents? When in the Rough Draft Jefferson said that men have a *right* to preserve life and liberty, and a right to pursue happiness, and when the final version asserted that men are endowed by their Creator with the rights more simply named "life" and "liberty," what was meant by the noun "rights"? Let me say very quickly that it will not do to dispose of this question by writing, as one eminent student of Jefferson has written, that "we can get at the heart of the matter if we regard the word 'rights' as merely the plural of the word 'right' and think of it in the moral sense. Rights, as the people in all ages understand them, are simply what is right."[1] First of all, the moral word "right" whose plural we are advised to form in order to get the Declaration's noun "rights" is an adjective and therefore, strictly speaking, has no plural. The adjective is a word which is normally applied to an action, as when we say that Brutus's stabbing of Caesar was right. Consequently, I do not think, as Dumas Malone does, that according to the Declaration "rights are simply what is right," and my reasons for objecting are more than grammatical. For one thing, *"a* right" refers to an entity that *may be exercised* in actions, whereas the adjective "right" characterizes actions themselves. For another, in exercising *a* right we do not necessarily do what *is* right because on *some* occasions it may not be right to exercise that right. Thus the right to rebel might be exercised prematurely or without reason, and hence the rebellion be condemned as not right.

In addition, we must remember that a statement that every man has a certain right is connected in several ways with the laws of nature, which express duties. First of all, the statements in the Declaration of *our* rights are deducible from statements of *our corresponding* duties, or duties to do that which *we* are said to have a right to do. Secondly, each such statement of a right implies that *every other* man has at least a duty not to prevent our exercise of the right in question. And, thirdly, our right to do something cannot conflict with our duties as expressed in natural law. Consequently, a reader who wishes to understand what the signers of the Declaration

1. See Dumas Malone, writing in *The Story of the Declaration of Independence* (New York, 1975), p. 88.

meant when they said that every man has a certain right to do something, must understand what the signers understood by a duty of natural law.

What, then, *are* rights and how are they connected with powers? When we probe in this direction, we discover that the American revolutionaries were influenced by writers who distinguished sharply between *natural* power and *moral* power. In this context the word "natural" is treated as equivalent to "physical," and so Pufendorf tells us: "In man the power to act is twofold. One is the *natural* power to act (*potentia*), through which he is able by his natural strength to perform an action, or to neglect it, without considering whether it be right or not."[2] Consequently, Pufendorf adds that natural power consists in being "able in fact to do things forbidden by laws, and to neglect their precepts."[3] By contrast, Pufendorf continues, *"moral* power in man is that whereby he is able to perform a voluntary action legitimately and with a moral effect, that is to say, so that this action shall harmonize with the laws, or at least be not repugnant to them, and be able to produce moral effects in others. Now a man is judged to have authority to do all that which can be done by him through the exercise of his natural power, whatever, namely, is not forbidden by the laws, or is also enjoined by the same, or else left indifferent."[4] Pufendorf was so preoccupied with the distinction between moral power conceived as a right and mere natural power (*potentia*) that he made a further distinction between having authority (*potestas*) and having a right (*ius*) by pointing out that when we are said to have authority over persons or things, it is not always clear how we have acquired the things. On the other hand, when we speak of having a right over them, this

2. *Elementorum Jurisprudentiae Universalis,* Book I, Definition XIV, p. 168 of Oldfather's translation.

3. *Ibid.*

4. *Ibid.*

"clearly indicates that this authority has been acquired properly and is now also properly held." Therefore, when Pufendorf says of a right that it is a "moral quality by which we properly either command persons or possess things, or by which things are owed to us," he conceives of a right as something that is doubly removed from mere natural or physical power but which does not for this reason cease being a physical power. It is a species of power to use one's strength in a manner which is morally approved.[5]

The idea that a right is a moral power is also emphasized by Burlamaqui, who may have had more influence on some American revolutionaries than Pufendorf had.[6] Burlamaqui defines a right as a power or a faculty which a man has to use his liberty and strength (*ses forces naturelles*) in a particular manner either in regard to himself or in respect to other men, so far as this exercise of his liberty and strength is approved by reason.[7] Because Burlamaqui emphasizes a distinction between physical power and right which will help us clarify what some of the colonists said about rights and dispel some confusion that commentators on Colonial writings may sometimes create, I shall quote a passage from the *Principles of Natural Law* in which he reveals basic agreement with Pufendorf:

> We must not therefore confound simple power with right. A simple power is a physical quality; it is a power

5. Pufendorf, *op. cit.*, p. 58. It may be helpful to note that Pufendorf uses *"potentia"* for natural power, *"potestas"* for a moral power to do something (*potentia moralis activa*), and *"ius"* for a moral power properly acquired. The logical path from *"potentia"* to *"ius"* is by way of adding two moral differences to the genus of natural power.

6. I have in mind here the disappointment which James Otis felt when he read Grotius and Pufendorf on the rights of colonists in general. See B. Bailyn, ed., *Pamphlets of the American Revolution, 1750–1776*, Volume I (1750–1765), p. 436. The passage appears in Otis's *The Rights of the British Colonies Asserted and Proved* (1764).

7. *Principles of Natural Law*, Part I, Chapter VII, Section II.

of acting in the full extent of our natural strength and liberty; but the idea of right is more confined. This includes a relation of agreeableness to a rule, which modifies the physical power.[8]

It is imperative to observe, therefore, that although a right conceived as a power is distinguished from power understood as unqualified physical strength, it is distinguished from it because a moral right is a power to use physical strength in conformity with, or not in violation of, natural law. When we view it in this way, we may distinguish physical strength as a morally neutral thing from its use in a morally acceptable way and from its use in a morally *un*acceptable way. Physical strength may, to put the matter simply, be used to good effect or ill effect. And from this it follows that many colonists who spoke of rights realized that a right was a power to effect something by the use of physical strength in what Burlamaqui calls a manner approved by reason. Consequently, they were not critical of the use of physical strength *as such*. Those who had studied *Cato's Letters* by Trenchard and Gordon would have read in Letter 25 that power conceived as physical strength is like fire because it warms, scorches, or destroys, according as it is watched, provoked, or increased. When such *physical* strength or power is used in certain morally objectionable ways by one man or by a few, it is called *despotic* power, *arbitrary* power, or dominion over other men. When it is used in morally objectionable ways by the many it is called "license."[9]

8. *Ibid.*, Part I, Chapter VII, Section III. Burlamaqui's reference to Pufendorf is to the latter's *De jure naturae et gentium*, Book I, Chapter I, Section 20, where he says almost exactly what I have quoted above from his *Elementorum Jurisprudentiae Universalis*.

9. John Trenchard and Thomas Gordon, *Cato's Letters: Essays on Liberty, Civil and Religious, and Other Important Subjects*, 6th ed., corrected (London, 1755). I have used a reprint edition published in New York, 1971, of which see Volume I, pp. 184–194. See also Locke, *Second Treatise*, Section 6, where he contrasts liberty and license. For some Colonial ref-

This is quite evident in the Rough Draft of the Declaration, where the second occurrence of the word "powers" appears in the reference to the *"just* powers" that governments derive from the consent of the governed, where the third occurrence refers to the right, which the people may exercise after abolishing one form of government, to organize the new government's "powers in such form, as to them shall seem most likely to effect their safety and happiness," and where the fourth occurrence refers to the fact that a long train of abuses, etc., has evinced "a design to subject them to *arbitrary* power."[10] Clearly, this shows that powers could be *just,* that they could be organized in forms that would seem likely to effect the people's *saftey and happiness,* and that they could be *arbitrary.* Furthermore, it is noteworthy that the phrase "subject them to arbitrary power" was ultimately replaced by "reduce them under absolute despotism."[11]

As soon as one realizes that the American revolutionaries thought that physical power was neutral and that it was not

---

erences to morally objectionable uses of power, see, for example, Jonathan Mayhew, *A Discourse Concerning Unlimited Submission and Nonresistance to the Higher Powers* (1750), Bailyn, *Pamphlets,* Volume I, pp. 240–241, where "absolute uncontrollable power" and "arbitrary power" are mentioned; also James Otis, *Rights of the British Colonies,* Bailyn, *ibid.,* p. 468, where "unlimited power of taxation" is condemned; also Oxenbridge Thacher, *The Sentiments of a British American* (1764), Bailyn, *ibid.,* p. 495, where there is a reference to "exorbitant wanton power." It should be clear that these qualifications of power are what grammarians call "attributive" rather than "predicative" since the authors do not intend by the use of an expression like "exorbitant wanton power" to assert that *all* power is exorbitant and wanton. They merely wish to specify some uses of power which are exorbitant and wanton. Furthermore, when we find an expression like "power and liberty ever being *opponents,*" *A Letter to the People of Pennsylvania* (1760), Bailyn, *ibid.,* p. 257, we must understand that the word "power" is here being used elliptically for something like "arbitrary power" or "despotic power" because, as we have seen, "liberty" is itself defined as a species of power.

10. Boyd, *Declaration of Independence,* p. 19.
11. For an interesting account of the steps by which this change came about see Boyd, *ibid.,* pp. 22–23.

evil as such, one can see why it would have been impossible for them to have held—as Professor Bernard Bailyn says they held—that "the sphere of power" and "the sphere of right" were "innately opposed."[12] No Colonial revolutionary who accepted the main tenets of his moral and juristic mentors could have believed this. How could he if he wished to defend the right of armed revolution? The very right to abolish a bad government which is advocated in the Declaration is plainly a right or a moral power to exercise physical strength if necessary.

In reporting what the colonists and their mentors believed, I have quoted the Declaration, the widely read *Cato's Letters*, Pufendorf, and Burlamaqui. Now let me add that John Adams once wrote: "It is a maxim, that in every government there must exist somewhere, a supreme, sovereign, absolute, and uncontrollable power; but this power resides always in the body of the people."[13] The same Adams asserted many years later, in words that are quite in keeping with those he uttered before the Revolution, that "All that men can do, is to modify, organize, and arrange the powers of human society, that is to say, the physical strength and force of men, in the best manner to protect, secure, and cherish the moral, which are all the natural rights of mankind."[14] It should be noted that Adams explicitly allows that physical strength may be used in a morally beneficial manner. And in 1776 Adams had asserted: "Government is a frame, a scheme, a system, a combination of powers for a certain end, namely, —the good of the whole community."[15] He also said once that

---

12. Bernard Bailyn, *The Ideological Origins of the American Revolution* (Cambridge, Mass., 1967), pp. 57–58.
13. J. Adams, "Proclamation of the Great and General Court" (Winter 1775–1776?), *Works*, Volume I, p. 193.
14. Letter to John Taylor in 1814, *ibid.*, Volume VI, p. 458.
15. *Ibid.*, Volume III, p. 479. This passage appears in a letter written by Adams to the *Boston Gazette*, January 27, 1766, under the pseudonym, "The Earl of Clarendon." For the obvious idea that unobjectionable forms of

he agreed with Butler rather than Hobbes[16] on the nature of man, with the Bishop Butler who summed up one of the most important parts of his *Sermons on Human Nature* by writing: "All of this is no more than the distinction, which everybody is acquainted with, between *mere power* and *authority*."[17] And Butler did not think that it was always wrong to exercise physical power.

It is absurd, therefore, to suppose that Adams regarded power conceived as physical strength as necessarily or intrinsically in conflict with the rights of man, with natural law, or with liberty conceived as a natural right. On the other hand, *despotic* power, *arbitrary* power, and other varieties of abused and immoral uses of physical strength or power *were* thought by Adams and by other colonists to be in conflict with natural law and with natural rights. To say so, however, would be trifling, to use Locke's term. By definition, a morally reprehensible use of physical strength or power would violate moral law and invade moral rights. It would be a use of physical strength of which reason would disapprove. And so how could it *fail* to clash with natural law and natural right? In reading even the most emotional and rhetorical pamphleteers one sees that they grasped some of the fundamental definitions of the eminent jurists and philosophers

---

government exercise powers, see also Daniel Dulany, *Considerations on the Propriety of Imposing Taxes in the British Colonies* (1765), Bailyn, *Pamphlets*, pp. 618–620.

16. Adams, *Works*, Volume IV, p. 406.

17. Joseph Butler, *Fifteen Sermons Preached at the Rolls Chapel* (1726; London, 1949), Sermon II, Section 14, p. 57. In Otis's *Rights of the British Colonies*, Bailyn, *Pamphlets*, Volume I, p. 476, see the following sentence: " 'Tis hoped it will not be considered as a new doctrine that even the authority of the Parliament of *Great Britain* is circumscribed by certain bounds which if exceeded their acts become those of mere *power* without *right*, and consequently void." Here, as in Butler, "mere power" is used in condemnatory fashion because the power is not rightful. However, the English word "mere" is ambiguous and may sometimes carry no pejorative implication. "Mere power" is then understood as "neutral power."

whom they read, so in fairness to these pamphleteers, one should not saddle them with trifling, self-contradictory, or patently false views. Yet it *is* trifling to assert that a morally condemnable use of physical strength is in conflict with natural law; it *is* self-contradictory to suppose that the use of morally approved strength is in conflict with morality; and it *is* patently false that the use of physical strength is *inevitably* in conflict with natural law. In the light of this, I cannot agree with Bailyn's statement that the colonists saw the public world "divided into distinct, contrasting, and innately antagonistic spheres: the sphere of power and the sphere of liberty or right. The one was brutal, ceaselessly active, and heedless; the other was delicate, passive, and sensitive. The one must be resisted, the other defended, and the two must never be confused."[18]

Is there no way of interpreting this statement so that it represents the colonists' views on power more accurately? Let me answer this by returning to the figure of fire in the twenty-fifth of *Cato's Letters*. Power is there said to resemble fire in being both useful and dangerous. It is dangerous because it has a tendency to break bounds, and perhaps this conveys the element of truth in the statement that power was regarded by the colonists as "brutal, ceaselessly active, and heedless." Like everyone else, the colonists were acutely aware of what might happen if fire—and, in general, physical power—were placed in the hands of fallen, biased, unchecked human beings. But this does not mean that the colonists held that all power to use physical strength was brutal, despotic, arbitrary, or opposed to liberty and right, which are themselves powers to use physical strength in a reasonable way.

Since I believe that the colonists on the whole tended to regard power as morally neutral physical strength, as Pufendorf's *potentia*, I have grave doubts about the following statement by Bailyn: "The essence of what they meant by

18. Bernard Bailyn, *Ideological Origins*, pp. 57–58.

power was perhaps best revealed inadvertently by John Adams as he groped for words in drafting his *Dissertation on the Canon and Feudal Law*. Twice choosing and then rejecting the word 'power,' he finally selected as the specification of the thought he had in mind 'dominion,' and in this association of words the whole generation concurred. 'Power' to them meant the dominion of some men over others, the human control of human life."[19] I fail to see that Adams's twice choosing and then rejecting "power" in favor of "dominion" shows that he *identified* power and dominion over men. It could more plausibly be argued that it shows his refusal to identify them, a refusal made all the more understandable by some of the passages from Adams I have quoted above and by some of the passages I have quoted from Pufendorf and Burlamaqui. I agree with Bailyn that the colonists believed that a physical power and a right should never be "confused," but it does not follow from this that they regarded them as "antagonistic." They viewed a natural right as a moral species of power, but a species, though *distinct* from the genus of which it is a species, is not *antagonistic* to it. Let me now consider certain moral powers, or rights, that occupied a central position in the philosophy of the revolutionaries, namely, unalienable rights.

Is the Right To Believe Unalienable?

Many older treatises on natural law contain classifications of rights. For example, rights are described as perfect, imperfect, alienable, unalienable, or external; and some are said to be held by man in a state of nature because they come from the hand of God, whereas others are said to exist in adventitious states of society which are the products of man's own acts. I begin by discussing the notion of an unalienable right not only because it is mentioned in the Declaration but also be-

19. *Ibid.*, pp. 55–56. See Adams, *Diary and Autobiography*, Volume I, p. 255.

cause unalienable rights play a particularly important part in the argument for rebellion, which I shall consider in a later chapter. But before I discuss the notion of unalienable right in some detail, I want to dispose of the misconception that it is a right which "no man can *take* away."[20] Let me say at once, therefore, that the term "unalienable" does not refer to what cannot be *taken away* but rather to what cannot be *transferred* to another. "Alienable" is equivalent to "communicable" in one of Pufendorf's statements on the subject.[21] And Rousseau said "To alienate is to give or sell" in a passage[22] cited by James Otis.[23]

I shall begin my discussion of how the revolutionaries viewed *alienable* rights by turning first to the writings of Francis Hutcheson. What he has to say about rights and about their alienability and unalienability is, naturally, influenced by his special views in moral philosophy and to that extent cannot be attributed in its entirety to all of the revolutionaries. But in spite of that, most of what he says is quite illuminating for our purposes primarily because he is clearer and more philosophical than most American writers on the subject.[24] He treats this subject in at least three places: (1) in the

20. Malone, *op. cit.*, p. 88. The emphasis is mine.
21. *De jure naturae et gentium*, Book I, Chapter I, Section 19. In one of Jefferson's first legal arguments—that in the case o. Howell vs. Netherland—he uses the verb "alien" rather than "alienate" in referring to the transferring of a black. In this same argument, Jefferson writes: "Under the law of nature, all men are born free, every one comes into the world with a right to his own person, which includes the liberty of moving and using it at his own will." He also appeals to Pufendorf, *op. cit.*, Book VI, Chapter III, Sections 4 and 9, on certain aspects of the subject of slavery. This argument of Jefferson's appears in P. L. Ford's edition of the *Writings of Thomas Jefferson*, Volume I (New York, 1892), pp. 373–381.
22. *The Social Contract*, Book I, Chapter IV.
23. *Rights of the British Colonies* in Bailyn, *Pamphlets*, Volume I, p. 436.
24. In general, I have also found Hutcheson's discussion of the various kinds of rights more helpful than those of the jurists. Except for Burlamaqui's treatment of the *adventitious* right of property, to which I shall soon come, he is much less probing than Hutcheson in his discussion of the different

second treatise of his *Inquiry into the Original of Our Ideas of Beauty and Virtue* (1725), the second treatise being entitled *An Inquiry Concerning the Original of Our Ideas of Virtue or Moral Good*; (2) in his *Philosophiae moralis institutio compendiaria* (1742, first translated into English in 1747 under the title *A Short Introduction to Moral Philosophy*); and (3) in his posthumous *System of Moral Philosophy* (1755). The first treatment is more extended than the others so I shall concentrate on it.

Hutcheson says that in order to determine what rights are alienable we must ask two questions. First: Is the alienation within our natural power, meaning, is it "possible for us in fact to transfer our right"? If so, then we must ask whether it will "serve some valuable purpose" to transfer that right. And, Hutcheson holds, a right is said to be alienable if and only if both of these questions are answered in the affirmative.[25] It seems clear, then, that the first question is nonmoral insofar as it concerns what is possible, whereas the second might be called a moral question if "valuable" is construed as a moral term. Because Hutcheson's distinction between two kinds of unalienability—natural and moral—raises some difficult questions, I want to discuss the two kinds at some length. I begin with the notion of natural unalienability, which in the eighteenth century affects the whole idea of the right to believe.

Hutcheson points out that because alienability involves

---

kinds of rights (*Principles of Natural Law*, Part I, Chapter VII, Section 8), as are Pufendorf (*De jure naturae et gentium*, Book I, Chapter I, Section 19) and Grotius (*De jure belli ac pacis*, Book I, Chapter I, Sections 4–7). Locke presents no systematic discussion of the various kinds of rights, though, as we shall see, he says some very relevant things, especially on matters pertaining to belief and life.

25. *Inquiry Concerning the Original of Our Ideas of Virtue or Moral Good*, sometimes referred to as *Inquiry Concerning Moral Good and Evil*, 2nd ed., corrected and enlarged (London, 1726), Section VII, Part VII, pp. 282–283.

the passing of these two tests, a right may be said to be un-alienable (incidentally, he uses that spelling and not "*in*alien-able") if it fails the first test alone. Thus he maintains that "the right of private judgment, or of our inward sentiments, is unalienable" because "we cannot command ourselves to think what either we ourselves, or any other person pleases."[26] The basic idea here seems to be that one's judging truth or falsity is caused by what appears to be relevant evidence and therefore that one cannot judge as one pleases. *A fortiori,* one cannot judge as another person pleases and hence cannot transfer one's right of judgment. What Hutcheson says about the right to judgment is of special concern to us because it is closely related to what Jefferson says at the beginning of his "Bill for Establishing Religious Freedom," namely, that he is *well aware that the opinions and belief of men depend not on their own will, but follow involuntarily the evidence pro-posed to their minds.*"[27] I suspect that Jefferson would have agreed with Hutcheson that the right to judgment or belief is unalienable because Jefferson says in his bill *"that the opinions of men are not the object of civil government, nor under its jurisdiction"* and that the civil magistrate should not "intrude his powers into the field of opinion."[28] But if Jefferson agreed with Hutcheson, both of them created a puzzle which is best introduced by returning to what Hutche-son says about the unalienability of the right of judgment.

In the course of trying to show that this right is unalien-able according to his first mark, Hutcheson says—and we have seen Jefferson agreeing—that one cannot judge as one pleases because one's judgment is caused or determined by the evi-dence as it appears to one. But if Hutcheson holds that one's judgment is caused in this way, one might well wonder whether he can also hold that one *has* a right of judgment.

26. *Ibid.,* p. 283.
27. *Papers of Thomas Jefferson,* Volume 2, p. 545.
28. *Ibid.,* p. 546.

If one's judging takes place without any willing or choosing on one's part because it is caused by what strikes one as evidence—in short, if one lacks what William James called "the will to believe"—then how can one be said to *do anything voluntarily* when one judges? And if one doesn't *do anything voluntarily* when one judges, how can one be said to have a *right* to judge? Hutcheson regarded a right as a faculty to perform a voluntary action,[29] which suggests that any so-called right that is said to be unalienable on Hutcheson's first count is not a right at all. In other words, when a man is said not to have what Hutcheson calls the natural power to alienate a right, it would seem that this means that he *has no right* which he can alienate. The logic is that of the following exchange: (A): "You can't give that man the chicken"; (B); "Why?"; (A): "Because you don't have the chicken." This view of the logical situation is confirmed by Locke's statement in his first *Letter Concerning Toleration:* "It is absurd that things should be enjoined by laws which are not in men's power to perform; and to believe this or that to be true does not depend upon our will."[30] This clearly implies that it is not in men's *power* to believe because believing does not depend on their wills. But if they have no natural power to believe, Locke quite properly says that they should not be commanded to believe, which means that they have no duty to believe. But the very consideration which leads Locke to say that they have no duty to believe should also lead one to say that they have no *right* to believe. Yet Hutcheson does not say that they have *no* right to judge: he says that they have a right to judge which is unalienable. And Jefferson does not say that they have *no* right to believe, he says that they are free to believe, which means that they have a right

29. Pufendorf defines a moral power as one whereby a person is able to perform a *voluntary* action, namely, one which it pleases him to perform. See the passage cited in note 4 above.
30. Locke, *Works,* Volume VI, pp. 39-40.

to believe. So there is no doubt in my mind that Jefferson succeeded in confusing some of his most careful and sympathetic readers, one of whom maintains that Jefferson's bill "asserted the natural right of a person to choose his beliefs and opinions free of compulsion."[31] But this does not square with Jefferson's own previously quoted statement that "the opinions and belief of men depend not on their own will, but follow involuntarily the evidence proposed to their minds." Obviously, if the opinions and belief of a man do not depend on his will then he *cannot* choose his beliefs and opinions, and it is hard to see how he has a *right* to choose them. The dictum, usually attributed to Kant, that "ought" implies "can" has a counterpart in the case of rights, for if a man has a right to perform a certain action, then it is also true that he can perform the action.[32] Therefore, if we deny that a man can perform an action, we should deny that he has a right to perform it. And if he has no right to perform it, he *lacks* a right which he can alienate or transfer to another.

Hutcheson does not seem to be able to escape this predicament, but Jefferson seems to have tried to escape it.[33] After he

---

31. Boyd, *Papers of Thomas Jefferson,* Volume 2, p. 547.

32. Hutcheson writes: ". . . There can be no *right, claim,* or *obligation* to impossibilities," *Inquiry Concerning Moral Good and Evil,* p. 293.

33. It is interesting that Jefferson does not seem to have availed himself of some of Burlamaqui's views on this question. Although Burlamaqui held that when the mind was forced by the evidence to believe a proposition, the will could play no part, he added that "the same cannot be affirmed in regard to things, that have less perspicuity and evidence for in these things the use of liberty displays itself in its full extent," by which he meant that "the obscurer things are, the more we are at liberty to hesitate, to suspend, or defer our determination," *Principles of Natural Law,* Part I, Chapter II, Section IV. Burlamaqui went even further and held that even in the case of so-called evident propositions, the will may play a part because "we are always at liberty to open, or to shut our eyes to the light; to exert, or relax our attention," *ibid.,* Section V. Had Jefferson taken this more seriously, he would not have accepted without qualification the view of Locke and Hutcheson.

asserts that the opinions of men do not depend on will but follow involuntarily the evidence proposed to their minds, he declares "that Almighty God hath created the mind free, *and manifested his Supreme will that free it shall remain by making it altogether insusceptible of restraint.*"[34] According to Jefferson, then, God did at least two things in this area. First, he created the human mind free in the sense of making its opinions not depend on the will, and secondly, he manifested his supreme will that the mind *should* remain free by so arranging things that all attempts to influence the mind by temporal punishments, burdens, or "civil incapacitations" would tend to produce habits of hypocrisy and meanness. Now God's willing that the mind *shall remain* free is crucial for Jefferson's escaping what I have called his predicament because God's willing—however it is manifested—means that God has imposed a duty on men to desist from *trying* to alter the fact that human opinions are necessarily brought about by what is taken to be evidence. And that duty implies a *right* on the part of all men to continue without punishments, burdens, or civil incapacitations in that state of forming their opinions only on the basis of what they regard as evidence. The effect of God's imposing this duty is not to endow man with a right to do the impossible, namely, perform a voluntary act of belief, or an act of belief which he chooses to perform. Rather, God wills that one man, *A,* has a duty not to *try* to get another man, *B,* to *try* to form his opinions by appealing to anything but the evidence as *B* sees it. However, the fact that we all have a right not to be molested by such attempts by *A* does not contradict my earlier statement that *we have no right* of private judgment if our belief or judgment is caused directly by the evidence and is not dictated by our will. And if we have no such right, then the only sense in which this so-called right could be said to be

34. *Papers of Thomas Jefferson,* Volume 2, p. 545.

naturally unalienable would be that in which it is impossible to give what we do not have.

But what about the Jeffersonian right not to be molested by those who would *try* to get men to adopt beliefs not supported by evidence? Is this naturally unalienable? Although I find no discussion of this point in Jefferson, it is hard to see how such a right could be naturally, or non-morally, unalienable. *B*'s complicated right *not* to be subjected to *A*'s effort to get *B* to believe propositions not supported by what *B* regards as evidence is what we must wrestle with. Does *B* have the natural power to transfer that right to another person? We must remember that the whole notion of a naturally alienable right is obscure, so we must proceed warily. We must ask, if I understand Hutcheson, whether *B*'s right not to be subjected to any effort like *A*'s can be transferred by *B*'s letting *C* rather than *B* himself be the beneficiary, so to speak, of the mentioned right not to be bothered by *A* and all other men or governments. I must confess that I am inclined to think that *B* does have the *natural* power to transfer this right to another, so we may now ask whether the right is *morally* alienable. The answer, I think, is that the right is *not* morally alienable according to those who speak in these terms. Since God imposed a duty on all men not to make an attempt like that of *A*, *B*'s right to be free of *A*'s intrusions would seem to be morally unalienable. Conversely, *A* has a similar right to be free of *B*'s intrusions. No man, as I shall explain later, can alienate or renounce a right which derives from a duty imposed by God on all men. I hope this will become clearer when I deal in greater detail with rights said to be unalienable on moral grounds, especially with rights whose names contain the word "life"—not only the direct right over one's life but the right to preserve one's life, the right to hazard one's life under certain circumstances, and the right to pledge one's life—all of which figure in eighteenth-century juristic and moral discussions.

Which Rights Involving Life Are Unalienable?

In "A Bill for Establishing Religious Freedom," Jefferson was not primarily concerned to establish the freedom of religious *belief* but rather the freedom of religious *worship,* and this makes all the more interesting the fact that in illustrating rights which are unalienable because they fail to satisfy what Hutcheson calls the "second mark"—the one I have called moral—Hutcheson presents "our right of serving God in the manner in which we think acceptable." However, it is important to observe that this right passes Hutcheson's first test. According to Hutcheson's view, the right to worship God in the manner in which we think acceptable is without doubt naturally alienable. Hutcheson's basis for distinguishing between our right to serve or worship God in the manner which we think acceptable and our right of private judgment in religion is that he thinks of the act of worship as one we *can* command ourselves to perform, whereas he thinks of believing as something we *cannot* command ourselves to perform. And since he thinks that we have the natural power to transfer our right to worship, he must go on to his second test in order to declare this right unalienable by claiming that it would serve no valuable purpose to alienate it. Hutcheson also says that "a direct right over our lives and limbs, is not alienable to any person" on the second, or moral, count.

Before I go on to consider the unalienability of this as well as some other rights which have something to do with life, I want to try to clarify what Hutcheson says about rights which he regards as unalienable on his second count by focusing on the unalienability of the right to worship God. This right would best be labeled in full as "the right to serve God in the manner in which *we* think acceptable." In that case, one may ask what transferring this right would amount to if it *were* transferred. It looks as though it would amount to telling another person that, beginning at a certain time, *his* judgment of what was an acceptable manner of worship *for us* would dictate the manner of *our* worship. In that case, of course, the overt act of worship would still be ours to perform. The other person or alienee would not be *doing* our worshipping after the alienation but would simply be dictating the manner of our worship. On the other hand, when Hutcheson says that our "direct right over our lives and limbs, is not alienable to any person, so that he might at pleasure put us to death or maim us," he seems to be saying that transferring *this* right would involve not only putting the transferee or alienee in a position to *choose* that we should be put to death or maimed but also in a position to perform the overt act of killing or maiming us. In general, then, it looks as though one's right to perform an action as one pleases may be alienated to another either in the case where one continues to perform the overt action but where the other person is the dictator of it, or in the case where the other person receives *both* the right to perform the overt action *and* the right to dictate its performance. I might add that although Hutcheson does not pursue the matter any further, I suspect that he would have allowed for a mode of alienating our direct right over our lives and limbs which would bring it closer to the mode in which he thinks of our alienating our right to worship. That might take place when the transferee receives the right to command the transferor to kill or maim himself. Here the transferor continues to perform the overt act while the transferee does the commanding.

We must remember, of course, that all of these modes of alienation are ruled out by Hutcheson on moral grounds. But our direct right over our life and limbs is so close to the right of preservation of life in the Rough Draft that we can profitably discuss the unalienability of the latter in the light of what has already been said about the former. Would the right to preserve one's life have passed Hutcheson's first, non-moral test? That is, did Jefferson think it within man's natural power to preserve his own life? It would seem that he did if he held with Burlamaqui and Locke that man has a moral *duty* to preserve his own life and that anyone who is obliged to do something *can* do it. Therefore, we must go on to test the right by using Hutcheson's second or moral mark of alienability. Would it serve a valuable purpose to transfer our right of self-preservation to another? I think that Jefferson would have rejected this version of the moral mark because it would have been at odds with his view that the right of self-preservation is derived from a duty of man which is established by Lockean reason and not by a Hutchesonian inquiry into whether anything served a valuable purpose. If it is our duty to preserve our life and therefore our right to preserve it, we would be violating that duty in transferring the right to another—that is how I think Jefferson would have formulated the moral argument for the unalienability of the right to preserve our life. In other words, he would have taken a view resembling that of Burlamaqui and of Locke's editor, Elrington, who, as we have seen, regarded a right that is derived from a duty as one that should not be renounced. Jefferson would have said that a right which is derived from a duty cannot be alienated because if God wills that a man should do something, that man can no more alienate the *right* to do that thing than he can renounce it.

The argument for this conclusion is as follows. If I alienate a right to someone else, then I no longer have the right to perform a certain action. But if I no longer have the right to perform that action because someone else now has the right to perform it, then I have a duty *not* to perform the action. Therefore, if I have a duty to *perform* the action, I will violate that duty if I put myself under a duty not to perform it. That is why having a duty to perform an action implies that

I *should not* alienate the right to perform that action. That is why a right to do something which is derived from a duty to do it is morally unalienable and unrenounceable.

Let me now turn to the right *of* life, which emerged in the final version of the Declaration as the successor to the *preservation* of life in the Rough Draft. It would appear from Boyd's[35] discussion that this substitution was made by Jefferson himself, a view which is compatible with the fact that Jefferson himself referred to the "rights of life and liberty" in what Adams called his philippic against slavery, the philippic that Congress omitted from the final version.[36] In my opinion, this was not a desirable change if, as I have argued earlier, Jefferson had, under the influence of Burlamaqui, believed that life was made part of the essence of man by God in creating him. We have seen that it is Burlamaqui's view that the *duty to preserve* life is derived from the fact that God made life an essential characteristic of man, in which case the *right to preserve* life would, he held, emerge from man's essence. And had Jefferson allowed "preservation of life" to stand, he might have avoided a certain anonymous criticism which appeared in *The Scots Magazine* in 1776.[37]

The critic in *The Scots Magazine* points out that since life or animation is of the *essence* of human nature, it is hard for him to understand what it means to say that every human being has the *right* of life because it is hard for him to understand the statement that a being which *has* life by definition also has a *right* to life. The point might be made by saying that if a man *must* be a living being, then it makes no sense to say that he has a moral *right* to be a living being; and that is why I believe that the Rough Draft was superior at this

35. Boyd, *Declaration of Independence*, pp. 29–31.
36. *Ibid.*, p. 20, p. 33.
37. *The Scots Magazine*, XXXVIII (August 1776): 433–434; reprinted in *A Casebook on the Declaration of Independence*, ed. R. Ginsberg (New York, 1967), pp. 6–8.

point to the final version. It is easier, even though one holds that man is by definition a living being, to make sense, à la Burlamaqui, of the statement that a man has a right to *preserve* his life. In that case one does not assert that one has a right to *have* an attribute that one has of necessity. One rather asserts that one has a right to *preserve* an attribute that has been put into one's essence by God. On the other hand, an alternative interpretation of the statement that every living being has a right to live would be that every living being has a right to *continue to be* a living being. This is a more generous interpretation because even though life be of the essence of humanity, *continuing to live* is not logically necessitated by being alive. Its relation to being alive is like the relation of *preserving life* to being alive. A living being is not *logically* required to continue living just as a living being is not *logically* required to preserve its life. And, therefore, if one interprets the right to, or of, life in this way, one may fend off certain objections to it of the kind dealt with above. Additionally, speaking of the right to *preserve* one's life is not subject to those objections and is therefore not in need of the interpretation that one must offer in order to fend off the objection we have been considering.

I will make one more comment about a related argument used by the critic in *The Scots Magazine*. He writes: "Prior to my having any right at all as a man, it is certain *I* must be a man, and such a man *I* certainly cannot be if I have no life; and therefore if it be said that *I* have a right to life, then the word *I* must signify something without life; and, consequently, something without life must be supposed to have a property, which without life it is not possible it can have." This argument rests on the premise, supposedly established, that the statement "Every living being, as a living being, has a right to life" is defective. So the critic imagines that the defender of the Declaration will retreat in the face of the critic's attack and will cease to make that statement. In that case, the defender must attribute the right to life to a being *without* life and therefore to a being who cannot be supposed to have that right *as a man*.

My own view, in keeping with what I have already said, is that the defender of the Declaration's final version should assert that one who is necessarily alive has, as a man, a right to life in the sense of a right to continue to live. Interestingly enough, another British critic of the Declaration, one John Lind, credits the revolutionaries when they speak of the rights of life, liberty, and the pursuit of happiness with meaning the right to *enjoy* life, to *enjoy* liberty, and to *pursue* happiness.[38] And this emendation, I think, goes a long way in the direction of Jefferson's original reference to the *preservation* of life and of my proposal that the revolutionaries should have referred to the right to *continue* to live rather than to the right of life. The point is that such an approach treats the right as a power to *do* something about one's life and thereby removes the kind of objection leveled by the anonymous critic in *The Scots Magazine*. For once we think of a right as a right to do something about one's life, or more specifically as a right to do something voluntarily about one's life, we diminish the force of the argument that the right of life is absurdly attributed in the Declaration because man is necessarily a living being and therefore one who may not be said without absurdity to have a right *or a duty* to *be* that which he is necessarily.

I come now to another criticism of the reference to the right to life in the Declaration which merits our attention. In dealing with it we may clarify the document by appealing to ideas current in the eighteenth century. The gist of this criticism is that there is a contradiction between the statement that the right to life is unalienable and the statement made by the signers at the end of the Declaration that "we mu-

38. J. Lind, *An Answer to the Declaration of the American Congress* (London, 1776), p. 120; reprinted in part in Ginsberg, *op. cit.*, pp. 9–17.

tually pledge to each other our lives, our fortunes, and our sacred honor."[39] This complaint is not without force if directed against the final version of the Declaration when that is read in a certain way. For, after all, if we are said to have a right to life which is unalienable, a reader might infer that we cannot give our lives away. And if we cannot give them away, how can we *pledge* them if that is thought to be tantamount to giving them away? In this connection it might be helpful to point out that Hutcheson maintained, in spite of holding that our "direct right over our lives and limbs" is unalienable, that "we have indeed a *right* to hazard our lives in any good action which is of importance to *the public;* and it may often serve a most valuable end, to subject the direction of such perilous actions to the prudence of others in pursuing a *public good;* as *soldiers* do to their *general,* or to a *council* of *war:* and so far this *right* is *alienable.*"[40]

Therefore, if we identify the right to life with Hutcheson's *direct right over our lives* or with the Rough Draft's *right to preserve life,* it becomes easier to see why we may nevertheless have a *right to risk our lives* in a good cause and why *that* right may be alienated to others by pledging our lives in the manner described at the end of the Declaration. We may have an unalienable right to preserve our lives and yet not only have a *right* to risk them but an *alienable* right to risk them and therefore to pledge them to our fellow-revolutionaries who might be viewed by us as Hutcheson viewed the general and the council of war in his illustration. However, although I think that the reference in the Rough Draft to an unalienable *right* to *preserve life* comports more easily with the pledge at the end of the Declaration than does the reference in the final version to a right to, or of, life, even the final

39. This criticism was made in R. E. Selden, *Criticism on the Declaration of Independence as a Literary Document* (New York, 1846), p. 17; reprinted in part in Ginsberg, *op. cit.,* pp. 37–56.
40. Hutcheson, *Inquiry Concerning Moral Good and Evil,* p. 283.

version may be defended against the above criticism. For we may have an unalienable right to our lives and still have an alienable right to hazard them by putting ourselves under someone else in a battle or by mutually pledging our lives in the manner of the signers.

As I approach the end of my discussion of the unalienability of certain rights, I should like to say a few words about Locke's treatment of some of the matters with which I have been dealing. First, I want to remind the reader that in his first *Letter Concerning Toleration,* Locke was aware that if belief does not depend on will, then it is absurd to command belief. In that context he was not explicitly discussing the question whether the right to believe was alienable, but in other places he says things which make it reasonable to assume that, if asked whether the so-called right to believe were alienable, he would have replied that there was no such right to alienate. And in these other places, he is discussing a right involving life. I have in mind a passage in his *Second Treatise* where he tells us that "a man, not having the power of his own life"—by which he means a power or right *over* his own life which would imply a power or right to destroy his life—"cannot, by compact, or his own consent, *enslave himself* to any one, nor put himself under the absolute, arbitrary power of another, to take away his life, when he pleases."[41] I take Locke to mean here *not* that man *has* a power or right over his own life which he is obliged *not to alienate* but rather that man has *no* such power or right. "No body," Locke continues, "can give more power than he has himself; and he that cannot take away his own life, cannot give another power over it."[42] Thus, for Locke, a man does not *have* the "power of his own life" and therefore does not have it to alienate because only God, man's maker and owner, has the power of man's life.

41. Locke, *Second Treatise,* Section 23.
42. *Ibid.*

Having said this, I must quickly point out that Locke distinguishes between what he calls the power *of his own* life—a right which man does not have—and what he calls the power *to preserve his* life, a right which man most certainly does have. This second right Locke would have called "unalienable" had he used that term in this context because he holds that the right to preserve one's life follows from one's duty to preserve one's life. Moreover, preserving one's life is interpreted by Locke as including the defense of oneself against attack by attacking those who attack or threaten one. He says in this connection that I "have a right to destroy that which threatens me with destruction. For *by the fundamental law of nature, man being to be preserved,* as much as possible, when all cannot be preserved, the safety of the innocent is to be preferred."[43] Now since a right is a power, "the power of his own life" must be equivalent, according to Locke, to "the right of his own life." And since Locke implies that we do not have this right, we may say that if Jefferson had followed Locke more closely (as well as Burlamaqui), he would not have eliminated the right of *preservation* of life from his Rough Draft in favor of the right of life. For the right of, or to, life was said by Locke to be unalienable only in the peculiar sense in which a right we do not have is unalienable, whereas for him "the right of preservation of life" unambiguously refers to a morally unalienable right, indeed, to a right which follows in a trifling way from what Locke regards as the fundamental law of nature.

Having said all of this, I do not wish to imply that Jefferson was persuaded or bullied into transforming "preservation of life" into "life." We not only have evidence that he may have made this change himself but we also know that he spoke of the "sacred rights of life and liberty" in that part of the Rough Draft in which he inveighed against slavery. Besides, even though Locke and Hutcheson distinguished be-

43. *Ibid.,* Section 16. Note the gerundive, *"to be* preserved."

tween different rights involving life, eighteenth-century writers on this subject were not usually given to great precision. Hutcheson, in the Latin original of his *Short Introduction to Moral Philosophy*, spoke of a *"Jus ad vitam, et corporis integritatem,"* which his translator rendered as "a right *to* life, and to retain their bodies unmaimed," and this right seems to be the counterpart of Hutcheson's "direct right *over* our lives or limbs" in his *Inquiry Concerning Moral Good and Evil*. However, in the same so-called Latin *Compend* he distinguishes the *"Jus ad vitam"* from the *"Jus . . . in vitam suam,"* which his translator rendered as "a right *over* life." After that the translator rendered Hutcheson's explanatory Latin as follows, "so far that each one, in any honorable services to society or his friends, may expose himself not only to dangers, but to certain death, when such public good is in view as overbalances the value of his life."[44] Thus the translator's "right *to* life" seems to be the counterpart of Hutcheson's "right *over* lives" in the latter's *Inquiry* of 1725, whereas the translator's "right *over* life" seems to be the counterpart of Hutcheson's "right *to hazard* our lives" in the *Inquiry*. Nevertheless, in spite of this eighteenth-century indifference to the use of nicety in discussions of rights, I cannot help feeling that what Jefferson *intended* in the so-called philosophical part of the Declaration on the subject of life was better expressed in the Rough Draft than in the final version.

He meant that the right to preserve life was morally unalienable even though it was naturally alienable. And the same might be said for the right to preserve one's liberty. It too could, in the natural or physical sense of that word, be transferred to another, but once again the moral argument for its unalienability would, I think, have been the same as that used in the case of preserving life. But what about the right to pursue happiness? That is a more difficult matter.

44. Hutcheson, *Short Introduction to Moral Philosophy*, Book II, Chapter IV, Section III.

Consistency, of course, would demand that Jefferson argue for its unalienability in the same way, but that would require holding that it is naturally possible for a man to transfer his right to pursue his happiness to another. The argument would have to proceed as it did in the case of other rights. The assumption would be that the pursuit of happiness is like the pursuit of one's dog from a logical point of view, meaning that a man has a right to pursue happiness if he pleases and therefore that he is not caused or determined by something external to pursue it—as he is, according to Hutcheson, caused to judge that the sky is blue. In that case the right to pursue happiness would be regarded as alienable by Hutcheson's first test on the assumption that it is naturally possible for one to transfer to another one's right to pursue one's happiness just as it is naturally possible to transfer one's right to pursue one's dog. Therefore, I think Jefferson would have to treat it as unalienable on moral grounds, arguing that since it is our duty and therefore right to pursue happiness, we would be violating that duty in transferring that right to another.

Property as an Adventitious Right

Having discussed at length the philosophico-theological path which I think Jefferson used in arriving at the rights of individuals enumerated in the Rough Draft and in the final version of the Declaration, and having also discussed the unalienability of these rights, I now want to contribute something to the explanation of why the right to property in goods and estates is mentioned in no version of the Declaration. This was called an adventitious right—I shall explain that term soon—by many theorists of natural law, and the fact that it was so described will help us understand why it may not have been listed among those listed in the different versions of the Declaration. The absence of the right to property from Jefferson's list is conspicuous not only because it is so central in Locke's *Second Treatise,* upon which Jefferson drew so heavily in other respects, but also because several of Jefferson's American contemporaries were given to employing what V. L. Parrington has called the classical enumeration of "life, liberty, and property" when they were expounding "revolution principles." Parrington was so struck by Jefferson's failure to subscribe to this classical trinity of rights and by his substitution of the "pursuit of happiness" for "property" that he regarded Jefferson's approach as marking "a complete break with the Whiggish doctrine of property rights that Locke had bequeathed to the English middle class."[45]

Before I introduce the notion of an adventitious right in explaining this omission, I should like to make a few preliminary comments. One is that Jefferson could hardly have regarded the right to property in goods or estates as *unalienable.* Therefore, if Jefferson had been concerned to list only unalienable rights in the Declaration, that alone would have forced him not to include the right to property in his trio because the idea that one may alienate what one owns is at least as old as Aristotle,[46] who is cited by Grotius as his chief authority on this point.[47] Although R. F. Harvey has performed a service in stressing the likely influence of Burlamaqui on Jefferson in explaining his failure to mention the right to property in the Declaration, I think that it is incorrect to say, as Harvey does, that "the inalienable rights of man as enumerated by Locke were life, liberty and property," where "property" signifies a right to goods and estates.[48] Laslett is

45. V. L. Parrington, *Main Currents in American Thought* (New York, 1927, 1930), Volume I, p. 344.
46. *Rhetoric,* Book I, Chapter V, 1361 A.
47. See Supplementary Notes, Property and the Doctrine of Natural Law, p. 284.
48. R. F. Harvey, *Jean Jacques Burlamaqui: A Liberal Tradition in American Constitutionalism* (Chapel Hill, 1937), p. 121.

quite justified in saying what he says in the first—the fully comprehensible—sentence of the following passage: "The conventional judgment of Locke's view of property, that it described a natural, inalienable right, seems . . . to be exactly wrong. Property is precisely that part of our attributes (or, perhaps to be pedantic, that attribute of our attributes) which we can alienate, but only of course by our own consent."[49] And if it be asked *why* Jefferson wanted to list only unalienable rights, the answer is, as we shall see in the next chapter, that it was the British government's invasion of unalienable rights that gave the colonists one of their strongest arguments for resistance and rebellion. But leaving these preliminaries aside, I now come to a more complex argument for the view that the right to property—construed as the right to goods and estates—could not be listed as one of the trinity by Jefferson. The point is that it was not a *primitive* right but rather an *adventitious* right.

A distinction was made by some theorists of natural law between what is called the primary or primitive natural law, which, Burlamaqui says, "immediately arises from the primitive constitution of man, as God himself has established it, independent of any human act," and secondary natural law, which "supposes some human act or establishment."[50] The three states we spoke of earlier, namely, those which involved man's relation to God, to himself, and to other humans, are all called by Burlamaqui "primitive and original states . . . in which man finds himself placed by the very hand of God, independent of any human action." But, Burlamaqui goes on to say, "man, being naturally a free agent, is capable of making great modifications in his primitive state, and of giving, by a variety of establishments, a new face to human life. Hence those adventitious states are formed, which are

49. P. Laslett, Introduction to *Two Treatises of Government*, 2nd ed. (Cambridge, 1970), p. 102, note.
50. *Principles of Natural Law*, Part II, Chapter IV, Section XXIV.

properly the work of man, wherein he finds himself placed by his own act and in consequence of establishments, whereof he himself is the author."[51] One of these adventitious states is produced or constituted by the property of goods, says Burlamaqui. In general, such an adventitious state is established because man in his natural, original state is in a "state of indigence and incessant wants, against which he would be incapable of providing in a suitable manner, were he not to exercise his industry by constant labor," labor that is invited by his original, natural wants. It would appear from this that Jefferson in his letter to Dupont de Nemours was adopting some such doctrine as Burlamaqui's when Jefferson said that a right to property is founded in our natural wants and in the means with which we are endowed to satisfy these wants.[52] In turn, Burlamaqui seemed to adopt a doctrine of Locke when Burlamaqui wrote that the establishment of property "modifies the right, which all men had originally to earthly goods; and, distinguishing carefully what belongs to individuals, ensures the quiet and peaceable enjoyment of what they possess; by which means it contributes to the maintenance of peace and harmony among mankind. But, since all men had originally a right to a common use of whatever the earth produces for their several wants, it is evident that, if this natural power is actually restrained and limited in divers respects, this must necessarily arise from some human act; and consequently the state of property, which is the cause of those limitations, ought to be ranked among the adventitious states."[53]

We can now see what might have prompted Jefferson *not* to list the adventitious right to property in goods as one of his three in the Declaration: it did not immediately come from the hand of God. It could not be derived from *mere*

---

51. *Ibid.*, Part I, Chapter IV, Section II and Section VI.
52. *Ibid.*, Part I, Chapter IV, Section V. Jefferson, *Writings*, Volume XIV, p. 490, written in 1816.
53. *Principles of Natural Law*, Part I, Chapter IV, Section VII.

creation nor could it be derived from *equal* creation by way of corresponding duties. Although for Burlamaqui the *primitive* states and their attendant duties are annexed to the nature and constitution of man, "such as he has received them from God," and are "for this very reason, common to all mankind," the "same cannot be said of the adventitious states; which, supposing an human act or agreement, cannot of themselves be indifferently suitable to all men, but to those only, who contrived and procured them."[54] In short, any obligation which might arise in an adventitious state would have to arise only after the performance of a free human act, like the picking up of the acorns in Locke's *Second Treatise*.

Nevertheless, this is not to say that the right to property was not *natural* for Jefferson or for Burlamaqui. Nor is it to say that it was not, according to Jefferson, a right protected by civil government if Jefferson agreed with Burlamaqui, as I think he did. For Burlamaqui held that "the property of individuals is prior to the formation of states, and there is no reason, which can induce us to suppose, that those individuals entirely transferred to the sovereign the right they had over their own estates; on the contrary, it is to secure a quiet and easy possession of their properties, that they have instituted government and sovereignty."[55] The adventitious state of property and its corresponding right is *natural* for Burlamaqui, but it is a natural right which is derived from what Burlamaqui calls a *secondary* natural law. Such a natural law is only a *consequence* (*une suite*) of the primary natural law, "or rather," he says in a manner reminiscent of Aquinas, "it is a just application of the general maxims of natural law to the particular states of mankind and to the different circumstances, in which they find themselves by their own act."[56]

The fact that Burlamaqui distinguished between a natural

---

54. *Ibid.*, Part I, Chapter IV, Section XII.
55. *Principles of Politic Law*, Part III, Chapter V, Section IV, Item 3.
56. *Principles of Natural Law*, Part II, Chapter IV, Section XXIV.

right and a *primitive* natural right has not been sufficiently
noticed by commentators. Thus Harvey confines himself to
quoting what Burlamaqui says about natural rights in only
one passage of *The Principles of Natural Law,* namely: "rights
are natural, or acquired. The former are such as appertain
originally and essentially to man, such, as are inherent in his
nature, and which he enjoys as man, independent of any particular act on his side. Acquired rights, on the contrary, are
those, which he does not naturally enjoy, but are owing to his
own procurement. Thus the right of providing for our preservation is a right natural to man; but sovereignty, or the
right of commanding a society of men, is a right acquired."[57]
Unfortunately, Harvey does not seem to have noticed that
even though the right to property is not natural in the sense
of primitively natural for Burlamaqui, it is a *natural* right for
him insofar as it is a right which is protected by the *secondary*
natural law.[58]

Moreover, Harvey does not recognize that a distinction
like Burlamaqui's between these two kinds of rights had been
made by a number of theorists of natural law.[59] Burlamaqui's

57. *Ibid.,* Part I, Chapter VII, Section VIII.

58. Wiltse, in his *Jeffersonian Tradition in American Democracy* (p. 74), also
    fails to see that, according to Burlamaqui, the adventitious state of society
    in which property first exists antedates civil society. He also fails to point
    out that in such an adventitious state the right to property is regarded as
    natural by Burlamaqui. These failures may lead him to suppose that Jef-
    ferson denied that property was a natural right.

59. Harvey writes that, excepting what he calls a "rather vague statement by
    Lord Kames," "Burlamaqui was the only recognized authority who had
    advanced an idea similar to that of Paine and Jefferson" (*op. cit.,* p. 123),
    meaning the idea that natural and acquired rights are to be distinguished.
    The fact is that not only Grotius and Pufendorf, as we shall see below,
    distinguished between natural and adventitious rights but so did Hutche-
    son in his *Short Introduction to Moral Philosophy* (Book II).

    Harvey's reference to Paine requires some comment. He reproduces on
    pp. 122–123 part of a passage by Paine, which is quoted in full by Gilbert
    Chinard in the second, revised edition of the latter's *Thomas Jefferson:
    The Apostle of Americanism,* paperback ed. (Ann Arbor, 1957), pp. 80–82.
    According to Harvey, the doctrine there espoused by Paine was similar to

remarks about property being both adventitious and protected by natural law are based, it would seem, on similar remarks by Grotius and Pufendorf. Grotius maintains that "the law of nature deals not only with things which are outside the domain of the human will, but with many things also which result from an act of the human will. Thus ownership, such as now obtains, was introduced by the will of man; but, once introduced, the law of nature points out that it is wrong for me, against your will, to take away that which is subject to your ownership."[60] And Pufendorf, while commenting on this passage in Grotius, says that "the ownership of things does not come directly from nature, nor can any express and determinate command be alleged for its introduction, yet it is said to spring from natural law."[61] So, although it might be argued that the omission of property from Jefferson's famous trio might be traced to earlier theorists of natural law, I am inclined to agree with Harvey that Burlamaqui was the more direct source of Jefferson's ideas on this subject. I say this primarily because Burlamaqui did *two* things which seem to have influenced Jefferson's "replacement" of the right to

---

that of Burlamaqui in advocating a distinction between natural and adventitious rights. It should be noted, however, that Paine never uses the word "adventitious" and that he is discussing the distinction between natural rights and civil rights. Burlamaqui, I repeat, regarded the right to property in estates as natural in spite of being adventitious because it existed in a state of society which antedated civil government, was governed by the secondary natural law, and was a right which civil government was instituted to protect. I therefore think that Paine was making a distinction that was not identical with Burlamaqui's.

60. *De jure belli ac pacis*, Book I, Chapter I, Section X. It is significant that the law of nature is represented by Grotius as saying that it is wrong to take away what is owned by another. It might also be represented as prohibiting such an act, in which case we may think of a *natural adventitious right* to what one owns as inferable from a *natural adventitious duty* on the part of others not to take it away. See Burlamaqui, *Principles of Natural Law*, Part I, Chapter VII, Section 6, where he says that "right" and "obligation" are correlative.

61. *De jure naturae et gentium*, Book II, Chapter III, Section 22.

property by the right to pursue happiness: (1) Burlamaqui denied that the right to property was expressed in a primary natural law and hence denied that it was an inherent natural right given directly by God to man (and here he was in accord with Grotius and Pufendorf); (2) Burlamaqui also thought that the duty to pursue happiness *was* expressed in a primary natural law and therefore implied an inherent right to pursue happiness. It is true that Burlamaqui held that we have no reason to suppose that individuals entirely transferred to the sovereign the right they had over their own estates when civil government was formed, but he also held that the right of property was not in the same exalted position as the rights which are mentioned either in the Rough Draft or the final version of the Declaration. The latter Jefferson also put on a pedestal; they were preeminently the rights which, when invaded by a government, gave people the right to make a revolution. They were God-given, inherent, unalienable, and not adventitious. They were moral powers that no man *should* transfer to any person or any government.

The fact that these rights belonged to men essentially and as originally created by God meant that the violation of them should, in the revolutionaries' view, offend *all* mankind and not merely those parts of it which happened to be in some adventitious state of society. That is why the signers had such a "decent respect to the opinions of mankind" as to declare the reasons for their rebellion to *them* in their first paragraph. And that is why Jefferson could have consistently asserted what he did assert in the very first words of the passage on slavery that Congress omitted from the final version of the Declaration. Those words were: "He has waged cruel war against human nature itself, violating its most sacred rights of life and liberty in the persons of distant people who never offended him, captivating and carrying them into slavery in another hemisphere, or to incur miserable death in their transportation thither."[62] Here we see Jefferson treating the blacks as possessed of human nature and therefore of two rights which were primitively natural and sacred by virtue of having been given to them by God. Here we see no hesitancy of the kind that Jefferson came to express in his *Notes on Virginia* about whether blacks possess the essential features of human nature.

The Status of the Right to Property: More Significant Ambiguity

So far all major parts of this work have revealed what I have called, for want of a more felicitous word, "jokers" in the philosophy of the revolutionaries, and the present chapter is no exception. The epistemology of self-evident truth might permit some to "principle" others by claiming that only they themselves had the qualifications to see self-evidence, and even the allegedly democratic epistemology of the doctrine of moral sense required that the moral judge have certain qualities that could give title to the favored few who wished to establish superiority over others in making moral judgments. The concept of essence in Revolutionary metaphysics was also susceptible to this kind of treatment since, by regarding one attribute rather than another as the essence of man, a philosopher could "derive" one duty rather than another as essential; and when one sees that so-called essential rights were derived in turn from essential duties, it is obvious that one could set one's favorite rights upon a pedestal simply by fixing upon appropriate attributes as essential to man. In calling attention to these potentialities of certain ideas in epistemology and metaphysics, I am not accusing their advocates of deliberate intent to dominate by exploiting language which could be turned to the interest of one social group

62. See above, notes 35 and 36.

rather than another. But, believing as I do, that the concept of self-evident truth is obscure and that the qualifications for perceiving it are obscure, believing something similar about the operations of the moral sense as described by some of its advocates, and believing that almost any attribute of all and only men could be regarded as the essence of man, I also believe that these ideas were more *capable* of political manipulation than most concepts are. But what, one may ask, is the comparable idea that emerges in the present chapter? I think it will come as no surprise if I should answer that it is the idea of a natural right which can be either original or adventitious. For once the theorist of natural rights is armed with that bit of logomachy, he can say, in effect, that all natural rights are natural but that some are more natural than others. And once having arrived at that conclusion, the theorist of natural law is faced with the question: Where shall I put property in material goods or estates? Is it an original natural right given directly to man by God or is it an adventitious natural right? For, certainly, if the right to property in material goods or estates were to be listed in a trinity that included two unalienable rights involving life and liberty, property would hold a more important position in the system of natural law. It would be viewed as a direct gift from God rather than as the product of some human act. And once it is thought to be a primary, primitive, or original gift of God, it assumes an aspect of eternality, necessity, and immutability which it can never have if it is thought to be the outgrowth of a mere human act. So a lot hinged on the proper placement of property among natural rights.

We have already seen where Jefferson probably stood on this issue, but I should point out that he did not represent the only Colonial position on it. In fact, if one were to make a statistical study of how colonists concluded lists of rights that began with "life" and "liberty," one would find that most of them put "property" in third place rather than "the pursuit of happiness." Yet even when they did put "property" in third place, they could find themselves in an ambiguous position, especially if they relied on Blackstone's *Commentaries,* as James Otis did in 1765. In his *Vindication of the British Colonies,* he lists "the right of personal security, personal liberty, and private property"[63] as absolute, *primary* natural rights, and after doing so refers us to the authority of Blackstone, who characterizes these three rights as follows: "By the absolute *rights* of individuals we mean those which are so in their primary and strictest sense; such as would belong to their persons merely in a state of nature, and which every man is entitled to enjoy, whether out of society or in it."[64] So far, then, it would appear that Otis and his mentor Blackstone think of all three of these rights as "primary." When we read Blackstone further we find that, according to him, life is the immediate gift of God and that this gift is the main basis for the right of personal security.[65] He also tells us that the right of personal liberty is "strictly natural."[66] But when he comes to property, although he begins bravely enough by saying that "the third absolute right, inherent in every Englishman, is that of property," he finds it necessary to make the qualified statement that "the original of private property is *probably* [my emphasis] founded in nature."[67]

When Blackstone elaborates on this statement in a later passage that is reminiscent of Locke and Burlamaqui, Blackstone asserts that the earth and all things in it were immediately given by God to man as his "general property" or as something to be held in common by all men. Blackstone adds that this communion of goods in the earliest of ages was ac-

63. Bailyn, *Pamphlets,* Volume I, p. 558.
64. Blackstone's *Commentaries on the Laws of England,* reprint of Philadelphia edition of 1803 (New York, 1969), Volume II, p. 123.
65. *Ibid.,* p. 129.
66. *Ibid.,* p. 134.
67. *Ibid.,* p. 138.

companied by a transient right on the part of an individual
to possess a given thing only so long as he used it. But this
transient individual right and the original right of *common*
ownership are the only Blackstonian rights which stand on a
par with the rights to personal security and personal liberty.[68] They are, therefore, the only Blackstonian rights of
ownership in material things which could also be called primary in the Burlamaquian sense. Otis would have known this
had he read on in Blackstone and therefore, since he probably did read on, it is fair to infer that he was not, to say the
least, eager to expound in full Blackstone's distinction between the right of property and the other two personal rights.
In fact, Otis misrepresented Blackstone when Otis called the
right to property a primary right without adding Blackstone's explanation that what was primary, or immediately
from the hand of God, was the right of common ownership,
and a transient individual right only during use or occu-
pancy. The point is that Otis was not interested in urging the
primacy of those examples of property rights. *He* was interested in what Burlamaqui would have called the non-primary,
adventitious right to one's land, to one's house, and to one's
gold watch.

I grant, of course, that Blackstone was partly responsible
for all of this misrepresentation because Blackstone did list
the right to property as one of the absolute rights of individuals in the "primary and strictest sense," meaning that it was
"such as would belong to their persons merely in a state of
nature, and which every man is entitled to enjoy, whether
out of society or in it." And it was, admittedly, several hundred pages later in his *Commentaries* before Blackstone began to make the qualifications that revealed his attachment
to something like Burlamaqui's idea that the right to a gold
watch was not a primary natural right. Indeed, Blackstone's
views were so close to Burlamaqui's that Sir Henry Maine

68. *Ibid.*, Volume III, pp. 2-4.

once claimed that the central statements about natural law "may be read in the introductory chapters of our own Blackstone, who has transcribed them textually from Burlamaqui."[69] Maine, however, should have added that, on the subject of property, Blackstone's transcription of Burlamaqui was much more evident in Book II of the *Commentaries* than in the opening chapters of Book I.

By contrast to all of those thinkers who put "property" where Jefferson put "the pursuit of happiness" when they believed that the right to property was an adventitious right, Jefferson appears as a more honest and more precise thinker: more honest because he must have known that if he had written "property" in that controversial third place, he would have been construed as meaning material property in goods and estates; more precise because he was committed to listing only what Burlamaqui called primitive rights, which were given immediately to man by God. Yet one cannot deny that there were some thinkers who, even though they accepted the distinction between primary and adventitious natural rights, fought their hardest to put the ownership of goods into the former category. For example, an editor of Blackstone believed that "the notion of property is universal, and is suggested to the mind of man by reason and nature, prior to all positive institutions and civilized refinements" and went on to say that he knew of "no other criterion by which we can determine any rule or obligation to be found in nature, than its universality; and by inquiring whether it is not, and has not been, in all countries and ages, agreeable to the feelings, affections, and reason of mankind." From this statement it is clear that the author was aware of the distinction between a

69. H. S. Maine, *Ancient Law,* reprint of the 10th ed. (London, 1924), pp. 123–124. See Harvey, *op. cit.,* p. 124, for references to other writers, for example, S. G. Fisher and E. S. Corwin, who have noted similarities between Blackstone and Burlamaqui; also Chapter 5 of the same work for a discussion of the impact of Burlamaqui's ideas on Revolutionary America and for references to a number of authors who have described this impact.

primary and an adventitious right and that he was flatly opposing Burlamaqui and Blackstone. For Burlamaqui had
said at the conclusion of a discussion of the distinction between primitive and adventitious states "that the former being annexed as it were, to the nature and constitution of man,
such as he received them from God, are for this very reason,
common to all mankind. The same cannot be said of the adventitious states." It is hard to avoid the conclusion, then,
that being primitive or immediately received from God was
thought to be a virtue by some theorists of natural law simply because they regarded such rights as more firmly established. And for them the universal prevalence and approval
of such a right would be evidence of its primitiveness in Burlamaqui's sense. By contrast, if a right were adventitious and
hence the outgrowth of a free human act, it must have seemed
to that extent shaky and insecure. All the more reason, from
such a point of view, to show that the right was primitive.
For, after all, if an adventitious state was the product of a free
human act, a free human act could destroy that state. And if
the very existence of an adventitious right presupposed a human act or agreement, another act or the undoing of that
agreement might be thought to destroy the right. I have
pointed out that Grotius, Pufendorf, and Burlamaqui all insisted that an adventitious right was also protected by the
natural law and hence by God's will. Indeed, the very social
contract which formed civil society was the product of free
acts of will that established certain obligations. But nevertheless, other things being equal, if one thought one had a natural right in the eighteenth century, one would rather that it
be a direct gift of God than adventitious no matter how many
times one might be told that adventitious rights were also
rights by the secondary natural law. For this reason, then, I
regard the distinction between a primitive and an adventitious right as the ethical counterpart of self-evidence in Revolutionary epistemology and of essence in Revolutionary meta-

physics. If one really wished to be sure of a right, it was
advisable to show that it came directly from the hand of God;
and therefore it would be worth a lot of intellectual effort to
show that one had a primitive right to property in goods.

Moreover, it is not surprising that James Wilson, one of
the ablest Revolutionary lawyers and a disciple of Burlamaqui, should have tried to accomplish this with very little intellectual effort. In his *Lectures on Law,* while repeating most
of what he had learned from his master, Wilson blandly disre-
garded what the master had said about property. Wilson did
this in the course of a statement about natural rights, every
sentence of which but the last might have been written by
Burlamaqui:

> Those rights result from the natural state of man;
> from that situation, in which he would find himself, if
> no civil government was instituted. In such a situation, a
> man finds himself, in some respects, unrelated to others;
> in other respects, peculiarly related to some; in still other
> respects, bearing a general relation to all. From his un-
> related state, one class of rights arises: from his peculiar
> relations, another class of rights arises: from his general
> relations, a third class of rights arises. To each class of
> rights, a class of duties is correspondent; as we had occa-
> sion to observe and illustrate, when we treated concern-
> ing the general principles of natural law.
>
> In his unrelated state, man has a natural right to his
> property, to his character, to liberty, and to safety.[70]

Had Burlamaqui been alive when the lecture containing
these words had been delivered and if he had heard them, he
might well have criticized his admirer for listing the right to
property along with the right to safety and liberty without
pointing out that property appears in an adventitious state
of society and that it is not a right which comes immediately

70. Wilson, *Works,* Volume II, p. 592.

from the hand of God. Burlamaqui might also have reminded Wilson that even Jefferson, a more wayward pupil of Burlamaqui's, had taken care not to put property on a par with liberty and safety in the Declaration.[71]

71. Those concerned with the history of what I have called the sacred trinity of rights might be interested in a remark by C. F. Mullet on p. 47 of his *Fundamental Law and the American Revolution, 1760–1776* (New York, 1933) about Francis Bacon's views. Mullet cites a passage in Bacon's *Works*, eds. J. Spedding et al. (Boston, 1861), Volume XV, p. 225, in which Bacon lists three things that "flow from the law of nature," namely, "preservation of life, natural; liberty, which every beast or bird seeketh and affecteth, natural; the society of man and wife, whereof dower is the reward, natural." Upon this passage Mullet comments: "Students of constitutional history and political theory may find in those phrases of Bacon more than a fanciful resemblance to Jefferson's 'life, liberty, and the pursuit of happiness.'" Pressing this resemblance fancifully would require an identification of the pursuit of happiness with sexual intercourse or with marriage—a rather narrow view of happiness—but it is interesting that Bacon should speak of "dower" as the *reward* of the society of man and wife, since Jacob Viner reports in his review of Macpherson's *Political Theory of Possessive Individualism* that "dower" often appears in the history of this subject as a replacement for "estate" in the stock phrase "life, liberty, and estate," *Canadian Journal of Economics and Political Science* 29 (1963): 554. I might add that for Burlamaqui marriage is an adventitious state, just as property is, so that the Baconian trio would, by Burlamaqui's standards, consist of two primary natural rights and one secondary or adventitious one. Of course, Burlamaqui holds that nature "invites" human beings to form marriages, but marriage is nonetheless an adventitious state.

· 6 ·

"Rebellion to Tyrants
Is Obedience to God"

I have analyzed the basic epistemological, theological, meta-physical, and moral ideas of the leading American revolution-aries, and so it remains for me to present the moral argument that they offered for their rebellion against Britain and the moral criteria which they thought any government, especially a new government, would have to meet. Having retraced the path they followed from their belief in God to their belief in unalienable rights, I now come to the ultimate step on that path, the one that brought the signers from their belief in the individual's unalienable rights mentioned in the Declaration to their belief that they, as a people, had a right—in fact a duty—to alter or abolish the government under which they had been living. The notion that they had a *duty* to rebel is extremely important to stress, for it shows that they thought they were complying with the *commands* of natural law and of nature's God when they threw off absolute despotism. This was in keeping with the strong language of the Virginia Bill of Rights of June 1776, according to which a majority of the community has, under certain circumstances, "an indubitable, inalienable, and indefeasible right to reform, alter, or abolish [the government] in such manner as shall be judged most conducive to the public weal." On the very plausible assumption that this passage, which appeared less than a month before the Declaration, had exerted great influence on Jefferson,[1] it is easy to see that the connection between a duty and an unalienable right was conceived by the revolutionaries as I have said they conceived it. An unalienable right to alter or abolish a government was unalienable because it was derivable from a duty to do the same. In short, the colonists thought that their rebellion was more than morally possible: it was morally necessary.

The Revolutionaries Were Not Utilitarians

However, this moral necessity, duty, or obligation was not, according to them, based on utilitarian considerations as the word "utilitarian" is generally understood. I have pointed out that Locke was not a utilitarian, and now I want to show why the colonists should not be called utilitarians in spite of their tendency to speak so much about pursuing happiness, a tendency which they shared with Burlamaqui, who, as we know, regarded the pursuit of happiness as a God-imposed duty along with other God-imposed duties, like the duty to preserve our lives and the duty to perfect our understandings. By regarding it as a duty he departed from the theorists of natural law who tended to regard as obligatory only specific actions, such as the preservation of life, the honoring of engagements, the honoring of parents, refraining from lying and stealing, and so on, in the manner of the Decalogue, which contained no such commandment as "Thou shalt pursue happiness." As we have seen, happiness was rather viewed by Pufendorf and Locke as a state to be achieved in *causal consequence* of carrying out duties which followed from the

1. Boyd, *Declaration of Independence,* pp. 12–14.

nature of man. These duties were perceived, therefore, by the exercise of intuitive or discursive reason and not by discovering empirically that carrying them out would cause us to be happy. Therefore, Burlamaqui's incorporation of the duty to pursue happiness into the body of natural law represented a significant change in the doctrine. He puts this duty on a par with the duty to preserve life and liberty, and by doing so he makes the principle that all human creatures should pursue happiness a rational principle of natural law. Witherspoon summed up an analogous view by announcing that *"reason* teaches natural liberty, and *common utility* recommends it."[2] And when reason *teaches* that the pursuit of happiness is a duty and a right, it does so by showing that the proposition that all human creatures ought to pursue happiness is self-evident or demonstrable. The moment a moralist takes this intuitionistic view of the way in which we *know* that a moral principle is true—whether it dictates the pursuit of happiness or the preservation of liberty—that moralist cannot be called a utilitarian in the normal sense of that technical term.[3]

As we have seen in our discussion of Locke, a utilitarian is normally regarded as a philosopher who thinks we can establish a moral principle by showing empirically that adopting and acting on it will in fact maximize happiness or pleasure. And when the utilitarian advances this view of how we can establish, for example, the moral principle that every man has a duty not to put his fellow-man in a state of subjection, the utilitarian usually also asserts or implies that such a principle cannot be established either by intuition, or by deduc-

2. Witherspoon, *Lectures on Moral Philosophy*, p. 90.
3. John Stuart Mill, in Chapter 1 of his *Utilitarianism,* makes clear that the epistemological contrast between the "intuitive" and the "inductive" schools of ethics underlies the issue about whether to reject or accept utilitarianism, the latter being the doctrine of *his* inductive school of ethics. He also points out that these two schools differ with regard to the evidence for "the same moral laws."

ing it from other intuitively known truths, or by deriving the duty it expresses from the essence or nature of man. These methods, being nonempirical, nonfactual, rationalistic methods of establishing a moral principle, are avoided by the utilitarian on that ground alone. That is why it is often said that a utilitarian cannot be an intuitionist and that an intuitionist cannot be a utilitarian—that the term "intuitionistic utilitarian" is virtually a contradiction in terms. And that is why it is incorrect to call the signers of the Declaration utilitarians in spite of their espousal of the duty and right of individual men to pursue happiness and the duty and right of a people to abolish or alter a government which does not effect its happiness.[4] The fact that these duties and rights concern *happiness* in no way eliminates, for the utilitarian, the epistemological taint which they receive from being expressed in self-evident principles, or the metaphysical taint which they receive from being derived from the essence of man. The utilitarian need not deny that men have a right to pursue happiness nor that governments have a duty to promote happiness, but he does deny that these rights are established in the manner described by the doctrine of natural law.

To defend what I have been saying I want to turn once again to the Declaration itself. It must be recalled that there

4. Of course, if one thinks of the fundamental thesis of utilitarianism, or of any other thesis in philosophical ethics, as an *analysis* of a concept like *good, right, true moral principle, etc.*, then any such thesis might be called rationalistic or intuitionistic if one holds that its truth is discovered by the use of intuitive reason. This would, as a consequence, show that there is a sense in which *all* philosophical ethical theories might be regarded as intuitionistic and that the expression "intuitionistic utilitarian" is therefore not a contradiction in terms. Alternatively, if one thinks of utilitarianism as the second-order moral principle that one should accept only ordinary moral principles conducive to utility, and one regards this second-order moral principle as intuitively known, then the expression "intuitionistic utilitarian" is, once again, not a contradiction in terms. However, I want to repeat that no American revolutionary was an intuitionistic utilitarian in the senses just explained.

are two contexts in which the word "happiness" enters the Declaration. The first is that in which the *individual's* moral right to pursue happiness is asserted and the second is that in which Jefferson speaks of the happiness of *the people*. This distinction was also made explicit by John Adams when in the winter of 1776 he wrote his "Thoughts on Government" to George Wythe and maintained that "upon this point all speculative politicians will agree, that the happiness of society is the end of government, as all divines and moral philosophers will agree that the happiness of the individual is the end of man."[5]

Let us first focus on the question whether it is correct to call Jefferson a utilitarian with regard to the moral principles of individual human behavior, especially those in the Declaration which assert the rights of individual men. In my opinion, Jefferson was not a utilitarian *when he wrote the Declaration,* even though he accepted the moral principle that every man has a duty and a right to pursue happiness. The crucial point is that he held that this duty followed from the essence of man and therefore defended the principle by appealing to intuition. He did not defend it on the ground that adopting and acting on it would *maximize the happiness* of individual men. Since Jefferson held with Burlamaqui that the duty and right to pursue happiness is based on the fact that God made the pursuit of happiness an end of man by incorporating a desire for happiness in man's essence, Jefferson needed no utilitarian justification of the right to pursue happiness. Adams defended the right to knowledge in the same non-utilitarian way when he asserted that the people "have a right, from the frame of their nature, to knowledge, as their great Creator, *who does nothing in vain* [my emphasis], has given them understandings, and a desire to know."[6]

5. Adams, *Works,* Volume IV, p. 193.
6. *Ibid.,* Volume III, p. 456, *Dissertation on the Canon and the Feudal Law.* Also see above, Chapter 4, note 32.

Adams certainly does not justify the right to knowledge by saying that having it would maximize happiness. What about two other moral principles maintained in the Rough Draft of the Declaration, namely, that all human creatures have a right to preserve their lives and that all human creatures have a right to preserve their liberty. Are *they* defended by asserting that man's possession of such rights will maximize happiness? Not at all. These two principles of individual morality are also thought to be self-evident or undeniable, and the rights they express are also said to be derived from man's created essence.

Now let us turn to the moral *principles* governing the actions of a *people* in order to see whether *they* are defended by an appeal to their tendency to promote happiness. We must not forget that the following truth was held to be self-evident or undeniable in the Declaration: "That whenever any form of government becomes destructive of these ends, it is the right of the people to alter or to abolish it, and to institute new government, laying its foundation on such principles and organizing its powers in such form, as to them shall seem most likely to effect their safety and happiness."[7] It will be noted that *two* rights of the people are asserted in *this* self-evident or undeniable proposition: the first that of altering or abolishing a government when it becomes destructive of certain ends mentioned earlier, the second that of forming a new government in such a way as shall seem most likely to the revolutionaries to effect their "safety" and "happiness." But these two rights of a *people* are not justified by asserting that if a people exercises such rights, it will *in fact* maximize its happiness. Because they are asserted in a principle which is said to be a self-evident or undeniable truth, such an appeal to what would in fact happen if such rights were exercised was at the least superfluous.

Jefferson and his co-signers claim that the principle which

7. Becker, *Declaration of Independence,* p. 186.

asserts these rights *of the people* is undeniable or self-evident, and thereby avoid an appeal to utility in justifying the principle, because they accepted a conception of the state or of government like that of Burlamaqui, namely, that it is "a society, by which a multitude of people unite together, under the dependence of a sovereign, in order to find, through his protection and care, the happiness, to which they naturally aspire."[8] Therefore, a government which fails to give that which it is government's purpose to give, is a degenerate government just as men who have lost their reason are degenerate, according to Locke, beings who have dropped out of their species—which is what "degenerate" means.[9] If a government is made by men with the purpose of promoting their happiness, when it fails to promote that end, it violates its duty just as an individual violates his duty when he fails to preserve his life and liberty or when he fails to pursue his own happiness. And when government fails to do its duty of promoting happiness, then those who have made it may alter it, or they may abolish it altogether. But the crucial thing to keep in mind is that *these* moral truths about the duty and right to alter or abolish a government which is not happy-making are not *themselves* supported by utilitarian arguments. They are supported by peering into the idea of government and asserting that it is self-evident that a government which fails to attain the end of happiness for which it was instituted may be altered or abolished.

It might be said in reply that John Adams was a utilitarian because he was more given to using the language of utilitarians than some of his fellow-revolutionaries. Let us consider two passages which might be thought to support this view. One appears in his "Thoughts on Government," where he not only says that the happiness of society is the end of government but also goes on to infer "that the form of govern-

8. *Principles of Politic Law,* Part I, Chapter IV, Section IX.
9. *Second Treatise,* Section 10.

ment which communicates ease, comfort, security, or, in one word, happiness, to the greatest number of persons, and in the greatest degree, is the best."[10] Even though he uses a stock utilitarian phrase in this passage—"happiness to the greatest number of persons, and in the greatest degree"—he is relying on a proposition I have already discussed in my earlier remarks on the Declaration, namely, that since men proposed social happiness as an end of government, government has a duty to promote social happiness. This supposedly self-evident truth is analogous to Burlamaqui's proposition that since God proposed individual happiness as an end of man, man has a duty to pursue his own happiness. Leaving aside the fact that in one case God makes man whereas in the other man makes government, and also the fact that happiness is an end in both cases, we are faced in both cases with instances of the following general proposition: *If the maker of a thing (like a man or a government) proposes a certain end for it, then it has a duty to attain that end—and the more successful it is in attaining that end, the better it does its duty.* I believe that Adams must have regarded this as a self-evident truth which is reminiscent of the so-called primary truths that Hamilton announced in Federalist Number 31. But when we focus on the consequent of Adams's instance of this general self-evident truth—"government has a duty to promote social happiness and the more social happiness it promotes, the better it does its duty"—we see that Adams can assert this categorically only if men did indeed propose social happiness as the end of government. Therefore, the statement that the government which promotes the happiness of the greatest number of persons, and in the greatest degree, is conditional upon the truth of a highly debatable proposition about the *end* for which government was formed. Adams's *so-called* utilitarianism, therefore, is unable to stand on its own legs, unable to serve as a test of good government

10. Adams, *Works,* Volume IV, p. 193.

without depending on an allegedly self-evident conditional statement and the highly debatable antecedent of that statement. In short, Adams's so-called utilitarianism with regard to government is as much dependent on a thesis within the doctrine of natural law as Burlamaqui's doctrine that individual men have a duty to pursue happiness. Both of them must therefore appeal to some form of intuitionism, the traditional philosophical enemy of utilitarianism. Neither one of them can dispense with an appeal to allegedly preestablished ends that allegedly create duties in a way that utilitarianism is committed to avoiding. The very principles which assert that men have a duty and a right to pursue happiness and that governments ought to promote the happiness of the greatest number of people were supported in a manner that utilitarianism was dedicated to abandoning because of its aversion to rationalism and *natural* rights, which Bentham called nonsense on stilts.

I now come to a second passage in which we find Adams using utilitarian terminology while thinking in terms of natural law. In his *Defence of the Constitutions of Government of the United States of America,* he begins a sentence (whose ending is of no relevance here) by writing, "As the end of government is the greatest happiness of the greatest number, saving at the same time the stipulated rights of all. . . ."[11] Here we see that quite apart from the question whether the achievement of the greatest happiness of the greatest number is said to be the test of the goodness of government in a self-evident or demonstrated proposition—which is what I have been focusing on up to now—Adams does not advocate a full-fledged utilitarian test of the goodness of a form of government. The crucial phrase in this passage is "saving at the same time the stipulated rights of all." Adams inserts it because he takes for granted that men have certain natural rights which are God-given and that an inquiry about social

11. *Ibid.,* p. 318.

happiness can never, *whatever its outcome,* support the invasion or abridgment of those rights. In short, he would not be willing to have a government invade those rights even if it could be shown that invading them would lead to the greatest happiness of the greatest number. He believes there are essential natural rights which are impervious to the outcome of any calculation about social happiness, and his belief that *there are* such rights shows that he is not a utilitarian in the ordinary sense of that philosophical term.

In spite of all that I have said, I can imagine someone wondering why we should not say that a *utilitarian* appeals to the nature of man while justifying a moral principle. After all, it might be urged, when the utilitarian shows that acting on a certain moral principle leads to happiness, he shows something about the nature of man. He shows that it is a fact of nature that man will gain happiness, pleasure, or well-being from acting on that principle. He shows something in the *natural* science of psychology or of sociology when he reports that man is made happy by acting in a certain way. What is to be said in response to this? Something that exposes the ambiguity of the expression, "the nature of man," and something that exposes the obscurity of the doctrine of natural law. If a philosopher who holds that doctrine maintains that all men *by nature* have a duty to act in a certain way, he means that this duty and the corresponding right follow from man's essence. But if someone who is not a theorist of natural law asserts that man is *by nature* a being who becomes happy by acting on a certain moral principle, this more innocent statement is not intended as a statement about man's *essence*. It merely asserts that men, who are parts of nature, are made happy by doing certain things. Clearly, then, the phrase "by nature" is ambiguous. The philosopher of natural law uses it in one way; the imaginary reader who thinks that the utilitarian speaks about man's nature uses it in another way. And the reason why the American revolutionaries were not utilitarians is that they thought that man had certain duties and rights by nature in the sense of "essence," whereas the utilitarian did not think he was extracting something from man's essence in asserting that man *by nature* becomes happy by acting on certain principles. The utilitarian merely meant that, *as a matter of fact* which was not to be extracted from man's essence, acting on these principles would make men happy. However, the utilitarian's matter-of-fact statement about nature was not enough for revolutionaries who subscribed to the doctrine of natural law. They thought their duties and rights *followed* in what we have seen was an obscure sense from that obscure entity, the essence or nature of man. They insisted that these duties and rights followed from the nature of man, and therefore they thought that their moral principles were necessarily true and immutable. That is why they were not content with maintaining a utilitarian theory according to which man's duties and rights were expressed in contingent principles which were true or acceptable merely because acting in accordance with them happened to make men happy. Even the principle that every man had a duty and right to pursue happiness had to be extracted from man's essence; and the principle that every government had a duty and right to promote the happiness of the people also had to be extracted from the essence of government. These principles could not be allowed to depend on the way the world happened to wag, for they had to be immutable, necessary, self-evident, sacred, and undeniable truths.

From the Unalienable Rights of Men to the People's Right To Rebel

Now that we have disposed of a possible misunderstanding of just how the duty and right to pursue happiness fits into the Revolutionary philosophy, it is time to turn to a network

of rights that linked the unalienable rights of individuals
with the people's right to rebel. In the background there is
the basic idea that a social contract of some sort had been
made in which the people transferred certain rights to government in return for something. What the government was
supposed to have given is not unambiguous, and later in this
chapter I shall have something to say about the ultimate ambiguity in the Revolutionary philosophy when I concentrate
in greater detail than I have so far on the ends of government
as viewed in the Declaration. What rights the people transferred is less important than the rights they did *not* transfer
because they were not transferable, that is to say, unalienable. Unalienable rights were thought to be held under *any*
form of government so that when a government merely
showed signs of wishing to invade these rights, it could be
regarded as intending to reduce the people under absolute
despotism. And when the people were sure that the government had this intention or design, that assurance was enough
to justify resistance. Now our task is to develop some of the
finer points of this argument by explaining the different
kinds of rights that are mentioned in some philosophical
treatments of this subject.[12]

We find discussions of it not only in the textbooks of jurists
like Pufendorf and Burlamaqui but also in those written by
moral philosophers like Hutcheson and Witherspoon, so that
we can infer that they were commonplace in the eighteenth
century. Such discussions appeared in those parts of the textbooks that also contained definitions of unalienable and adventitious rights, which we have already examined. Let us
turn to two other commonly made distinctions between
rights.

12. James Otis, in *The Rights of the British Colonies*, Bailyn, *Pamphlets*,
Volume I, p. 434, quotes Section 149 of Locke's *Second Treatise*, which
contains the argument some refinements of which I am about to present.
Also see Bailyn, *ibid.*, p. 477, for a related comment by Otis.

The first is that between *perfect* and *imperfect* rights. According to Witherspoon, a perfect right is one which we may use force to maintain, whereas an imperfect right is one that we may not use force to maintain.[13] The question is simply whether we may or may not use force in seeing to it that we are not prevented from exercising a right. Self-preservation is considered a perfect right, whereas the right to gratitude for a favor is imperfect.

I now come to a kind of right called "external," which is sometimes defined as a right the exercise of which is "contrary" to an imperfect right of another person. Thus, if one person has done a favor for another, and hence has an imperfect right to the other's gratitude, the other has an *external* right to withhold his gratitude. For that reason the exercise of the external right of the beneficiary to withhold gratitude from his benefactor is "contrary" to the imperfect right of the benefactor to receive it. At one point Hutcheson speaks contemptuously of this as "an external shew of right," though he insists that it should not be denied.[14]

We are now in a position to understand a statement by Hutcheson about all "human power, or authority" of the kind that is vested in government. Before quoting this statement, I should, with due recollection of our earlier discussion of power and right, call attention to Hutcheson's putting "authority" in apposition to "power," thereby showing that *power* was not only not *contrasted* with the moral concept of

13. Witherspoon, *op. cit.*, p. 70. For other philosophical discussions of this distinction, see Hutcheson's *Inquiry Concerning Moral Good and Evil*, Section VII, Part VI; his *Short Introduction to Moral Philosophy*, Book II, Chapter II, Section III; and his *System of Moral Philosophy*, Book II, Chapter III, Section III. For a legal discussion of a perfect right, see Pufendorf's *Elementorum*, Book I, Definition VIII. The difference between a perfect moral right and a perfect legal right involves the distinction between what can be done in a state of nature and what can be done in civil society.

14. Hutcheson, *Short Introduction, loc. cit.*; also *System of Moral Philosophy, loc. cit.*, where the phrase "shadow of right" is used.

authority but it was often identified with the latter. Hutcheson says that all such power or authority consists "in a *right transferred to any person or council, to dispose of the alienable rights of others.*"[15] It should be observed that a government's power or authority is, first of all, transferred, that is to say, alienated to it by others. Secondly, this alienated right is a right to dispose of the *alienable* rights of those others, which means that the government may exercise, or do what it will with, the alienable rights. But, Hutcheson goes on to say, "there can be no government so absolute, as to have even an *external right* to do or command everything. For wherever any invasion is made upon *unalienable rights,* there must arise either a *perfect,* or *external right* to *resistance.*"[16]

The first part of this passage shows that no government can be so absolute as to have even an *external* right—the weakest kind of right—to do or command *everything.* This is because the people never transferred to the government *all* of their rights and because a government can have no rights except those transferred to it by the people. The second part of the passage shows that when a government tries to do or command *everything* and in consequence invades the people's unalienable rights, the people have either a perfect or an external right to resist. Now why is the right to resist said to be perfect *or external?* The reason for the addition of "or external" becomes clearer in a subsequent passage where Hutcheson says that there are two moral restraints upon the right of subjects to resist. First of all, there is the restraint imposed by the subjects' realization that if they are too weak, they may cause more harm than good by their resistance. And, secondly, there is the restraint imposed by their realizing that governors who are on the whole good may have done some injury which is too small to outweigh the advantages of their administration or the evils that resistance would

15. *Inquiry,* Section VII, Part VII, p. 294.
16. *Ibid.*

occasion. In such cases, even though an invasion of an unalienable right has occurred, the subjects have only a "show
of right" or an external right to resist.

I want to remark here that although Hutcheson's treatment of rights is, in general, more utilitarian than that of the
Lockean and Burlamaquian colonists, what he says about
weighing harm and good in exercising the right to resist is
not so utilitarian as to be incompatible with the intuitionistic
Declaration precisely because one of the self-evident or undeniable duties of the people *is* to take account of their own
happiness when contemplating a revolution. The right to reform, alter, or abolish a government is said to be an inalienable right in the Virginia Bill of Rights, but it must be exercised in such a manner "as shall be judged most conducive to
the public weal." So, plainly, the right or duty to resist must
be exercised with due attention to the public weal even according to those who enunciate the duty or right in a self-
evident or undeniable principle.

I also lay stress on this idea that the right to resist a government which has invaded an unalienable right *may be* external because it bears closely on a part of the Declaration in
which the signers speak of a dictate of *prudence* that governments long established should not be changed for "light and
transient causes." This is the passage which concludes with
the reference to "the patient sufferance of these colonies" and
is consonant not only with Hutcheson's idea that subjects
who contemplate resistance should keep in mind certain restraints which would make their right to resist merely external rather than perfect but also with more psychological remarks that Locke makes about revolution in the *Second
Treatise*. He observes, while discussing the dissolution of
government that "such *revolutions happen* not upon every
little mismanagement in public affairs. *Great mistakes* in the
ruling part, many wrong and inconvenient laws, and all the
slips of humane fraility will be *born by the people,* without

mutiny or murmur." And not only does Locke strike that note of "patient sufferance" but he does so just before he uses words which are astonishingly close to Jefferson's. Locke says: "But if a long train of abuses, prevarications, and artifices, all tending the same way, make the design visible to the people, and they cannot but feel, what they lie under, and see, whither they are going; 'tis not to be wonder'd, that they should then rouse themselves, and endeavour to put the rule into such hands, which may secure to them the ends for which government was at first erected."[17]

The Rights of Men, the Ends of Men, and the Ends of Government

In the passage above, Locke concludes with a phrase of considerable importance, namely, "secure to them the ends for which government was at first erected." What were these ends as conceived by the American revolutionaries? What was government supposed to do according to the contract whereby the people gave up certain rights? What was it obliged to do? What omissions on the part of the government would justify patient people in rousing themselves against it? I said earlier that the answer to this was not unambiguous, but I went on to say that there was one thing that government was clearly obliged *not* to do. It was obliged not to invade the unalienable rights of the people on pain of being resisted. But was this the sum total of the government's obligation? Was this the only duty or end of government? It might

17. Locke, *Second Treatise*, Section 225. See also Sections 210 and 230 as well as P. Laslett's reference to the similarities between Locke and the Declaration in Laslett's note to Section 225. Bailyn has noted James Otis's echoing of Section 225. See Otis, *Rights of the British Colonies* in Bailyn's *Pamphlets*, Volume I, p. 429 and Bailyn's note 7 on p. 720. E. S. Corwin had observed that in the Declaration Jefferson had repeated Locke's language about a long train of abuses, *The "Higher Law" Background of American Constitutional Law*, p. 82, note 119.

be added that government was also obliged to guard those rights against invasion by other people. But should one stop there? Clearly not, for even though the invasion of *unalienable* rights constitutes one of the greatest sins, there are *alienable* rights, like the right to estates and goods, which government would also be obliged not only not to invade but also to guard. So far, however, we have talked only of government's obligation not to invade and its obligation to guard the rights of people. Can we go any further in the sequence of which *not invading* and *guarding* are the first two members? For example, is the government obliged to aid and abet people in the exercise of the unalienable rights (which, as we have seen, are derived from duties) listed in the Declaration? Concerning that profound question there may have been differences among the American revolutionaries and doubt in the mind of Jefferson himself.

In order to try to answer this question, I want to compare Jefferson's Rough Draft with the final version of the Declaration. I have already called attention to the removal of Jefferson's statement that certain rights were *derived from equal creation*, to the removal of the word "inherent" as a characterization of those rights, and to the shift from speaking of the preservation of life, the preservation of liberty, and the pursuit of happiness to speaking of life, liberty, and the pursuit of happiness. Now I wish to discuss the fact—perhaps of greatest significance for political philosophy—that Jefferson in the Rough Draft, just after listing *its* trio of rights, goes on to write: "that to secure these *ends* [my emphasis] governments are instituted among men, deriving their just powers from the consent of the governed," whereas in the final version the word "ends" is replaced by the word "rights."

Because I think the reader will be able to follow my argument more easily with verbatim texts available, I reproduce first a part of the Rough Draft which is long enough to show the crucial section in its full context:

We hold these truths to be sacred & undeniable; that all men are created equal & independant, that from that equal creation they derive rights inherent & inalienable, among which are the preservation of life, & liberty & the pursuit of happiness; that to secure these ends, governments are instituted among men, deriving their just powers from the consent of the governed; that whenever any form of government shall become destructive of these ends, it is the right of the people to alter or to abolish it, & to institute new government, laying it's foundation on such principles & organising it's powers in such form, as to them shall seem most likely to effect their safety & happiness. prudence indeed will dictate that governments long established should not be changed for light & transient causes: and accordingly all experience hath shewn that mankind are more disposed to suffer while evils are sufferable, than to right themselves by abolishing the forms to which they are accustomed. but when a long train of abuses & usurpations, begun at a distinguished period, & pursuing invariably the same object, evinces a design to subject them to arbitrary power, it is their right, it is their duty, to throw off such government & to provide new guards for their future security. such has been the patient sufferance of these colonies; & such is now the necessity which constrains them to expunge their former systems of government. the history of his present majesty, is a history of unremitting injuries and usurpations, among which no one fact stands single or solitary to contradict the uniform tenor of the rest, all of which have in direct object the establishment of an absolute tyranny over these states.[18]

Now I reproduce the corresponding part of the final version:

We hold these truths to be self-evident, that all men are created equal, that they are endowed by their Creator with certain unalienable Rights, that among these are

18. See Boyd, *Declaration of Independence,* p. 19.

Life, Liberty and the pursuit of Happiness. — That to secure these rights, Governments are instituted among Men, deriving their just powers from the consent of the governed, — That whenever any Form of Government becomes destructive of these ends, it is the Right of the People to alter or to abolish it, and to institute new Government, laying its foundation on such principles and organizing its powers in such form, as to them shall seem most likely to effect their Safety and Happiness. Prudence, indeed, will dictate that Governments long established should not be changed for light and transient causes; and accordingly all experience hath shewn, that mankind are more disposed to suffer, while evils are sufferable, than to right themselves by abolishing the forms to which they are accustomed. But when a long train of abuses and usurpations, pursuing invariably the same Object evinces a design to reduce them under absolute Despotism, it is their right, it is their duty, to throw off such Government, and to provide new Guards for their future security. — Such has been the patient sufferance of these Colonies; and such is now the necessity which constrains them to alter their former Systems of Government. The history of the present King of Great Britain is a history of repeated injuries and usurpations, all having in direct object the establishment of an absolute Tyranny over these States.[19]

In the Rough Draft, when Jefferson writes "to secure these ends governments are instituted among men" immediately after the phrase "the preservation of life, & liberty & the pursuit of happiness," to what does the phrase "these ends" refer? I think it refers to three Burlamaquian ends of man: the preservation of life, the preservation of liberty, and the pursuit of happiness. Now let us ask what the word "secure" means here. I believe that it is synonymous with the word "attain" in this context, being influenced as I am not only by

19. Becker, *Declaration of Independence,* pp. 186–187.

the fact that this makes grammatical sense when speaking of ends, but also by certain views which Burlamaqui advances about civil government. He calls it an adventitious though natural state; he also holds with Locke that human society is originally and in itself a state of equality and independence, and that the institution of sovereignty destroys this independence. *But* he affirms resolutely that this institution does not subvert natural society. On the contrary, he says, it contributes to strengthen and cement it. Therefore, Burlamaqui says, to form "a just idea of civil society we must call it natural society itself, modified in such a manner, that there is a sovereign presiding over it, on whose will whatever relates to the welfare of the society ultimately depends; to the end that, by these means mankind may attain, *with greater certainty* [my emphasis], that happiness to which they all naturally aspire."[20]

In order to lend further support to my hypothesis that Jefferson was using the word "secure" to mean *attain* the goals of *preserving* life and liberty, and of *pursuing* happiness, I call attention to the fact that Burlamaqui holds that when a man has a natural right, "other people ought not to employ their strength and liberty in resisting him in this point; *but on the contrary, . . . they should respect his right, and assist*

20. *Principles of Politic Law,* Part I, Chapter I, Section III. The French passage which is translated by the matter following the semicolon is: *"afin que par ce moyen les hommes puissent se procurer d'une manière plus sûre le bonheur auquel ils aspirent naturellement."* The verb *"procurer"* is to be noted here. Elsewhere Burlamaqui is translated as follows: "Government . . . was intended to enable us the better to discharge the duties, prescribed by natural laws, and to attain more certainly the end, for which we were created." Here the French reads: *"On a voulu mettre les hommes plus en état de s'acquiter des devoirs que les loix naturelles leur prescrivent, & de parvenir plus sûrement à leur destination,"* Principles of Natural Law, Part II, Chapter VI, Section II. He also writes in the *Principles of Natural Law,* Part II, Chapter VI, Section III, that in civil society the sovereign acts "to the end that, under his protection and through his care, mankind may surely attain (*procurer*) the felicity (*bonheur*), to which they naturally aspire."

him in the exercise of it, rather than do him any prejudice [my emphasis]." Reason, he goes on to say in the same vein, "obliges every body to favor and abet" those who exercise these rights.[21] And this favoring and abetting of right-holders in the exercise of their rights would be in keeping with the idea that civil society or government has as *its* end the assisting and abetting of men who wish to exercise the inherent rights of preserving their life, preserving their liberty, and pursuing their happiness.

Supplied with this information, let us see what happens when the phrase "these ends" is changed to "these rights" in the final version. The verb "secure" can no longer mean "attain" there. Rather it must have the meaning of "make secure" or "guard." Since the revision of the Rough Draft involved changing "the *preservation* of life" to "life" and "the *preservation* of liberty" to "liberty," when the final version goes on, after saying that all men are endowed by their Creator with the rights of life, liberty, and the pursuit of happiness, to say "that to secure these *rights,* governments are instituted among men," the final version has to construe "secure" as meaning *make secure* rather than *attain.* Why? Well, once we speak of *rights* as secured by government, and especially of rights with which men have already been endowed by their Creator, it is manifestly pointless to use the verb "secure" to mean *attain* since government need not be instituted to *attain* what people already have. It might be held that when the final version put "secure these *rights*" in place of the Rough Draft's "secure these *ends,*" no change in the meaning of "secure" became necessary, on the ground that the word "ends" in the Rough Draft referred to the *rights* previously mentioned in the Rough Draft, namely, rights of preservation of life, preservation of liberty, and pursuit of happiness. Therefore, this argument would run, when the final version

21. *Principles of Natural Law,* Part I, Chapter VII, Section V.

replaced "ends" by "rights" it was simply making more explicit what had been intended originally, namely, to assert that government was instituted to *guard* rights whose names were changed merely to simplify the prose. In reply I repeat that I do not think that in the Rough Draft Jefferson used the word "end" to refer to a right since it was more common in the literature of the period to speak, as both Burlamaqui and Locke did, about an *activity* as an end of man than it was to speak about a *right* as an end of man. Moreover, it hardly makes sense to speak of a right already possessed by man as an *end* which is to be secured in the sense of attained by government while it makes eminently good sense to speak of the activity of preserving one's life as an end to be attained. But even more persuasive, I think, is the fact that my interpretation of the referent of "these ends" is in accord with what I take to be the Burlamaquian tendency of Jefferson's philosophical thinking at the time he wrote the Rough Draft. Consequently, I think that what looks on first sight like a mere verbal change, in which the word "rights" replaced the word "ends" while maintaining the same referent as "ends," might have altered the fundamental purpose of government as Jefferson conceived it in the Rough Draft. That purpose was, I believe, to *aid and abet men in attaining ends proposed by God:* the preservation of life, the preservation of liberty, and the pursuit of happiness. But in the final version of the Declaration the purpose of government must be understood as merely that of *making secure rights which have been given by God,* which means making them secure against invasion.[22]

In the light of what I have said, I cannot avoid the conclusion that somewhere between the Rough Draft and the final version certain philosophical changes were made which were not "merely verbal" and which were not made simply out of

22. See Supplementary Notes, Further Remarks . . . , p. 285.

concern for style.[23] On the contrary, these changes reveal a tendency on the part of Jefferson, or of others to whose wishes he acceded, to dilute the purpose of government to the point where it ceases to be an *abettor* of men in the active attainment of three Burlamaquian ends proposed by God and becomes only a *protector* of certain rights. Consequently, in the final version we are not presented with a moral basis for altering or abolishing a government which fails to *increase* the probability that mankind will attain the happiness to which all persons naturally aspire. Rather, we are only presented with a basis on which we may alter or abolish a government which *decreases* the probability of our attaining that happiness. And that may well have been the purpose of the transformation of the first occurrence of "these ends" to "these rights," a transformation which forced "secure" to mean *guard* rather than *attain*.

The changes I have mentioned and the problems they raise give one the feeling that Jefferson may have been wobbling on a fundamental question in the philosophy of government. And his wobbling may well be connected with something that puzzled Gilbert Chinard fifty years ago. Chinard wondered why Jefferson, while copying certain passages from James Wilson's *Considerations on the Nature and Extent of the*

23. Jefferson described the changes made by Franklin and Adams before he showed it to the Committee of Five as "merely verbal." See Jefferson's letter to Madison, August 20, 1823, *Writings,* Volume XV, p. 461. On the merit of certain changes I cannot agree with Becker. He thinks, for example, that " 'they are endowed by their creator' is obviously much better than 'from that equal creation' "—on stylistic grounds. Perhaps it is, but it obscures Jefferson's reliance on Locke's view of the connection between equal creation and liberty. Becker also writes: "Why say 'the preservation of life'? If a man has a right to life, the right to preserve life is manifestly included" (*op. cit.,* pp. 198–199). But the elimination of "equal creation" and "preservation of life" obscures the connection between Jefferson's views and Burlamaqui's and therefore prevents us from seeing the intended progression from the created essence of man to his God-proposed ends, his God-ordained duties, and to his unalienable rights.

Legislative Authority of the British Parliament into his own *Commonplace Book,* failed to reproduce a passage of Wilson which said, among other things, that those who are subject to government had given their consent to being governed "with a view to *ensure and to increase* [my emphasis] the happiness of the governed above what they could enjoy in an independent and unconnected state of nature." In this passage Wilson cites Burlamaqui, and the crucial reference for us is to *increasing* as well as to *ensuring* happiness. On the other hand, Jefferson *did* quote Wilson when Wilson asked rhetorically, by way of testing the legitimacy of Parliament's possessing a supreme, irresistible, uncontrolled authority over the American colonies: "Will it then ensure and increase the happiness of the American colonies?"[24]

In my view, ambiguity about whether the end of government is merely to protect certain rights or whether government was to go further and *encourage* man's exercise of those rights is intimately connected with the question whether government was not only to ensure but "to *increase* the happiness of the governed above what they could enjoy" in an independent and unconnected state of nature. Only some seriously divided person, or some seriously divided Committee, could have produced a final Declaration which bore the marks of both these philosophical conceptions of the ends of government since Congress, we are assured, did not concern itself with the more philosophical parts of the Declaration except for deleting "inherent" as applied to rights.[25]

The importance of calling attention to these two conceptions of government between which Jefferson himself may have oscillated is underscored when we find one student of

24. See Chinard's Introduction to his edition of the *Commonplace Book,* pp. 39-44.
25. Boyd, *op. cit.,* p. 32. See C. M. Wiltse, *The Jeffersonian Tradition in American Democracy,* Chapters VII and VIII, *passim,* for a discussion of certain political acts of Jefferson that may have reflected the intellectual division I have been discussing.

Jefferson, Daniel Boorstin, arguing, mainly on the basis of the Declaration, that "the Jeffersonian natural 'rights' philosophy was thus a declaration of inability or unwillingness . . . to face the need for defining explicitly the moral ends to be served by government."[26] This statement, however, is directly controverted by Jefferson's statement in the Rough Draft that governments are instituted among men to secure *the ends* listed there. Furthermore, the statement would also be controverted if Jefferson believed that the purpose of government was to increase as well as to ensure the happiness of society. It might be said in reply that, according to Jefferson, active governmental intervention would not always be necessary to increase the happiness of society because under certain conditions it would be increased by individuals without governmental aid. This idea was expressed in Jefferson's First Inaugural when he wrote that a wise and frugal government will restrain men from injuring one another but leave them otherwise free to regulate their own pursuits of industry and improvement. On the other hand, Jefferson once said that if the advantage of the people could be increased by executive intervention, the executive would not only have a right to intervene but a duty. This emerges clearly in a letter of September 20, 1810, where Jefferson is imagining that the executive might, while pursuing his duties, buy the Floridas cheaply without Congressional approval if he expected that such approval would be forthcoming when Congress met.[27]

Boorstin has also said that Jefferson was not concerned with duties because he failed to make explicit the moral ends of government. But if I am right in supposing that the rights in the Rough Draft were advocated by Jefferson as logical consequences of Burlamaquian duties, then Jefferson believed in man's duty to attain certain moral ends and that

---

26. Daniel Boorstin, *The Lost World of Thomas Jefferson* (New York, 1948), p. 195.
27. *Writings,* Volume XII, p. 418, Letter to J. B. Colvin.

government should aid man in that pursuit. It is true, as Boorstin says,[28] that in asserting a right we imply what the community *cannot* do, but in asserting a right in the spirit of Burlamaqui we imply that every one ought to favor and abet the exercise of the right, and to that extent we prescribe what the community and every individual in it *must* do. Therefore, I cannot accept the statement that Jefferson's " 'natural rights' theory of government left all men naturally free from duties to their neighbors: no claims could be validated except by the Creator's plan, and the Creator seemed to have made no duties but only rights."[29] This, I believe, can be maintained only if one neglects the Lockean and Burlamaquian roots of Jefferson's thinking which *require* reference to duties not mentioned in the Declaration but implicit in Jefferson's telescoped derivation of rights. Jefferson never could have derived his rights from equal creation without statements of God-imposed duties of natural law as intermediate steps.

Furthermore, Jefferson wrote the economist J. B. Say that the laws of nature "create our duties."[30] Indeed, Boorstin quotes this letter; and to make more ironical his view that, according to Jefferson, God made no duties for man, Boorstin tells us that the motto which Jefferson chose for his seal, "Rebellion to Tyrants Is Obedience to God," comes close to summing up his whole political philosophy.[31] But how could Jefferson have spoken of *obedience* to God if he had thought that God had laid no duties on man? And what about the Lockean passage in the Declaration—not very different from its ancestor in the Rough Draft—which I have previously mentioned and which says that "when a long train of abuses and usurpations, pursuing invariably the same Object evinces

28. Boorstin, *op. cit.*, p. 195.
29. *Ibid.*, p. 196.
30. *Writings,* Volume XI, p. 3; February 1, 1804.
31. Boorstin, *op. cit.*, p. 203.

a design to reduce [the people] under absolute Despotism, it is their right, *it is their duty* [my emphasis] to throw off such Government"?

I emphasize that much of my interpretation relies on the Rough Draft, where the influence of Burlamaqui and even that of Locke is more evident than in the final version. However, if Jefferson himself made the changes in the Declaration that pointed toward a less affirmative view of the role of government, it becomes interesting to ask why Jefferson decided to alter it so as to give the impression that governments are instituted to *secure* in the sense of *guard* certain *rights* rather than that they are instituted to *secure* in the sense of *attain* certain *ends*. To this question I cannot present an answer that satisfies me. But I cannot resist expressing the *opinion*— and I underscore that word—that two warring philosophical souls dwelt within Jefferson's breast and that one of them may have triumphed before he showed his draft of the Declaration to anyone. The victory did not go to the Jefferson who thought that the government should actively encourage the attainment of certain human ends proposed by a God who gave man a certain nature, and it did not go to the Jefferson who thought that government should not only ensure but increase the happiness of the people through favoring and abetting the exercise of their rights. Rather, the victory went to the Jefferson who thought that government should merely see to it that man did not enjoy *less* happiness than he could enjoy in what James Wilson called "an independent and unconnected state of nature." The same Wilson continued to sound the same Burlamaquian note in his *Lectures on Law,* delivered in 1790, for there he affirmed: "Government, in my humble opinion, should be formed to secure and to enlarge the exercise of the natural rights of its members; and every government, which has not this in view, as its principal object, is not a government of the legitimate kind."[32] But the

32. Wilson, *Works,* Volume II, p. 592.

idea that government is formed "to *enlarge* the exercise of the natural rights" as well as "to secure" or guard them does not come through in the final version of the Declaration. Therefore, we may describe this difference between Wilson and the Declaration he signed as evidence of what I have called the ultimate ambiguity of the American revolutionary mind: its failure to come to a single conclusion on the role of government with regard to man's natural rights. Was it merely to guard them, to see to it that they were not invaded? Or was it to abet and favor the people in attaining certain God-proposed ends? The revolutionaries who signed the final version of the Declaration seemed to answer the question in the first way, but they also left signs of an inclination to answer it in the second way. The Republic would spend the next two hundred years trying to answer it in its own way.

Epilogue
Man's Glassy Essence:
The Murky Mirror of Morality

> ". . . man, proud man,
>   Drest in a little brief authority,
>   Most ignorant of what he's most assur'd,
>   His glassy essence, like an angry ape,
>   Plays such fantastic tricks before high heaven,
>   As make the angels weep. . . ."
>
> *Measure for Measure,*
> I.i.33

It is often pointed out in studies of the *Federalist Papers* that the task of constructing a new government was very different from that of overthrowing an old one and that therefore the ideas employed in those papers were significantly different from those that I have been examining. I agree with this to some extent, and that is why I have not studied concepts like faction, separation of powers, and checks and balances. Such concepts were tools of the constitution-makers who tried to construct a government that would achieve the ideals that the revolution-makers had extracted from the essence of man as they saw him. I agree therefore with Arthur O. Lovejoy, who said that "The ablest members of the Constitutional Convention were well aware that *their* task—unlike that of the Continental Congress in 1776—was not to lay down abstract principles of political philosophy, not to rest the system they were constructing simply upon theorems about the 'natural rights' of men or of States, though they postulated such rights. Their problem was not chiefly one of political ethics but of practical psychology, a need not so much to preach to Americans about what they *ought* to do, as to predict successfully what they *would* do. . . ."[1] However, Lovejoy seems to couple this attribution of what is sometimes called "realism" to the constitutionalists of 1787 with a suggestion that whereas they were tough, shrewd psychologists who saw men as lower than the angels, the revolutionaries of 1776 viewed men as residents of Carl Becker's "Heavenly City of the Eighteenth-Century Philosophers." And it is with this suggestion that I wish to take exception on the basis of what I have shown in earlier chapters.

For one thing, it is clear that those who believed in self-evident moral truth and those who believed in the existence of the moral sense did not think all men were of celestial caliber. If they had, they would not have acknowledged with Locke and Aquinas that some men are incapable of seeing the truths of natural law, they would not have asserted that the perception of moral truth could be and was often blinded by vice, corruption, prejudice, ignorance, and stupidity, and they would not have taken pains to point out that the reliable moral judge must have qualities that many human beings do not have.

The fact that the rationalistic followers of Locke made an Aquinas-like distinction between truths self-evident *in themselves* and truths self-evident *to the learned* showed little faith in the capacity of *all* the people to absorb the moral truths to which the revolutionaries appealed. It is worth pointing out, therefore, that when Alexander Hamilton employed a version of that distinction to beat down political enemies in Federalist Number 31,[2] he was not inventing an idea that was not available to him in the 1770's, when he was wrapped up in the Revolutionary philosophy I have been ex-

1. A. O. Lovejoy, *Reflections on Human Nature* (Baltimore, 1961), pp. 46–47.
2. See above, Chapter 2, section entitled "Hamilton and Self-evidence."

amining in this book. Nor did Hamilton have to wait until 1787 to learn how to defend a practice which dramatized his lack of faith in *all* of the people—the requirement of property qualifications for voting. Hamilton indirectly gave his approval to that practice in *The Farmer Refuted* (1775), one of his early pamphlets that was full of natural law and Revolutionary sentiment. Hamilton extracted what he must have at that time regarded as the best defense of that practice from the following passage in Blackstone's *Commentaries:*

> The true reason of requiring any qualification, with regard to property, in voters, is to exclude such persons as are in so mean a situation that they are esteemed to have no will of their own. If these persons had votes, they would be tempted to dispose of them under some undue influence or other. This would give a great, an artful, or a wealthy man, a larger share in elections than is consistent with general liberty. If it were probable that every man would give his vote freely and without influence of any kind, then, upon the true theory and genuine principles of liberty, every member of the community, however poor, should have a vote in electing those delegates, to whose charge is committed the disposal of his property, his liberty, and his life. But, since that can hardly be expected in persons of indigent fortunes, or such as are under the immediate dominion of others, all popular states have been obliged to establish certain qualifications; whereby some, who are suspected to have no will of their own, are excluded from voting, in order to set other individuals, whose wills may be supposed independent, more thoroughly upon a level with each other.[3]

Hamilton quoted from this passage mainly to show that the opulent as well as the indigent American colonists were worse off than the meanest Britisher. He did not condemn the view that the meanest Britisher should not be entitled to

3. Blackstone's *Commentaries,* Volume II, pp. 170–171.

vote, nor did he quarrel with Blackstone's view that such people did not possess independent wills. On the contrary, Hamilton noted with approbation that the poor in England

> compose a part of that society, to whose government they
> are subject. They are nourished and maintained by it,
> and partake in every other emolument, for which they
> are qualified. They have no doubt, most of them, rela-
> tions and connexions, among those who are privileged to
> vote, and by that means, are not entirely without influ-
> ence, in the appointment of their rulers. They are not
> governed by laws made expressly and exclusively for
> them; but by the general laws of their country; equally
> obligatory on the legal electors, and on the law makers
> themselves. So that they have nearly the same security
> against oppression, which the body of the people have.
>
> To this we may add, that they are only under a con-
> ditional prohibition, which industry and good fortune
> may remove. They may, one day, accumulate a sufficient
> property to enable them to emerge out of their present
> state.[4]

Hamilton's willingness to accept the idea of property qualifications for voting in a pamphlet dominated by Lockean
moral philosophy, shows that the eleven years separating the
Declaration and the Constitutional Convention did not witness a transformation in which ardent lovers of the common
people were altogether replaced by shrewd observers of their
limitations. On the contrary, the idea that the indigent were
not men of independent will was as commonplace in pre-
Revolutionary years as Locke's idea that dairy-maids could
not detect self-evidence and Jefferson's fear that blacks might
not possess that degree of rational power which would give
them the same essence and therefore the same position in the
scale of being as whites.

Since we have seen in earlier chapters that the ignorant

4. *Papers of Alexander Hamilton,* Volume I, p. 107.

and the stupid were regarded by major theorists of natural law as lacking the *understanding* to grasp the ideas contained in the natural law, it should not surprise us to find Blackstone denying some people the right to vote on the basis of a defect in their *wills*. For just as many moralists of 1776 held that only a certain kind of person could see that he had certain natural rights, so Blackstone held that only a certain kind of person was fit to elect those who would run the government that would do what it was obliged to do concerning those rights. Blackstone's argument, tacitly accepted by Hamilton in 1775, was that an indigent person was not fit to vote. And this lack of fitness was said to rest on considerations which are *analogous* to those adduced when blacks, insane people, children, and women were held not to be fit. I say "analogous" because when those individuals were deprived of a right to vote, they were deprived of it because they allegedly lacked, had lost, or had failed to attain *rationality*, whereas Blackstone's argument concerning the poor rested on their alleged lack of *a will* of their own, or of an *independent* will. And his main evidence for this is that they are prone to sell their votes to the rich. If, therefore, an indigent man were prevented from having a vote to sell to a rich man, then the rich man, Blackstone maintained, will be prevented from having a larger share in elections "than is consistent with general liberty," and all individuals, "whose wills may be supposed independent" will be "more thoroughly" set "on a level with each other." However, Blackstone did not seem to worry about whether the voters would deprive the voteless of their natural independence in Locke's sense. If he had been asked about this, I suspect that he would have said that taking the vote away from a poor man would be less likely to interfere with "general liberty" than giving him the vote would.

Behind this preoccupation with *general liberty* there stood a distinction between various liberties of individuals and the liberty of a civil society or state—a distinction which is made clear in Richard Price's pamphlet, *Observations on the Nature of Civil Liberty, the Principles of Government, and the Justice and Policy of the War with America* (1776). Whereas what Price calls physical liberty, moral liberty, and religious liberty are attributed to *individuals*, "*civil liberty* is the power of a *civil society* or *state* to govern itself by its own discretion, or by laws of its own making, without being subject to the impositions of *any* power, in appointing and directing which the collective body of the people have no concern, and over which they have no control."[5] It would appear, however, that Price thinks of the "collective body of the people" as composed only of what he calls "independent agents," namely, those of us who possess what he calls physical liberty, spontaneity, or self-determination "which gives us a command over our actions, rendering them properly *ours,* and not effects of any foreign cause."[6] Therefore, although a state can vary in its degree of liberty, it sinks to the lowest degree of it if "the majority of its representatives are always elected by a handful of the meanest persons in it, whose votes are paid for; and if also, there is a higher will on which even these mock representatives themselves depend, and that directs their voices: In these circumstances, it will be an abuse of language to say that the state possesses liberty."[7]

Here we see a philosophical rationale for property qualifications in a free society. The whole society or state can be free if and only if its "independent agents" elect representatives, and the indigent are, for Price, definitely not independent agents. What has happened, however, is that a metaphysical conception of independence espoused by Price—according to which a man's actions are *his* only when he has willed them through an undetermined volition of his own—has been sophistically transformed into an economic conception of inde-

5. Richard Price, *Observations on the Nature of Civil Liberty,* p. 3.
6. *Ibid.*
7. See Supplementary Notes, Richard Price on the Dependent Voter, p. 289.

pendence. For, clearly, a man who accepts a bribe to vote in a certain way *is* an independent agent by Price's definition. He has command over his action in accepting the bribe and in voting; both actions *are* properly *his*. Yet Price tries to persuade us that the action of voting is not *his* when he has voted as directed by someone who has paid him. By that argument, one might show that if *A* is *persuaded* by *B* to vote in a certain way by *B*'s eloquent appeal to *A*'s self-interest, *B* is *directing A*'s actions. Yet Price surely cannot hold that *A* and others like him would be so lacking in independence as to make us call the state in which they live and vote a free state only by an abuse of language.

I do not wish at this late stage to enter into a full discussion of free will, but I think it is clear that Price misused his powers as a philosopher when he suggested that the indigent should be disenfranchised for lacking what *he* calls "physical liberty" or the "independence" of an agent whose actions are his own. The poor lack money, but if they are said to lack independence on this score and are therefore to be disenfranchised, then I believe that the number of voters in Price's free society would shrink to zero if his argument were consistently applied. For who is not moved to vote by considerations which, even though they are not financial, are nevertheless similarly effective in getting us to vote as another man votes?

If I have succeeded in showing anything in this look forward to the Constitutional Convention, it is that the most subtle argument for property qualifications was not a merely political one devised by "realistic" psychologists, but was rather formulated in 1776 by a friend of the Revolution and an acute moral philosopher who fallaciously identified poverty and metaphysical bondage within his own system. This is enough to show at least two things: (1) that high-powered metaphysics rather than political argument was sometimes employed in the effort to deny a poor man the right to vote;

and (2) that the revolutionaries of 1776 did not fail to see man's limitations. It is worth noting that John Adams in his defense of the state constitutions of the United States wrote that "our friend Dr. Price has distinguished very well, concerning physical, moral, religious, and civil liberty" in a reference to the work by Price that I have just been discussing; and one might conclude from this alone that Adams in his capacity as constitutionalist was prepared to accept Price's argument for property qualifications.[8]

Such a conclusion is supported by a letter written by Adams to James Sullivan from Philadelphia on 26 May 1776, a place and date which make abundantly clear that those who were fomenting the Revolution were able to be "realistic" well before they were obliged to make the Constitution of the United States of America. Sullivan had written a letter on May 6 to Elbridge Gerry that Gerry had given to Adams, and this letter prompted a response by Adams to Sullivan on a wide range of important topics. In his reply, Adams worries about the reason why the majority may govern the minority, why men may govern women without their consent, and why the old may bind the young without theirs. He answers that necessity requires that the majority have a right to govern and that the minority have a duty to obey: "there can be no other rule." Women are excluded from the governing class, he continues, because "their delicacy renders them unfit for practice and experience in the great businesses of life, and the hardy enterprises of war, as well as the arduous cares of state. Besides, their attention is so much engaged with the necessary nurture of their children, that nature has made them fittest for domestic cares." And children, says Adams as he explains *their* exclusion, "have not judgment or will of their own."[9]

8. Adams, *Works*, Volume IV, p. 401.
9. *Ibid.*, Volume IX, pp. 375–376.

When—at this point in his argument—Adams comes to the thorny question of property qualifications, he contends that a combination of the reasons he has given for denying votes to women and children will also apply in the case of men "wholly destitute of property." Like women, they are too little acquainted with public affairs to form a right judgment; and like children, they are "too dependent upon other men to have a will of their own." Summing up this point, Adams writes: "If this is a fact, if you give to every man who has no property, a vote, will you not make a fine encouraging provision for corruption, by your fundamental law? Such is the frailty of the human heart, that very few men who have no property, have any judgment of their own. They talk and vote as they are directed by some man of property, who has attached their minds to his interest."[10]

This, however, is not the end of Adams's thinking about property qualifications. Like any intelligent reader of Blackstone's reasons for that institution, Adams was aware that someone might ask why, if differences of property cause some men to be dependent, their dependency should not be *eliminated* rather than used as a basis for denying the vote to them. Adams offers this comment on the subject: "Harrington has shown that power always follows property. This I believe to be as infallible a maxim in politics, as that action and reaction are equal, is in mechanics. Nay, I believe we may advance one step farther, and affirm that the balance of power in a society, accompanies the balance of property in land. The only possible way, then, of preserving the balance of power on the side of equal liberty and public virtue, is to make the acquisition of land easy to every member of society; to make a division of the land into small quantities, so that the multitude may be possessed of landed estates. If the mul-

10. *Ibid.,* p. 376.

titude is possessed of the balance of real estate, the multitude will have the balance of power, and in that case the multitude will take care of the liberty, virtue, and interest of the multitude, in all acts of government."[11]

We are still not finished with Adams's discourse on property qualifications, for he now becomes more practical and writes: "I believe these principles have been felt, if not understood, in the Massachusetts Bay, from the beginning; and therefore I should think that wisdom and policy would dictate in these times to be very cautious of making alterations. Our people have never been very rigid in scrutinizing into the qualifications of voters, and I presume they will not now begin to be so. But I would not advise them to make any alteration in the laws, at present, respecting the qualifications of voters."[12] And then he ends with a warning: "Depend upon it, Sir, it is dangerous to open so fruitful a source of controversy and altercation as would be opened by attempting to alter the qualifications of voters; there will be no end of it. New claims will arise; women will demand a vote; lads from twelve to twenty-one will think their rights not enough attended to; and every man who has not a farthing, will demand an equal voice with any other, in all acts of state. It tends to confound and destroy all distinctions, and prostrate all ranks to one common level."[13]

In sum, the philosophy of the *American Revolution* contained much theoretical ammunition that the so-called political psychologists who wrote the Constitution could have used if they wished arguments for disenfranchising blacks, women, and poor people. A supposed deficiency in the power to use reason was thought by some philosophers to be enough to exclude blacks and women, and a supposed lack of will-power was thought sufficient to exclude the poor. Whatever the ad-

11. *Ibid.*, pp. 376–377.
12. *Ibid.*, p. 377.
13. See Supplementary Notes, Price's Measures . . . , p. 291.

mirable features of the philosophical ideas advocated in the Revolutionary era might have been, then, a faith in all of the people was not one of them. We can certainly see this if we probe deeply into the epistemology, the metaphysics, the philosophical theology, and the ethics of the American Revolution—which is what I have tried to do in this book.

The reader knows that I have concentrated on the theory of knowledge, the metaphysics, the philosophical theology, and the ethics used by theorists of the American Revolution. I have expounded in detail their views and those of their transatlantic mentors on self-evident truth, on the God-created essence of man, his God-proposed ends, his God-ordained duties, and his God-given rights. I have dilated on the nature of those rights, on their various kinds, and on the relationship of rights to powers; I have also pointed out that some rights were regarded as unalienable because they were derived from duties of natural law and that the people's right and duty to rebel was defended by arguing that the British monarch had shown an intention to invade their unalienable rights as individuals, an intention which entitled the colonists to believe that the social contract had been broken by the monarch before they had ever fired the shot heard round the world.

I have just sketched what may be called the analytical part of my inquiry, but the reader knows that I have also offered a number of reflections on those philosophical concepts which could be and were used for various political ends. My recent treatment of Price's views of the relationship between physical and civil liberty is, to some extent, an example of what I have tried to do in more detail at several earlier places in this book. In reflecting in this manner on ideas that I have also analyzed, I have, as I have previously indicated, done something similar to what Locke did when he remarked on the political potentialities of the doctrine of innate principles, and also something similar to what John Stuart Mill did when he assessed the political impact of intuitionism. We find similar reflections on the possible and actual impact of relatively abstract ideas of philosophy in the writings of those eighteenth-century moralists and their Colonial disciples who argued that a moral philosophy which made no room for a moral sense thereby showed itself indifferent to the powers and aspirations of ploughmen. However, my own claims in this area have been guarded. I have not said flatly that the doctrine of self-evident truth was inevitably a tool of haughty dictators of principles but rather that it *could have been* easily turned into one under certain circumstances, and that on occasion it was used in this way. An advocate of this doctrine could claim that those who did not agree with him on the self-evidence of some proposition were biased, incapable of using their reason, insistent upon not using it, ignorant, or prisoners of vice and blindness. And we have seen in one of our rare leaps forward to the *Federalist Papers* that Hamilton used the doctrine in this way while trying to bully some of his political opponents. By contrast, I have argued that although Jefferson subscribed to this epistemological doctrine, he was optimistic enough to think that the majority could and should be educated to the point where what was self-evident to him was also self-evident to them.

While pursuing such reflections I have also remarked that not only the theory of self-evidence could be, and was at times, used tendentiously but that the theory of moral sense, in spite of having been advertised as the democrat's answer to the alleged political defects of moral rationalism, also contained jokers. Thus, James Wilson, following Burlamaqui, was careful to point out that the moral sense to which we must appeal in showing that moral principles are true is not the moral sense of any person whatsoever—certainly not that of a savage—but rather that of a man in a perfect state, perhaps someone like the Stoic sage or the prudent man to whom Aristotle always appeals in a moral pinch.

Mentioning Aristotle leads me to remind the reader that

our Revolutionary theorists not only leaned on an epistemology of self-evident truth which was easily turned to political advantage but also relied heavily on eighteenth-century versions of Aristotle's concept of essence. And any thinker who professed to be able to penetrate man's mysterious essence thought he was in a position to extract certain duties and rights from it rather than others. If he were to say that possession of an opposable thumb differentiated man's essence from that of other beings, he could consider a life of thumb-opposing obligatory on man rather than a life of reason.[14] And, to take an issue which seriously divided modern theorists of natural law, it is worth recalling that one alleged penetrator of man's essence—Pufendorf—leaned heavily on Aristotle's statement that man was essentially a sociable animal, whereas another, Locke, seized on his statement that man was essentially a rational animal. Moreover, if Burlamaqui had not seen the *desire* for happiness in man's "glassy essence," Jefferson might never have regarded the *pursuit* of happiness as an unalienable right.

All of this, I should emphasize, is intended to show that because so much was thought to depend on what was inside so obscure a notion as man's essence—a notion which its greatest sponsors thought was difficult to analyze even when they insisted on its existence—those who claimed to penetrate it often saw what they *wanted* to see there because if they did not, how would they be able to arrive at all of those duties

14. See Aristotle's criticism of Anaxagoras' opinion that the possession of hands is the cause of man's being intelligent, it being Aristotle's view that man's possession of hands is *the consequence* of the fact that he is the most intelligent of all animals, *De partibus animalium,* 687 A 7–23. I am indebted to Professor Harold Cherniss for calling my attention to this passage, as I am for his calling my attention to, and helping me to understand, so many passages from classical philosophers. Although Aristotle does not speak here about man's possessing an opposable thumb, the passage serves, nevertheless, to illustrate the sort of debate about man's essence that reveals the obscurity of that doctrine as traditionally conceived.

and rights? As the reader may have gathered, I am not exactly sympathetic to the doctrine of essence, and whether I express my disapproval of it by saying that I do not understand the word "essence" or by saying that I do not think there are any essences, I am bound to conclude that those who think duties and rights follow from essences really come to their views on duties and rights in some other way. For some reason they *think* there are rabbits in a hat which doesn't contain them; and, to go further by means of this figure, they wrongly suppose that there is a *hat*.

I must conclude therefore that when some thinkers say that a certain right is derivable from the essence of man and others disagree with them, their differences must be explained in some other way on the supposition that each disputant has *some* reason for saying what he says. I take the same view of the dispute between those who think that the essence of government is to protect rights and those who think that it should not only protect them but also abet and favor the exercise of them. I take the same view of those who defend property qualifications for voting by declaring that an indigent man's bribed voting would not be *his* act because it is the essence of *his* act that it should not be "determined" by a cause outside of himself, as Price does in his most technical philosophical work, *A Review of the Principal Questions in Morals*.[15]

15. See pp. 181–182 of that work (Oxford, 1948) where the following passage appears:

> The *liberty* I here mean is the same with the power of *acting* and *determining:* And it is self-evident, that where such a power is wanting, there can be no moral capacities. As far as it is true of a being that he *acts,* so far he must *himself* be the cause of the action, and therefore not necessarily determined to act. Let any one try to put a sense on the expression; *I will; I act;* which is consistent with supposing, that the volition or action does not proceed from myself. Virtue supposes determination, and determination supposes a determiner; and a determiner that determines not himself, is a palpable contradiction. Determination requires an efficient cause. If this cause is the being himself, I plead for no

Before I conclude this set of reflections, I should point out
that although I have called *self-evident truth* epistemological
and *essence* metaphysical, we have seen that they are intimately connected in the minds of some theorists of natural
law. For example, Aquinas thought that one who did not
know the *essence* of man would not be able to see that the
proposition that man is a rational being is self-evident, and
Locke held that one who did not grasp the *ideas* that made
up the proposition "creatures of the same species and rank
promiscuously born to all the same advantages of nature, and
the use of the same faculties, should also be equal one amongst
another without subordination or subjection, unless the Lord
and Master of them all, should by any manifest declaration of
his will set one above another, and confer on him by an evident and clear appointment an undoubted right to dominion
and sovereignty"[16] would not see that *it* was self-evident. But
if there are any two words which have been viewed suspi-
ciously in the history of philosophy, it is "essence" as used by
Aristotle and "idea" as used by Locke. Here we are, however,
advised that if we do not see something to be self-evident, it
is because we have not grasped an essence or an idea. So, since
our failure to see as self-evident what the great theorists of
natural law regarded as self-evident depends on our failure to

---

more. If not, then it is no longer *his* determination; that is, *he* is
no longer the determiner, but the motive, or whatever else any
one will say to be the cause of the determination. To ask, what effects *our* determinations, is the very same with asking who did an
action, after being informed that such a one did it. In short; who
must not *feel* the absurdity of saying, *my* volitions are produced
by a *foreign* cause, that is, are not *mine;* I determine *voluntarily,*
and yet *necessarily?*—We have, in truth, the same constant and
necessary consciousness of liberty, that we have that we think,
chuse, will, or even exist; and whatever to the contrary any persons may say, it is impossible for them in earnest to think they
have no active, self-moving powers, and are not the causes of *their
own* volitions, or not to ascribe to *themselves,* what they must be
conscious *they* think and do.
16. *Second Treatise,* Section 4.

know what Aristotelian essences and what Lockean ideas are, we may say that the potentiality for political abuse in the doctrine of self-evident truth in part depends on the darkness surrounding Aristotle's *essences* and Locke's *ideas*. He who does not know what they are cannot honestly agree with any assertions of self-evidence and is therefore put in an awkward position. If he hypocritically assents to them without understanding them, he would earn the contempt of the Jefferson who wrote "A Bill for Establishing Religious Freedom," but if he does *not* assent to them, he would earn the contempt of the Jefferson who wrote the Declaration of Independence. It is clear to me which contempt it would be better to earn, and I hope it is the same contempt as that which my readers would prefer to earn, however much they admire the Republic that was born when the Declaration of Independence was signed.

Supplementary Notes

Moral Rationalism in Jefferson,
*Bolingbroke, and Locke**

Some evidence for believing that Jefferson subscribed to moral rationalism when he wrote the Declaration may be derived from a commonplace book of Jefferson's which has been edited by Gilbert Chinard under the title, *The Literary Bible of Thomas Jefferson: His Commonplace Book of Philosophers and Poets* (Baltimore, 1928). In it Jefferson copied a passage from Bolingbroke which reads as follows:

> It is not true that Christ revealed an entire body of ethics, proved to be the law of nature from principles of reason, and reaching all the duties of life. If mankind wanted such a code, to which recourse might be had on every occasion, as to an unerring rule in every part of the moral duties, such a code is still wanting; for the gospel is not such a code. Moral obligations are occasionally recommended and commended in it, but no where proved from principles of reason, and by clear deductions, unless allusions, parables, and comparisons, and promises and threats, are to pass for such. Were all the precepts of this kind, that are scattered about in the

* Page 77.

whole new-testament, collected, like the short sentences of ancient sages in the memorials we have of them, and put together in the very words of the sacred writers, they would compose a very short, as well as unconnected system of ethics. [p. 50]

When Chinard comments on this excerpt from Bolingbroke, Chinard never tells us that it immediately follows a passage in which Bolingbroke is attacking the latter part of Locke's *Reasonableness of Christianity* (see above, Chapter 1, notes 31–36 and the material in the text associated with them). Bolingbroke mistakenly thought, as I have indicated, that Locke believed that the Gospel contained a demonstrative system of morality and that is why Bolingbroke felt obliged to write the passage which Jefferson copied and which is reproduced above. It is probable that Jefferson excerpted that passage from Bolingbroke partly because Jefferson was sympathetic at the time to the view that morality *could be* a demonstrative science.

The larger passage in Bolingbroke from which Jefferson excerpted the passage I have reproduced above reads as follows:

. . . The great book of nature lies open before us, and our natural reason enables us to read in it. Whatever it may contain, that cannot be thus read, cannot be called natural religion with any precision of ideas, or propriety of words; nor will the example, that has been brought, of men who assent readily to truths consonant to their reason, which they receive from others, and would have found it hard to discover themselves, be made applicable to the present case, so as to destroy the distinction. Mr. Locke should have seen this sooner than any man, and one would think a reflection so obvious should escape no man. He did not, or he would not, make it. He seems to me, in the latter part of his treatise concerning the reasonableness of Christianity, not only to confound the want of sufficient means to propagate, and the want of

that the principles of Aristotelian logic could serve as the first principles or axioms upon which a science like that of mathematics could be erected. See, for example, his *Essay,* Book IV, Chapter VII, Section 11. One wonders what he would have said if he had been confronted with systems of modern logic.

Moral Sense and Reason in Hutcheson, Butler, and Kames*

See Raphael, *The Moral Sense,* pp. 15–16. Also see W. R. Scott, *Francis Hutcheson* (Cambridge, Eng., 1900), Chapter XII. Scott emphasizes the impact on the later Hutcheson of Stoicism as well as that of Butler. Although Raphael (*op. cit.,* p. 16, note 1) cites a passage from Hutcheson's *System of Moral Philosophy* (London, 1755), Volume I, p. 58, in which Hutcheson says that the moral sense "may be a constant settled determination in the soul itself, as much as our powers of judging and reasoning," Hutcheson immediately adds that " 'tis pretty plain that *reason* is only a subservient power to our ultimate determinations either of perception or will. The ultimate end is settled by some sense, and some determination of will: by some sense we enjoy happiness, and self-love determines to it without reasoning. Reason can only direct to the means; or compare two ends previously constituted by some other immediate powers." It would seem, therefore, that Hutcheson's later blurring of the distinction between the moral sense and reason is not as plausibly associated with the passage quoted by Raphael as it is with passages discussed by Scott (*op. cit.,* p. 247) in his linking of the later Hutcheson with the Stoic doctrine of "right reason."

Since I am concentrating on Hutcheson's views on moral sense, I want to mention certain views about the moral sense held by Bishop Butler and Lord Kames in order to contrast

* Page 100.

the views of each of them with the view of the early Hutcheson. It is worth noting that Butler was prepared to assert the existence of a moral sense provided that he was not obliged to identify it flat-footedly with reason or sense, and provided that he was not obliged to say, with Hutcheson, that benevolence was the whole of virtue. In Butler's *Dissertation of the Nature of Virtue,* appended to his *Analogy of Religion,* he avoided arguing about whether the moral faculty was to be identified with a sense or with reason by saying: "It is manifest, [that a?] great part of common language, and of common behavior over the world, is formed upon supposition of such a moral faculty; whether called conscience, moral reason, moral sense, or divine reason; whether considered as a sentiment of the understanding or as a perception of the heart, or, which seems the truth, as including both." And in that same *Dissertation* Butler further disassociated himself from Hutcheson by writing: "benevolence, and the want of it, singly considered, are in no sort the whole of virtue and vice." Like Butler, Lord Kames rejects Hutcheson's views on the role of benevolence in moral judgment but Kames insists that it is a moral *sense* which tells us what our moral duty is because he agrees with Hutcheson that there is a nonrational faculty. The authority of our moral sense or conscience, Kames says, "arises from a direct perception, which we have upon presenting the object, without an intervention of any sort of reflection. And the authority lies in this circumstance, that we perceive the action to be our duty, and what we are indispensably bound to perform. It is in this manner that the moral sense, with regard to some actions, plainly bears upon it the marks of authority over all our appetites and passions. It is the voice of God within us, which commands our strictest obedience, just as much as when his will is declared by express revelation" (*Essays on the Principles of Morality and Religion,* 3rd ed. [Edinburgh, 1779], pp. 43–44).

*Jefferson on Ignatius Sancho**

The Letters of the Late Ignatius Sancho, to which Jefferson refers, were first published (posthumously) in two volumes (1782). The fifth edition of 1803 in one volume has been reprinted in facsimile, with an Introduction by Paul Edwards (London, 1968), and my references will be to this edition. Upon reading it, I am struck by the weakness of Jefferson's use of it to support his suspicion that blacks were inferior to whites in rational power as opposed to moral feeling. The work is a collection of letters written to friends in unbuttoned moods and rarely provide Sancho with an occasion for what Jefferson rather pompously refers to as "demonstration." It is true, as Jefferson says, that they "breathe the purest effusions of friendship and general philanthropy," but their author is quite aware of his own tendencies in this regard, referring at one point to "the simple effusions of a poor Negro's heart" (p. 179) and at another to "the warm ebullitions of African sensibility" (p. 205). Those effusions lead Sancho to fill his pages with the word "heart" but he is also given to *commenting* on both the heart and head as faculties —as Jefferson is—and with about the same degree of consistency. In a letter recommending books to a young man, Sancho writes much as Jefferson was to write five years later to Carr (see Chapter 3, note 35): "Two small volumes of Sermons useful—and very sensible—by one Mr. Williams, a dissenting minister—which are as well as fifty—for I love not a multiplicity of doctrines—A few plain tenets, easy, simple, and directed to the heart, are better than volumes of controversial nonsense" (p. 152). And, like Jefferson, Sancho also admired the work of Laurence Sterne, with whom he corresponded. Writing to a Mr. M——— in 1777, Sancho says: "You have read and admired Sterne's Sermons—which chiefly

* Page 115.

inculcate practical duties, and paint brotherly love and the
true Christian charities in such beauteous glowing colours—
that one cannot help wishing to feed the hungry—clothe the
naked, &c. &c.—I would to God, my friend, that the great
lights of the church would exercise their oratorical powers
upon Yorick's plan:—the heart and passions once lifted under
the banners of blest philanthropy, would naturally ascend to
the redeeming God—flaming with grateful rapture.—Now I
have observed among the modern saints—who profess to pray
without ceasing—that they are so fully taken up with pious
meditations—and so wholly absorbed in the love of God—
that they have little if any room for the love of man" (pp. 84–
85). In the same vein, he writes to another young man in
1780: "My dear youth, be proud of nothing but an honest
heart" (p. 302).

In other moods, Sancho, like Jefferson, praised the *combination* of head and heart—as when he speaks with approval of
"the head and heart of Addison's Sir Roger de Coverley" (pp.
247–248); or when he says to a correspondent that a certain
proposal "did honor to your heart, and credit to your judgment" (p. 197); or when he speaks of a man "whose looks and
address bespeak a good heart and good sense" (p. 193); or
when he writes: "I would wish you to note down the occurrences of every day—to which add your own observation of
men and things—The more you habituate yourself to minute
investigation, the stronger you will make your mind—ever
taking along with you in all your researches the word of God
—and the operations of his divine providence" (p. 188).

After reading through these letters I can sympathize with
Jefferson's judgment of their general merit—Mr. Paul Edwards, who edited them, says that "the reader should not expect to find anything remarkably original" in them—but it is
hard to see how they support the view that Sancho or blacks
in general are inferior to whites in rational power. Perhaps
Jefferson was affected by some of Sancho's remarks on the

American Revolution. See, for example, his remark on November 5, 1777, about the good news of "the defeat of Washintub's army—and the capture of Arnold and Sulivan [sic] with seven thousand prisoners—thirteen counties return to their allegiance" (p. 117).

Jefferson, Scientific Inquiry, and Ranking Blacks in Intelligence*

Jefferson's diffidence about advancing more than a "suspicion" of the inferiority of blacks in rational power was based on more than what he took to be the difficulties of establishing this scientifically. It was also based on his awareness of what was riding on the outcome of such a scientific inquiry, namely, the possibility that it "would degrade a whole race of men from the rank in the scale of beings which their Creator may perhaps have given them" (*Writings,* Volume II, p. 200). Jefferson's maintaining their rank in the scale of beings as possessing reason in a certain degree might bear on being able to defend their rights on the basis of the "equal creation" from which Jefferson had *derived* these rights in the Rough Draft of the Declaration. It should be noted that in the *Notes on Virginia* Jefferson does not deny that blacks are *men* just as Aristotle had not denied manhood to his natural slaves. Furthermore, Jefferson was prepared to say that "It is not against experience to suppose that different species of the same genus, or varieties of the same species, may possess different qualifications" (*ibid.,* p. 201), thereby echoing to some degree Aristotle's notion that the natural slave "participates in reason to the extent of apprehending it in another, though destitute of it himself" (*Politics,* 1254 B 13, Barker's translation). Aristotle, however, placed his slaves above animals, "which do not apprehend reason, but simply obey their in-

* Page 116.

stincts" (*ibid.*, 1254 B 13–14). By "apprehending reason," Aristotle meant that slaves could understand the commands of their masters even though they could not use reason to originate such commands.

Jefferson's concern about the rank of the American black in the scale of being or nature was not unrelated to earlier concerns of Bishop Berkeley as indicated by a sermon preached by Berkeley about some of his experiences in Rhode Island. He reports, in a sermon preached in London in 1732, "an irrational contempt of blacks, as creatures of another species, who had no right to be instructed or admitted to the sacraments" (*Works of George Berkeley,* ed. Fraser, Vol. IV, p. 405).

Hutcheson's Appeal to Aristotle's Moral Philosophy*

I add this note for the reader who may be interested in Hutcheson's use of Aristotle, as indicated in his *System of Moral Philosophy*—particularly in those parts of that work to which Wilson refers us.

Among the references to Aristotle given by Hutcheson we find one to the last chapter of Book II of the *Nicomachean Ethics*. There Aristotle, after a discussion of his concept of the mean, tells us that, after all, no general rule will tell us what to do in specific cases. There he also says, in a passage which is attractive to Hutcheson for obvious reasons, "But up to what point and to what extent a man must deviate before he becomes blameworthy it is not easy to determine by *reasoning* [my emphasis], any more than anything else that is perceived by the *senses* [my emphasis]; such things depend on particular facts, and *the decision rests with perception* [my emphasis]" (Ross's translation in Volume IX of the Oxford

* Page 135.

Works of Aristotle, 1109 B 20–26). This is one of the passages on the basis of which Hutcheson claims the support of Aristotle for Hutcheson's own statement that "many points in morals, when applied to individual cases cannot be exactly determined; but good men know them by a sort of *sensation.*" However, the passage which Hutcheson, by his method of quotation, leads us to think follows immediately afterwards in Aristotle's text does *not.* To find the statement, "The good man is thus the last measure of all things," or something like it, we must go to another place in Aristotle cited in Hutcheson's text, namely, to Book III, Chapter 4, of the *Nicomachean Ethics.* There Aristotle is discussing the relationship between wishing and the good. After he tells us that some people think we wish for the good and others think we wish for the apparent good, and after he points out difficulties in both of these views, he begins to consider a third possibility and in the course of that says something that is to Hutcheson's taste: "If these consequences are unpleasing, are we to say that absolutely and in truth the good is the object of wish, but for each person the apparent good; that that which is in truth an object of wish is an object of wish to the good man, while any chance thing may be so to the bad man, as in the case of bodies also the things that are in truth wholesome are wholesome for bodies which are in good condition, while for those that are diseased other things are wholesome—or bitter or sweet or hot or heavy, and so on; since the good man judges each class of things rightly, and in each the truth appears to him? For each state of character has its own ideas of the noble and the pleasant, and perhaps the good man differs from others most by seeing the truth in each class of things, being as it were the norm and measure of them" (Ross's translation of 1113 A 23–35).

I think this passage is to Hutcheson's taste not only because of its reference to the good man being the norm or measure but because of Aristotle's references to bitterness and heat, which are, of course, *sensed*. For the same reason Hutcheson is drawn, as we have seen, to the last chapter of Book II of the *Nicomachean Ethics,* where there is also emphasis on perception by the senses. What Hutcheson does not say, however, is that Aristotle's reference in the last chapter of Book II is to the perception of facts concerning the deviation of acts from the mean, and not to the perception of goodness or badness, rightness or wrongness.

Property and the Doctrine of Natural Law*

The word "property" is notoriously vague as well as ambiguous in the literature of natural law. Often, therefore, some right associated with property *is* said to be unalienable by some writers. Thus, John Adams writes: "All men are born [equally] free and *independent,* and have certain natural, essential, and unalienable rights, among which may be reckoned the right of enjoying and defending their lives and liberties; that of acquiring, possessing, and protecting [their] property; in fine, that of seeking and obtaining their safety and happiness" (*Works,* Volume IV, p. 220). And Benjamin Franklin writes: "If the British subjects, residing in this island, claim liberty, and the disposal of their property, on the score of that unalienable right that all men, except those who have justly forfeited those advantages have to them, the British people, residing in America, challenge the same on the same principle" (*Papers,* Volume 17, p. 7). If the word "their" in the passage from Adams—which, like the other bracketed words above, was deleted by the convention on a Constitution for Massachusetts—is allowed to remain, then these passages together seem to assert the unalienability of the rights to possess, protect, and dispose of one's property *while it is one's own*. Such unalienability is, so to speak, asserted in

* Page 214.

a trifling proposition since if one at a certain time does hold a piece of land as property, it is logically impossible to alienate one's right to possess, protect, and dispose of the land *while owning the land*. Nevertheless, this trifling kind of unalienability is compatible with the alienability of the land itself. If, on the other hand, one strikes the word "their" from Adams's statement, one seems to be left with an assertion of the unalienability merely of the right *to be a property-holder*, which is also compatible with the alienability of the land itself. Insisting upon the unalienability of the right *to be a property-holder* is comparable to insisting on the unalienability of one's right to be a free man as opposed to a slave.

Puzzles about Locke's seemingly shifting use of the word "property" are debated by J. Viner and C. B. McPherson in the *Canadian Journal of Economics and Political Science,* Volume 29 (1963): 548–566. Since I need not become involved in that controversy, I am inclined to say only this: that Locke, instead of being charged with *ambiguity* or with using different senses of "property" because in some places in the *Second Treatise* he refers to life, liberty, and estates as property whereas in others he refers only to estates as property, might better be understood as using *one* sense of the word "property" but illustrating it differently in different contexts. It should be remembered that in the *Essay,* Book IV, Chapter III, Section 18, Locke identifies the idea of property simply with the idea of a right in order to establish the proposition that wherever there is no property, there is no injustice since injustice is simply the violation of a right.

Further Remarks on "these ends" and "these rights"*

If we seek a full explanation of why this change from "these ends" to "these rights" was made, it is impossible, I think, to

* Page 250.

find one with the evidence now at our disposal. Julian Boyd's careful analysis in *The Declaration of Independence: The Evolution of the Text* (pp. 28–31) suggests that Jefferson himself made this change since Boyd believes that it was not made by anyone else on the Committee of Five or by the Congress, which concentrated on making others when it, as someone said, mangled Jefferson's draft. But I have found nothing in the writing of commentators nor in Jefferson's own writing which illuminates the change in a specific manner. To make matters more confusing, we discover that in spite of getting rid of "these ends" in favor of "these rights" at one place in the document, Jefferson, the presumed eliminator of "these ends" at its first occurrence in the Rough Draft, allowed it to remain in the immediately ensuing "self-evident truth," that is to say, in the clause "that whenever any form of government becomes destructive of *these ends* [my emphasis], it is the right of the people to alter or abolish it." To what does the phrase "these ends" which Jefferson allowed to remain in the Declaration refer? If it refers back to the textual successors of Jefferson's *rights* in the Rough Draft, namely, to the right to life, to the right to liberty, and to the right to pursue happiness, one wonders what the "destruction" of *them* could possibly mean. *Can* a government *destroy* a God-given *right?* One would not have thought so. Such rights are supposedly immutable and therefore indestructible. If, on the other hand, the second occurrence of "these ends," which was allowed to remain in the final version, refers to what were sometimes called "the objects" of rights, that would permit the ends to be destructible and also support my view that in the Rough Draft both occurrences of "these ends" referred to the preservation of life, the preservation of liberty, and the pursuit of happiness as objects of rights and not as rights. It would, as a consequence, also support my view that government was, in the Rough Draft, thought to be instituted to *attain* these objects of rights and not the rights themselves, and that it could be abolished when it either destroyed or failed to attain these objects. Such objects of rights may be plausibly spoken of as attained and also as destroyed when the rights of which they are objects are invaded. Therefore, had the Rough Draft's rights been allowed to remain in the final version, the occurrence of the phrase "these ends" which stayed on would have made more sense. In addition, the Declaration would have been clearer, more coherent, and more Burlamaquian. "These ends" would have been ends proposed by a Creator who thereby created obligations which implied that individual men had rights to strive for certain ends; government would have been understood to have been instituted in part to *help men* as they strove for those ends; bad governments would have been clearly viewed as destroyers of those *ends;* and such bad governments would have been more clearly seen as institutions which men had a right, *nay a duty,* to alter or abolish.

Now that I have employed the distinction between a right and its object, I must consider another possibility. Consider the right of preservation of one's life, or the right to preserve one's life. I have spoken as though the object of this right were the preservation of life, as though the object of the right to preserve liberty were the preservation of liberty, and as though the object of the right to pursue happiness were the pursuit of happiness. But why, it might be asked, can't we think of the objects of these rights, respectively, as life, liberty, and happiness, the things preserved and pursued? Let us, therefore, consider the possibility that in the Rough Draft the objects of the rights and the ends to be secured by government are life, liberty, and happiness not conceived as rights. Plainly, this will have an absurd consequence in the case of life if we read "secure" as meaning *attain* in the Rough Draft, because government could not have been thought of as instituted to *attain* life. But what if we read "secure" as meaning *make secure,* or *guarded,* in the Rough Draft? I still see difficulty in referring to life, liberty, and happiness as *ends* and also as things to be *guarded* for we simply don't speak of guarding ends, but there is another objection to it which derives from the philosophical tradition upon which the signers drew. I have in mind Aristotle's distinction between *doing* and *making.* In the *Nicomachean Ethics* (1140 B 6–7) he says: "Doing and making are generically different, since making aims at an end distinct from the act of making, whereas in doing the end cannot be other than the act itself: doing well is in itself the end." The same distinction is also present in the *Politics* (1254 A), one of the books on public right to which Jefferson refers when he speaks of the various ideas he was trying to harmonize while writing the Declaration. I am inclined to think, therefore, that the rights enunciated in the Rough Draft and in the final version were rights to *do* or to *act* in Aristotle's sense. And if the Declaration's rights were rights to *do* or *act,* then actions were the ends to which Jefferson referred whenever he spoke of "these ends." In that case we can rule out the possibility that life, liberty, and happiness were the ends which could be secured in the sense of attained. Only acts could serve in that capacity, a conclusion which is further supported by the tendency of most eighteenth-century jurists and moralists to define a right as a power to *act,* as we have previously seen. Furthermore, only acts could be destroyed in the sense required by the phrase "whenever any form of government becomes destructive of these ends." So, when this occurrence of "these ends" was allowed to remain even after the first occurrence had been removed, it could now only refer in an incomprehensible way to *the rights* of life, liberty, and the pursuit of happiness whereas in the Rough Draft it could meaningfully refer to the *acts* of preserving life, preserving liberty, and pursuing happiness.

Richard Price on the Dependent Voter*

To the word "meanest," Price attaches a footnote that reads: "In Great Britain, consisting of near *six millions* of inhabitants, 5723 persons, most of them the lowest of the people, elect one half of the *House of Commons;* and 364 votes chuse a ninth part. This may be seen distinctly made out in the *Political Disquisitions* [by James Burgh], Volume I, Book 2, Chapter 4, a work full of important and useful instruction."

This idea was of some importance to Price because, in his later pamphlet, *Observations on the Importance of the American Revolution and the Means of Making It a Benefit to the World* (New Haven, 1785), Price writes as follows in a footnote to a remark in the text where he refers to "abuses so gross as to make our boasts of liberty ridiculous": "The majority of the British House of Commons is chosen by a *few* thousands of the dregs of the people, who are constantly paid for their votes" (p. 54). This reference to "the meanest persons" and "the dregs of the people" is very interesting in a writer who is preoccupied with the civil liberty of the state, who virtually identifies it with a pure, majoritarian democracy, and who is willing to settle for a representative democracy as the next best thing. Note that he seems to worry about the dangers of vote-buying and giving the "dregs of the people" power only when he comes to discussing a *representative* democracy, and that what he also fears there is the relative *fewness* of these mean people who manage to acquire power out of proportion to their numbers. But it would be interesting to know whether the possibility of a *majority* of these "dregs" having power in a pure democracy worried him. Presumably votes can be bought in a *pure* democracy and presumably the majority of *its* members could be mean and dregs.

* Page 262.

I now turn to what Price had in mind when he cited Burgh. In Book II, Chapter IV of his *Political Disquisitions,* Burgh cites certain statistics which are intended to show "the monstrous irregularity of parliamentary representation." He says that he relies on "the learned and indefatigably laborious Brown Willis, Esq; in his NOTIT PARLIAM" and infers from these statistics that 254 members of the House of Commons—almost a majority—were elected by 5,723 votes. Burgh's method is to take first Wallingford, for example, which sends 2 members who are chosen by 76 people, which is a majority of the 150 electors. He uses 76 as the number of what he calls the *efficient* votes on the theory that anyone elected by 76 "is as effectually elected as if he had the whole 150." Thus Burgh seems to disregard the *actual* vote for the 2 members, arguing that 76 *could and therefore do* elect the 2 members. He continues in this way, adding all the members to get 254, and adding all the bare electing majorities to get 5,723. Burgh remarks that the 254 members constituted nearly a majority of the 502 who voted in "the most numerous meeting of the commons ever known"—in the debate on Walpole in 1741. And, continuing with his reasoning about *efficient* numbers, he says that this 254 "comes very near . . . the *whole acting* and *efficient* number" (*ibid.,* p. 45) in the House of Commons. In connection with Price's remark about "dregs," we should observe that Burgh confines himself to saying of the 5,723: "And the greatest part of these illustrious 5723 who have the power of constituting lawgivers over the property of the nation, are themselves persons of no property" (*ibid.,* pp. 45–46).

It is interesting that although Price cites Burgh in support of a view that Price shared with Blackstone about the importance of limiting the voting of the poor, Burgh thought that Blackstone was not sufficiently aroused by defects of the system of voting and representation in England at the time. See a note to Blackstone's *Commentaries,* Volume II, p. 172, in which Burgh's criticisms are reproduced by the editor. They are taken from Burgh's *Political Disquisitions,* Volume I, pp. 80–81. It might be argued that American thinkers believed their own country to be one in which the class of indigent people was relatively small but that belief was compatible in their eyes with accepting the idea of property qualifications and certain philosophical defenses of them. Adams quoted with approval Harrington's saying that "he who wants bread, is his servant that will feed him" *(Works,* Volume IV, p. 427), and spoke glowingly of the equality that prevailed in the colonies in 1765 *(Diary and Autobiography of John Adams,* Volume I, p. 278), but he was all for assuring the continuation of an independent electorate in Price's sense. Moreover, Jefferson's life-long celebration of the independent yeoman was linked with Harrington's views about establishing one's independence by the acquisition of real estate. See James Harrington, *Oceana,* ed. S. B. Liljegren, (Lund and Heidelberg, 1924), especially where Harrington writes: "equality of estates causeth equality of power, and equality of power is the liberty not onely of the *Commonwealth,* but of every man" (p. 21).

Price's Measures for Discouraging Inequality of Property*

I might add here that Richard Price, in spite of supplying some metaphysical support for property qualifications, was willing to recommend to the Americans certain measures for preventing too great an inequality of property, for example, the discouragement of primogeniture. He thinks that "the disposition to raise a name, by accumulating property in one branch of a family, is a vanity no less unjust and cruel, than dangerous to the interest of liberty; and no wise state will

* Page 266.

encourage or tolerate it" (*Observations on the Importance of the American Revolution,* pp. 60–61). Indeed, Price went so far in the same work as to suggest that the establishment of a community of goods and the annihilation of property advocated by Plato and Thomas More were not "wholly impracticable" (*op. cit.,* p. 59). Price reports, in a letter to Jefferson, that his pamphlet had been reprobated in South Carolina because of its remarks on preventing too great an inequality of property and its attack on slavery, *Papers of Thomas Jefferson,* Volume VIII, p. 258. There is a striking resemblance between what Price says in the *Observations* just mentioned and what Jefferson says in a letter to James Madison about a year after Price's *Observations* had first appeared, and after an extended correspondence between Price and Jefferson. Jefferson's letter to Madison is dated October 28, 1785, and concerns the economic situation in France. At one point it reads: "I am conscious that an equal division of property is impracticable. But the consequences of this enormous inequality producing so much misery to the bulk of mankind, legislators cannot invent too many devices for subdividing property, only taking care to let their subdivisions go hand in hand with the natural affections of the human mind. The descent of property of every kind therefore to all the children, or to all the brothers and sisters, or other relations in equal degree is a politic measure, and a practicable one" (*Papers,* Volume VIII, p. 682).

Index